apr
May
June
Jly
Ag

2

6

8

2

Son 1/77

D1419652

PRINCESS MARINA
HER LIFE AND TIMES

Portrait sketch by Philip de Laszlo

Reproduced by kind permission of H.R.H. Prince Michael of Kent

PRINCESS MARINA

HER LIFE AND TIMES

STELLA KING

CASSELL · LONDON

CASSELL & COMPANY LTD
35 Red Lion Square, London, WC1
Melbourne, Sydney, Toronto
Johannesburg, Auckland

First published 1969

S.B.N. 304 93460 7

Printed in Great Britain by Cox & Wyman Ltd,
London, Fakenham and Reading

Contents

CONTENTS

List of Illustrations

The three genealogical tables which appear in the book were drawn up by Patrick Montague-Smith, Editor of Debrett's Peerage.

Acknowledgements

It would have been impossible to write this book without the guidance, help and advice of many people, and I am extremely grateful to all those who have assisted me.

I should particularly like to thank the following: Lady (Hilary) Baker; Mr Cecil Beaton, C.B.E.; Miss Dorothea Blaker; Count and Countess Alexis Brobrinskoy; Mrs Tamara Bruce (Karsavina); Mr G. Canellos; the Dowager Marchioness of Cholmondeley, C.B.E.; the Misses I. L. and R. Cook; Mr H. I. David, Chairman All England Lawn Tennis and Croquet Club; H.H. Prince Dmitri of Russia; Mrs M. Ellison; Mrs Marie Empson,; Mr Douglas Fairbanks, K.B.E., D.S.C., Mrs Esta Foster, M.B.E.; Mr John Gordon; Mr Christopher Halkias; Mrs M. R. Harlip; Mr Norman Hartnell, M.V.O.; Mr Stelios Hermouzias; Commandant Marion Kettlewell, C.B.E., Hon. A.D.C. Director W.R.N.S.; Countess Kleinmichel; Mr Nicolas de Komstadius; Mr James Loring, Director of the Spastics Society; Mrs Kathleen Lumley; Mrs N. Micrulachi; Major A. D. Mills, Secretary All England Lawn Tennis and Croquet Club; Lady Rachel Pepys, C.V.O.; Mrs Zoia Poklewska; Mrs Lilia Ralli; Miss Kay Riley; Mrs E. St Leger Moore; Mr W. D. Short, formerly of H.M. Factory Inspectorate; Mr and Mrs Peter Stephens; Count Soumarokoff–Elston; the Hon. Sir Steven Runciman, F.B.A., M.A.; Miss Anita Stubbs; Chief Officer Mary Talbot, M.A., Assistant Director W.R.N.S.; Mrs Helen Vlachos–Loundra; Mr Sophocles Vamvakos; Dame Jocelyn Woollcombe, D.B.E.; and others.

I am indebted to those of Princess Marina's relations and others close to her who prefer to remain anonymous but whose contributions have been invaluable.

I am very grateful indeed to Lady (Ingra) Aylwen for her kind assistance and to Mr John Stuart, whose enthusiasm and help has, in every conceivable way, played a large part in the construction of this book.

I should also like to thank officials of the following embassies, ministries, firms and organizations who have, each in their own way, helped so much: Royal Aero Club; Australia House; British European Airways; the Belgian Embassy; Christie Manson & Woods Ltd; Ministry of Defence; the Foreign Office; H.M. Factory Inspectorate; the Greek Embassy; the Home Office; the Metropolitan Police; the Norland Nursing Training College; Ministry of Employment and Productivity; Sotheby & Co.; J. Walter Thompson & Co. Ltd.; the Treasury; Westminster Bank Ltd.

Also Mr E. Merritt, Chief Librarian Express Newspapers; Mr C. Blackwell, head of the Royal Library Express Newspapers; and Mr A. Eke, head of the Photo Library Express Newspapers; and the staff of the British Museum Library, the British Museum Newspaper Library, the London Library and the Public Records Office for their patience and helpfulness.

My gratitude to Miss Sylvia Adburgham and Miss Susan Raymond who have helped so much with the research; to Mrs D. N. Floyd and Mrs E. M. Wallis who have so cheerfully done the typing; and to Mrs Irene McCarthy for her valuable contribution.

And my special thanks to my mother, my son Michael, and my husband Robert Glenton, who have all consistently helped and encouraged me in so many ways.

Before 1918 both Russia and Greece used the Julian Calendar which in this century was thirteen days behind the Gregorian calendar used today. When it is necessary to use the old style dates they are indicated (O.S.).

Introduction

This book was begun long before the death of Princess Marina. It was originally intended as a biography of Princess Marina and her sisters, Princess Paul of Yugoslavia and Countess Toerring. It was to be called *The Three Sisters*, a Chekhovian title which was not inappropriate because by birth the three princesses were predominantly Russian.

This is not an authorized biography. One is not likely to appear—if at all—for another ten or fifteen years. Although I have often seen Princess Marina, and been present at both formal and informal functions she has attended, I have never met her.

The basic research was nearly completed before Princess Marina's life ended in such a tragic and untimely way and much of the material I had gathered is included in this story of her life and times. I have had no access to family papers but some unpublished material has been made available to me which I have made full use of and found very helpful. I have also talked to many of the people who knew her, including some of her family and closest relations. I have visited Athens and other places where she lived or stayed and I have tried to cover as many aspects of her life as I can.

The first part of the book goes into a great deal of her family background. It is impossible, in my opinion, to write about her without doing this. Her family, both before and after she married, was the main pivot of her existence. Between the Princess, her parents, her sisters, her husband and her children, was a bond of loyalty and affection rarely found in such strength. And this close family tie had an enormous influence on her life—whatever affected a member of her family also affected her.

This applied, too, to the times in which Princess Marina lived. She was mainly an onlooker; but personal and historical events in which her relations were involved—often to an extent which was largely unnoticed—were to alter her whole way of living. The way in which she lived and the times in which she lived help to explain her personality. Princess Marina had a complex character. Her friends and relations are often contradictory when they talk about her, although they all agree on the fundamental qualities which she possessed. I have tried to do her justice. I hope I have succeeded.

The last glimpse most people had of Princess Marina was on television on Saturday 6 July 1968, when she presented prizes at the first Open Lawn Tennis Championship at Wimbledon. She seemed very animated and gay. There was no sign that anything was wrong. But in fact she was having trouble with a painful left leg and sometimes stumbled involuntarily, as though she had slipped. 'Look at me. I'm getting old,' she joked.

On 16 July she went into hospital for six days for an examination and was afterwards advised to rest and have electrical treatment. She was not told that tests had revealed an inoperable brain tumour and she had, at the outside, six months to live; only her children knew this. The following month, at 11.40 a.m., on 27 August at Kensington Palace, Princess Marina died. She was sixty-one; but in death her face took on the youthful beauty which had captured Britain by storm more than thirty years before, when she came here as the prospective bride of King George V's youngest son Prince George, later the Duke of Kent. Princess Marina was mobbed and cheered then. Her pork-pie hat was copied and worn by a million women. Her name was given to a song, a flower, a tartan, a shade of peacock blue—and an enormous number of baby girls.

Though a Greek Princess, Princess Marina was three-quarters Russian, one-quarter Danish. Her father was Prince Nicholas of Greece; her mother the Grand Duchess Helen Vladimiróvna of Russia. Both her grandmothers were grand duchesses and her maternal grandfather was a grand duke. On her father's side her grandfather was Danish-born King George I of the Hellenes, whose sister was Queen Alexandra, the wife of King Edward VII.

1

The End of
an Era

1 | *The Greek Inheritance*

A curious set of circumstances brought Princess Marina's grandfather, George I, to the throne of Greece.

The story begins with the ending of the nine-year Greek War of Independence in 1830, which released Greece from Turkish rule for the first time in four hundred years. It became an autonomous state under the protecting powers of Great Britain, France and Russia. Their first task was to find a monarch for the country, for the last sovereign of Greece had been the Emperor Constantine XI, killed at Constantinople in the fifteenth century. By 1830 the dynasty was no longer in existence.

It is said that the three protecting powers, who had an uneasy alliance, were mainly influenced in their choice of king by the necessity of selecting a man who was not a particular favourite of any of them. The debate went on for two years, but eventually, after a tentative approach to Queen Victoria's uncle Leopold, who refused Greece but accepted Belgium, they decided on Prince Otto, the seventeen-year-old son of King Ludwig I of Bavaria. Prince Otto accepted and became King Otho I of Greece (the Greek spelling of Otto is Othon). He was honest, and well-meaning, passionately devoted to his adopted country but lacking in judgement and common sense. He ruled for twenty-nine stormy, difficult years, until 1862 when a successful military revolt overthrew the King for good. King Otho and his wife, Queen Amalia, were on a tour at the time of the rising, and when they tried to return to Greece they were

TABLE 1

**THE GREEK AND DANISH
ROYAL FAMILIES**

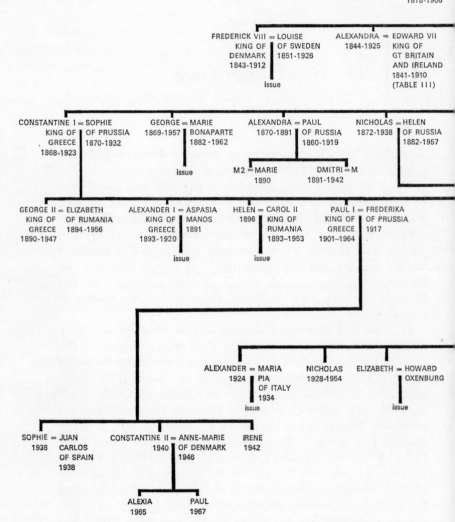

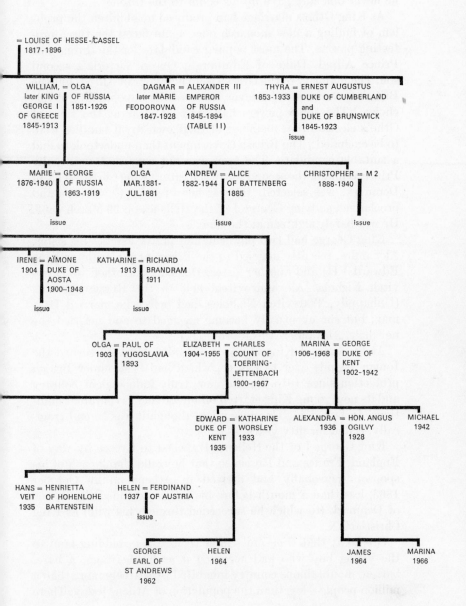

= LOUISE OF HESSE-/CASSEL
1817-1896

WILLIAM, = OLGA
later KING OF RUSSIA
GEORGE I 1851-1926
OF GREECE
1845-1913

DAGMAR = ALEXANDER III
later MARIE EMPEROR
FEODOROVNA OF RUSSIA
1847-1928 1845-1894
(TABLE II)

THYRA = ERNEST AUGUSTUS
1853-1933 DUKE OF CUMBERLAND
and
DUKE OF BRUNSWICK
1845-1923
issue

MARIE = GEORGE
1876-1940 OF RUSSIA
1863-1919
issue

OLGA
MAR.1881-
JUL.1881

ANDREW = ALICE
1882-1944 OF BATTENBERG
1885
issue

CHRISTOPHER = M 2
1888-1940
issue

IRENE = AÏMONE
1904 DUKE OF
AOSTA
1900–1948
issue

KATHARINE = RICHARD
1913 BRANDRAM
1911
issue

OLGA = PAUL OF
1903 YUGOSLAVIA
1893

ELIZABETH = CHARLES
1904–1955 COUNT OF
TOERRING-
JETTENBACH
1900-1967

MARINA = GEORGE
1906–1968 DUKE OF
KENT
1902-1942

EDWARD = KATHARINE
DUKE OF WORSLEY
KENT 1933
1935

ALEXANDRA = HON. ANGUS
1936 OGILVY
1928

MICHAEL
1942

HANS = HENRIETTA
VEIT OF HOHENLOHE
1935 BARTENSTEIN

HELEN = FERDINAND
1937 OF AUSTRIA
issue

GEORGE
EARL OF
ST ANDREWS
1962

HELEN
1964

JAMES
1964

MARINA
1966

B

prevented from landing. The King was thus given no choice but to leave Greece, but, though he only lived for five more years, he never officially gave up his claim to the throne.

As King Otho's marriage had produced no children the problem of finding a new monarch once again faced the three protecting powers. The most popular candidate for the throne was Prince Alfred, Duke of Edinburgh, Queen Victoria's second son. The majority of the Greeks were in favour of Alfred, but the British Government, however, asserted the impossibility of this choice. (The three powers had made it clear at the time of Otho's election that members of their own royal families were to be excluded.) The British Government then undertook to find a suitable candidate. The task was not easy, but eventually Prince William, the second son of the future King Christian IX of Denmark, was selected. He was accepted by the Greeks and proclaimed as King George I of the Hellenes on 30 March 1863. He was barely eighteen at the time.

King George had two powerful and pretty assets—his sister, Alexandra, recently married to the Prince of Wales (later King Edward VII) and another sister, Dagmar, betrothed to Tsarevitch Nicholas Alexandrovitch, heir to the Russian throne. (Unhappily, Tsarevitch Nicholas died before he married Dagmar; but she eventually became engaged to and married the new heir, Alexander Alexandrovitch.)

At the time of King George's accession England turned the Ionian Islands over to Greece, which had been under British protection since 1815. So the new, truly independent country and its new young King started off under very favourable conditions. In fact, King George's reign, though it was to end tragically, lasted for fifty years.

King George I of the Hellenes travelled to Greece by way of England, France and Russia so that he could thank each of his sponsors personally and arrived in Athens on 29 October 1863, less than a month before his father ascended the throne of Denmark (to which he succeeded through his wife) as King Christian IX.

Greece at that time must have seemed a forbidding land to the young boy who had accepted it as his heritage: a bare, barren, mountainous country inhabited by scarcely more than a million people—less than the population of Athens today. There

were no roads outside the capital and when King George wished
to travel anywhere it had to be by mule along rough tracks and
bridle paths. Few villages and towns had been re-built since the
devastation caused by the nine years of war, over thirty years
ago, and the peasants lived in mud huts which they had built
among the ruins and hung with lighted ikons. Two-thirds of the
population scratched a living from the dusty soil, the rest were
mostly fishermen or seamen: a clannish, patriotic, excitable,
quarrelsome, superstitious race, proud and quick to take
offence, inquisitive and lively, immensely hospitable and with
a passion for gambling and politics. They still sang songs about
Constantine XI, the last Byzantine Emperor; and in country
districts national costume, beautifully embroidered, was almost
universal—some of them bound themselves so tightly round
the waist with silk and wool girdles that their bodies were
permanently scarred and their livers deformed. Up in the
mountains hordes of brigands and nomads roamed, living in
caves and goat-hair tents.

In Athens less than two hundred houses had been left standing after the war and those were all huddled round the base of
the Acropolis. New houses, in classical style, had been built
during the reign of King Otho and in the glare of the sunshine
shone with dazzling whiteness. At the height of summer the
city was almost impossible to live in because of the dust-storms
which whirled the light soil from the Plain of Atticas with a
choking, blinding ferocity into the eyes, throats and noses of the
inhabitants, covering everything with a thick layer of dust
which was in turn churned up by every step they took. Herds
of goats, which roamed all over the city and were a common
feature of Athenian life, did nothing to improve the situation.
The dust penetrated everywhere and into every building, including the Royal Palace.

The Palace is a large, rectangular building which was designed by a Bavarian architect in the nineteenth century. It is
vaguely classical in style with its columned portico in the front,
its row of Doric-type columns at the back and its flat roof edged
by a frieze of acanthus leaves and relieved by two central pedi-
ments. Royalty has not lived in the Palace for many years.
Now it is the Greek Parliament building; some of the rooms
are government offices and it houses a huge and splendid library.

As a home the Greek Palace had its drawbacks. It was draughty, inconvenient and uncomfortable—bitterly cold in winter, dusty and hot in summer. Wind whistled down the endless corridors, wider than most of the city's streets, and up and down the wide marble staircase. Opinions differ as to whether there were one or two bathrooms among the 365 rooms, but everyone who stayed there is convinced that cockroaches rather than water ran out of the bath taps. So the bath (or baths) was left well alone and enamelled tin tubs were usually used instead, filled laboriously by innumerable jugs of tepid water. The Palace was also plagued by numerous unpleasant smells, which were mostly the result of poor sanitation. (Athens at that time possessed no drains.) But to those who lived in it it *was* a home, a home which was loved despite all its faults.

King George at that time was very slim—a feature he retained throughout his life. He had steady blue eyes which would suddenly sparkle with merriment and an enormously long moustache waxed to the thinness of fine twine for nearly three inches at either end. He was exuberant and not even the responsibilities of his precarious sovereignty could suppress his liveliness. A British diplomat in Athens, Sir Horace Rumbold, talking about the young king after he had been monarch for nine months, said: 'King George ... although still boyish in many ways, and with a flow of animal spirits that made it sometimes difficult for us, his daily companions, to maintain the respectful reserve and gravity due to his regal station, already showed much of the simple dignity and charm of manner which ... have made his sister the Princess of Wales the beloved of all England.' Sir Horace also added that the King, like King Leopold I of Belgium, 'kept a portmanteau ready packed' and was quite prepared to leave should his subjects wish to get rid of him. In fact, someone, probably his grandfather, had been so mindful of the precariousness of his position that the three protecting powers had been induced to guarantee an annuity of £20,000 should he be forced to give up his throne. But the Greeks had no desire to depose their King and Sir Horace commented, 'His truthfulness and straightforwardness united to form considerable firmness of character and personal courage, and assured him an exceptional position with his subjects.'

King George's family had never been rich—at one time his father had an income of only £800 a year, a pittance by royal standards—nevertheless he was used to a high standard of efficiency among palace officials and servants, and he found the slap-happy carelessness in the manner and behaviour of the Greeks a torment to his fastidious nature. He had not been in the Royal Palace very long before he entirely reorganized his household and personally trained his butlers, footmen, coachmen, grooms, aides and court functionaries himself.

It must have been an intriguing sight to watch the enthusiastic young monarch teach his butler to pour wine, show his footman how to wait at table and demonstrate the correct way to open a carriage door. Not content with this he arranged the menus, selected wines for any big dinners he gave and supervised the housekeeping. He was to do this for the rest of his life, even after he married. If there were any guests at the palace it was the King and nobody else who gave all the orders in connection with their visit.

When King George was twenty-two years old, he married the Grand Duchess Olga Constantinovna, a niece of Tsar Alexander II and the daughter of the Grand Duke Constantine Nicholaevitch, third son of Tsar Nicholas I (reputedly the richest of the Russian Grand Dukes) and Princess Alexandra of Saxe-Altenburg. He had first met her when he had visited Russia in 1863 on his way to Athens; she was then twelve years old. At their marriage in October 1867 she was barely sixteen and a juvenile sixteen at that. When she went to Greece as Queen there was a trunkful of dolls amongst her luggage.

The Grand Duchess Olga and her parents lived in what was known as the Marble Palace in St Petersburg (then the Russian capital), and, like other grand-ducal mansions, it was situated on one of the banks of the wide river Neva which runs through the city now known as Leningrad. The Grand Duke Constantine's country estate at Pavlovsk was about twenty miles from the capital and less than three miles from Tsarskoe Selo—the Russian equivalent of Windsor.

The Grand Duke Constantine was reputed to have a violent nature, but his daughter Olga was a very sweet-tempered person. She had a fair complexion and serene, deep-set, light blue eyes—a contemporary account describes her as 'one of the handsomest and most charming members of the Imperial Family'. She became a bit stout as she grew older and refused to go sea bathing because she did not feel she would look becoming in a bathing costume though she was always a very handsome woman.

It was in the Winter Palace, the Tsar's residence at St Petersburg, that the Grand Duchess Olga was married to the young King of Greece. The wedding was celebrated less than a year after King George's sister Dagmar, later known as Marie Feodorovna, married the future Tsar Alexander III.

Sixteen-year-old Queen Olga made a brave entry into Greece wearing a blue and white dress—the colours of the Greek flag chosen by King Otho—but for months she was extremely miserable. Later she never tired of telling her grandchildren how she would play with her dolls for hours instead of going to some public function and would frequently be found in some corner of that vast, uncomfortable palace overcome by intense homesickness. Hers was not the temporary affliction which affects nearly everybody away from home for the first time, but a permanent sense of loss. And it was not her family she missed so much but her country. She loved Russia with a depth of feeling which never abated; however much she tried she never had the same enduring affection for Greece.

But even child brides grow up and the following year, 1868, she gave birth to a son, who was called Constantine but who became universally known as Tino. Then, spaced over twenty years, came the rest of the family: George, Alexandra, Nicholas (Princess Marina's father), Marie, Olga, Andrew and Christopher.

The Greek royal children grew up in a happy, homely atmosphere and they were all very noisy and full of fun. They stripped the sides from four-wheeled carts and raced them downhill in a modified form of what is now go-kart racing; tormented the head gardener who had been in charge of the palace gardens since the time of King Otho; battled with swords made from fleshy, spiny aloe leaves (although they had the sense to remove the thorns first); and, led by the King himself, took part in hectic roller-skating and bicycle races on the parquet floors, in and out of the marble columns of the three big ballrooms which stretched right along the length of the Royal Palace. Nor did they tire of games like hide-and-seek and leapfrog, and playing practical jokes on their relations when they came to stay.

Meanwhile, as her children were growing up, Queen Olga assumed her role as consort with dutiful thoroughness. Within a year of her marriage she had been able to speak the difficult Greek language fluently. And her public duties consisted of going to orphanages, hospitals, sanatoriums and schools; visiting the sick; arranging loans for the sponge-fishers; and helping the poor. In particular she did her utmost to raise the standard of living for Greek women at a time when their status was low and their education was completely neglected.

King George, of course, was fully occupied with the affairs of his country. Greece under King George was a democracy under a King. His powers were considerable but strictly defined—he could not act without the advice and signature of his ministers, though he could appoint and dismiss them as he wished. When he was able to, he spent much of his spare time with his family.

One suspects that the King probably missed his homeland. He had a Danish-style dairy built in the grounds of his summer house at Tatoi, near Athens, and if a Danish ship berthed at Piraeus he would go on board, invite some of the officers and cadets to the palace and be inordinately delighted whenever he was presented with fresh-baked loaves of brown rye bread which was impossible to get in Greece.

But he was discreet and not nearly so enthusiastic about his homeland as Queen Olga was about hers. For example, when a Russian ship came near Athens the Queen would go down as often as four times a week to visit it and as most of her visits were unannounced they sometimes proved a little embarrassing and there would be a frantic scurry among officers and crew to provide her with a suitable welcome, and she would often stay so long they were at a loss to know what to do to entertain her. She, too, invited the crew to the palace where she gave them Russian tea and kept them talking for hours. She felt that they were her only link with Russia.

In the palace at Athens her own rooms were hung with so many ikons that one visitor said it was rather like entering a religious sanctuary. On the top floor a guest room was converted into an Orthodox Chapel where she and her family worshipped, and she organized a choir to sing the beautiful music which is so much a part of the Russian churches. The house at Tatoi

had been specially built to please the Queen—it was an exact
replica of a Victorian-style mansion which stood in the grounds
of the Grand Duke Constantine's country estate at Pavlosk.

This uninhibited devotion to Russia sometimes offended the
Greeks. A book published in 1905 commented: 'Queen Olga is a
kind-hearted, benevolent woman, deeply religious, and interested in all good works, particularly in hospitals and the relief
of the suffering. But like many other good people she is deficient
in tact; and although she has lived so many years in Greece, she
is just as Russian as when she first set foot on Greek soil. While
respecting her deep love of her own country, her subjects think
that it goes too far.'

Most members of her family felt the same way. In an effort to
fill them with the same enthusiasm Queen Olga talked so
constantly and so admiringly about her native land that she
made them all heartily sick of it. 'She rammed Russia down
her family's throat,' said one of her relations, 'and turned them
so much against it that they all became violently pro-Greek.'
So much so that one of Queen Olga's sons—Prince Philip's
father, Prince Andrew—refused to speak any other language.
Perhaps the only one who shared a portion of his mother's
worship of Russia was her youngest son Prince Christopher,
who, unlike the others, was born at Pavlovsk. And, although
three of them eventually married Romanovs, all King George's
children behaved as if they had been Hellenic for generations—
in spite of the fact that they had not a drop of Greek blood
between them.

Queen Olga of Greece

Prince Nicholas and the Grand
Duchess Helen of Russia on their
wedding day

Η ΔΟΛΟΦΟΝΙΑ ΤΗΣ Α.Μ. ΤΟΥ ΒΑΣΙΛΕΩΣ ΤΩΝ ΕΛΛΗΝΩΝ
ΓΕΩΡΓΙΟΥ ΤΟΥ Α. ΕΝ ΘΕΣΣΑΛΟΝΙΚΗ
ΕΓΕΝΝΗΘΗ ΤΗΝ 12ʰ ΔΕΚΕΜΒΡΙΟΥ 1845. ΕΔΟΛΟΦΟΝΗΘΗ ΤΗΝ 5ʰ ΜΑΡΤΙΟΥ 1913

L'ASSASSINAT DE S.M. LE ROI DES HELLÈNES
GEORGES I, A SALONIQUE
NÉ LE 12ᵐᵉ DÉCEMBRE 1845 · ASSASSINÉ LE 5ᵐᵉ MARS 1913

eft: Prince and Princess Nicholas, Princess Elizabeth, Princess Marina and Princess Olga *Right:* Prince and Princess Andrew, Princess Margarita and Princess Theodora

Princess Nicholas, a photograph taken in Paris

The Tsarina, Alexandra
Feodorovna

The Grand Duchess
Vladimir

The Grand Duke Vladimir

2 | *Prince Nicholas*

Prince Nicholas (who was to be the father of Princess Marina) was born in January 1872, the third of the five sons of King George I of Greece, and it was said that he was lucky to be alive at all because somebody accidentally tipped Queen Olga out of her bathchair in the courtyard of the Royal Palace two weeks before his birth. He had fine features, his mother's fair complexion, and inherited the same cheerful, good humour as his father.

In his autobiography, published in 1926, he tells how, as a child, he once filled an unsuspecting Orthodox priest's high hat with walnuts before putting it on the unfortunate man's head; he broke windows by aiming apples at them, and, egged on by his cousin 'Georgie' (the future King George V of England), shot a sleeping coachman with pellets from a toy pistol. He liked eating small live crabs and records how he gave one to a servant who did not have the young Greek prince's expertise in dealing with this unusual delicacy and had his tongue nipped. 'He was furious with pain and we laughed at his discomfort, which we knew how to avoid,' said Prince Nicholas. He was equally candid about his own misadventures and describes graphically an incident when his father enlisted the help of his sons in driving a hornet out of his study where it was nesting in a chandelier. They tried to chase the insect out with a broom because the tender-hearted monarch did not want it killed. The hornet swooped downwards, and, for fear of being stung, they all ducked. 'The next thing that happened was that our father, we, the broom and the chandelier, lay on the floor in the middle of the room, one on top of the other, in undignified confusion— whilst the hornet sailed gaily out of the window,' he said.

Prince Nicholas was taught by tutors and had hoped to go to Oxford, but, as far as possible, the King of the Hellenes preferred, that his sons should complete their education in Greece. Prince Nicholas, instead of going to university, became an officer in the Greek army. At this time he grew a jauntier, smaller, more military version of his father's long, waxed whiskers and, like the Greek sovereign, retained his boisterous humour. In addition he had a devastating aptitude for wickedly accurate mimicry. He managed to mimic without giving offence to his victims; a rare gift illustrated by an incident which took place when the Greek Royal family were on one of their visits to Denmark, and King George of the Hellenes, who was riding a bicycle one day in the rose garden at Bernstorff, one of the Danish Palaces, accidentally ran over a pekinese dog which belonged to his sister, the Princess of Wales. The dog was not badly hurt but it yelped with pain and the Princess who happened to be near, and was holding a tray with a jug of milk and some biscuits on it, dropped the tray and rushed to pick up her pet, screaming at the top of her voice: 'He has killed my dog. He has killed my dog. . . .'

When the panic subsided, Prince Nicholas, an amused spectator of all this, re-enacted the whole scene for his aunt's benefit, imitating her screams and even impersonating the limp with which Princess Alexandra, who had a stiff leg, always walked. The result was so funny yet so unmalicious that even his aunt laughed.

A commentator, writing about the Greek royal family at the beginning of the century, dismisses Prince Nicholas and his abilities in a few lines, saying only that he 'is credited with literary and artistic tastes . . . has written a comedy and plays lawn tennis . . .' In fact, he had a great talent for sketching, did much serious reading and later on his passion for the theatre led him to write several plays. He also fished, golfed and sailed, was a splendid horseman, a good bridge player, an accomplished dancer and an amusing raconteur of spicy stories.

Rather surprisingly he dreaded the formality of the annual Court Ball in Athens when the King and his family circled round the ballroom talking to guests. 'My parents were so used to these functions that they thought little about them and never found themselves at a loss to find an amiable word for everybody,' he said. 'We of the younger generation, however, were self-conscious and shy, and often used to torment ourselves beforehand as to what to say to this or that person.' But it seems he managed to conceal his diffidence—a male guest at one of those far-off balls recalls that 'Prince Nicholas . . . always had something terribly important and slightly "broad" in the shape perhaps of a limerick to communicate.'

The Greek prince was also an expert shot but his father, who did not share the same sporting instincts, refused to let him shoot the stags roaming Tatoi or the red-legged partridges which nested on some of the islands. Game in Greece was not very plentiful; but he found plenty of sport elsewhere. He hunted wild boar in various German duchies; went after auroch, the now extinct European bison, with the Tsar of Russia, and shot pheasants at Sandringham with the Prince of Wales— his 'Uncle Bertie'. Prince Nicholas was particularly impressed by the excellent shooting of his cousin Georgie whom he declared to be one of the finest shots in England.

Those who knew Prince Nicholas give similar descriptions of him—as 'a butterfly of a man', and it is true that at one time he flitted gaily from pleasure to pleasure round the Courts of Europe, sipping at the tables of his innumerable royal relations. He was a great traveller whenever he got the chance; as well as annual trips to Denmark, he journeyed regularly to Russia, many times to England, and often to such places as Paris, Berlin, Munich and Vienna.

But for a time his butterfly existence came to a stop. There had been trouble in Crete—the same trouble which continues in Cyprus today, a deep and everlasting feud between Greeks and Turks living on that island. Unwisely, in 1897, Greece declared war on Turkey, with disastrous results. As the Empress Frederick of Germany (Queen Victoria's eldest daughter) said: 'Of course, what has happened was only to be expected. Here were overwhelming numbers against a small army, inexperienced, untried, imperfectly organized, and, above all, not in the hands of the Military Commander but half dependent on political men in Athens . . . to think of all this bloodshed for nothing it is quite maddening, yet all Greece wished for war.' The Military Commander was Crown Prince Constantine and the Empress, giving a remarkably accurate and concise view of the situation, did not exaggerate the sentiments of the Greek population, though it seems to have been accentuated by what have been called 'patriotic hotheads'.

An onlooker in Athens at the time describes the people as 'possessed by the wildest war mania'. All the streets in the city were decorated and Constitution Square was a mass of blue and white flags as the Evzones in their colourful uniforms—dark blue jackets, white pleated skirts and tufted shoes—marched through it on their way to the Piraeus where they were to embark for the front, 'like a gigantic blue and white serpent' across the open square and through the billowy sea of shouting and gesticulating human beings.

In Thessaly, where the fighting took place, Prince Nicholas was in the thick of it. The war lasted only a month but was so bitter that even in hospitals, where wounded Greek and Turkish troops were kept in separate wards, sentries had to be posted to prevent patients from sneaking out and continuing to battle in their bandages.

It had a particularly depressing effect on Prince Nicholas. He watched the rout of Greek troops with deep despair and said afterwards, 'Unless one has been an eyewitness, it is impossible to picture to oneself the appalling impression produced by human beings running for their lives . . . it was a terrible sight.' For the first time in his life he experienced the fear and fatigue of battle, and long, drawn-out months of discomfort, dirt, hunger and a plague of malaria-ridden mosquitoes, while peace talks went on. 'Everything seemed to have collapsed; my hopes and dreams had vanished like smoke and I felt humiliated and ashamed,' he said.

He felt too that the King and Crown Prince Constantine were unjustly blamed for the disaster, although someone said at the time that the apathetic attitude of the Greek people towards their king was the result of their exhausted state. They accepted the monarchy as a useful institution, and it took an incident which happened early the following year to change all this: an attempt on the King's life.

One afternoon in February 1898, King George went for a walk on the sands at Phaleron with his daughter Princess Marie. When he was driving back to the Palace in an open carriage, with Princess Marie by his side, he was ambushed and shot at

by a spattering of rifle bullets. According to contemporary reports one of these smashed a carriage lamp, another went
through the coachman's hat, one grazed a footman's leg, some
hit the carriage, and yet another went through a harness-ring;
but the King and the Princess were unhurt. Queen Olga kept
the battered harness-ring as a souvenir of her husband's escape.

The attempted assassination of a King who had never in his
life had a bodyguard, jolted the Greeks out of their apathy.
They were not only indignant that such a thing could have
happened, but, as Prince Nicholas declared, 'the event completely
turned the tide of popular feeling in our favour'. Messages of
sympathy and congratulation on the escape poured into the
Royal Palace and a public subscription raised enough money to
build a church on the site of the ambush. In May, when Prince
Nicholas accompanied his parents on a tour of the provinces, he
reported that they were received everywhere with scenes of
wild enthusiasm. Flower arches, decorated houses and mounted
escorts welcomed them to even the smallest village and they
were pelted with flowers and sweetmeats, though the last were
not always appreciated. And the Royal party frequently heard
the loud crackle of rifle shots; but these were only the normal
joyous firings which always marked a special celebration in
Greece.

So the peaceful times, which Prince Nicholas once thought
had ended, returned. He went off on his travels again and was
back in London that summer for another season. England was
the place where, he said later, 'I have had some of the happiest
days of my life'. He stayed with his aunt and uncle, the Prince
and Princess of Wales, in Marlborough House where, he commented, 'nothing seemed to affect my aunt's appetite and good
spirits'. The Prince of Wales was not quite so sparkling in his
own home. 'Uncle Bertie never spoke much, and would sometimes be impatient when little details were not quite as he
expected them to be,' noted Prince Nicholas. 'He had ordered
pencils and paper to be in readiness in all the rooms in case he
needed to write, and when the servants forgot—they didn't
forget his annoyance.'

But however sour he might be to his household, the heir to
the British throne put himself out to be charming to his nephew
by marriage. He laughed heartily at the younger man's jokes,

saying in his gruff, guttural voice: 'That's a good one'—which, as Prince Nicholas said, 'encouraged one to further efforts'. And the Prince of Wales sent for his own tailor to make several suits for his nephew, taking care to choose the materials himself as he was of the opinion that Greek tailoring standards did not match up to the sartorial standards of Savile Row.

He did not go so far as to pay for them. 'The bill was a stiff one, and my allowance was small,' remarked Prince Nicholas afterwards, 'but I was too proud of my new clothes to complain'; and in fact he kept the same English tailor for the rest of his life.

Prince Nicholas first visited London in 1895 when he was twenty-three. He went to galleries, museums and exhibitions, rode in hansom cabs and on the top of a bus, and was fascinated by the orators at Speaker's Corner in Hyde Park. 'I could not help picturing to myself the impression such "spouters" would have produced in Athens,' he once said. 'The whole populace would either have joined the speakers in rebellion or stoned them to death.' After that first enjoyable visit, he always liked returning to London.

If the truth be told, Prince Nicholas liked staying at Sandringham better than anywhere; not only for the shooting which he thought stupendous after the scarcity of game birds in Greece, but because he liked the atmosphere and found his fellow guests 'easy to get on with'.

At one period he was rather fond of his English cousin Princess Maud, and was annoyed when she married his kinsman Prince Charles of Denmark, who eventually became King Haakon VII of Norway.

But this setback did not perturb him for long. He also enjoyed his visits to Russia. Little did he know that in the grandest Court of all he would find happiness, and that yet another grand duchess would be stepping bravely out on to the barren soil of Greece ready to start a new life as the bride of a Greek prince.

3 | *Russian Autocracy*

Prince Nicholas was half Russian and had been brought up to think of the Tsar as the Emperor and Autocrat of all the Russians, as indeed he was—he was the absolute ruler of 180 million people and his country covered more than a million square miles of land.

To most of his people the Tsar was a deity, the 'Little Father' of his subjects. They humbled themselves before him as they did to God, falling full length flat on the ground with their faces in the earth in the ultimate act of reverence and obeisance.

Even the mild and gentle Queen Olga had all the autocratic instincts of her dynasty which had ruled Russia since the beginning of the seventeenth century. Once, when Prince Nicholas teased her by saying that people must have a say in their own government, she replied, 'I would rather be governed by a well-born lion than by four hundred rats of my own class.' And there was no reason why she should think anything different. She had been brought up to believe in the inviolability of race backed by 'wealth and power in its most absolute form' which made the Imperial Court the most opulent in the world.

The children and grandchildren of the Emperor, ranked as grand dukes and grand duchesses, had a power and importance secondary only to the Tsar, and they were responsible only to him. They were immune from any form of arrest, invariably good-looking and immensely wealthy.

All of them had vast private fortunes involving huge estates and rich mines yielding ore, oil and precious stones. In addition they each received an annual income of 280,000 roubles (equivalent to more than £200,000 today) from the day they were born. This came from the Apanages, a fund set up for the

TABLE II

THE RUSSIAN IMPERIAL FAMILY

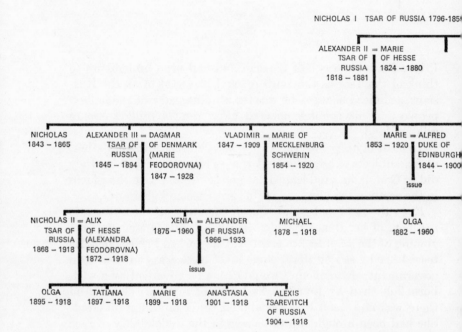

NICHOLAS I   TSAR OF RUSSIA 1796-185█

ALEXANDER II = MARIE
TSAR OF   OF HESSE
RUSSIA   1824 – 1880
1818 – 1881

NICHOLAS   ALEXANDER III = DAGMAR   VLADIMIR = MARIE OF   MARIE = ALFRED
1843 – 1865   TSAR OF   OF DENMARK   1847 – 1909   MECKLENBURG   1853 – 1920   DUKE OF
RUSSIA   (MARIE   SCHWERIN   EDINBURGH
1845 – 1894   FEODOROVNA)   1854 – 1920   1844 – 1900█
1847 – 1928
issue

NICHOLAS II = ALIX   XENIA = ALEXANDER   MICHAEL   OLGA
TSAR OF   OF HESSE   1875 – 1960   OF RUSSIA   1878 – 1918   1882 – 1960
RUSSIA   (ALEXANDRA   1866 – 1933
1868 – 1918   FEODOROVNA)
1872 – 1918
issue

OLGA   TATIANA   MARIE   ANASTASIA   ALEXIS
1895 – 1918   1897 – 1918   1899 – 1918   1901 – 1918   TSAREVITCH
OF RUSSIA
1904 – 1918

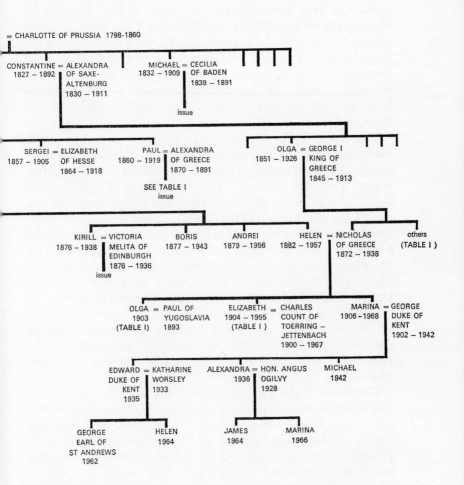

c

purpose by Emperor Paul I. It had a reserve of 60 million roubles and an estate which consisted of several million acres, said to be the greatest domain in Russia.

And, in the late nineteenth century, the grandest of them all by far was Princess Marina's maternal grandfather, the Grand Duke Vladimir Alexandrovitch, son of Tsar Alexander II, brother of Tsar Alexander III, and uncle of Tsar Nicholas II. He was the senior of the grand dukes and the most powerful man in Russia after the Tsar himself. He was Commander of the Imperial Guard as well as Commander of the St Petersburg Garrison—a job which was considerably more important than it sounds because its domain included such a vast stretch of territory that he was, in fact, Commander-in-Chief of the Russian Army.

The Grand Duke Vladimir was an impressive figure, tall, exceedingly good-looking and possessing a neatly-trimmed short beard and mutton-chop whiskers. He looked exactly like his father, Tsar Alexander II, the most liberal of the Russian Tsars, who freed the peasants from their feudal servitude and was on the eve of signing a document granting Russia a constitution for the first time in her history when he was blown up by a bomb in 1881. They both had the same elegant, aquiline profile which was to pass right down through three generations and be perfectly reproduced in the lovely features of the Grand Duke's great granddaughter, Princess Alexandra of Kent.

The Grand Duke Vladimir was the third of seven children— six of them boys. The oldest was the Tsarevitch, Nicholas Alexandrovitch, who died before he could be married to the Danish Princess Dagmar, and the second son was Alexander who became Tsar Alexander III.

The Grand Duke Vladimir possessed a loud, booming voice, which must have been the envy of any regimental sergeant-major who heard it and which nobody ever forgot. His shouts of 'Bravo' to ballerinas dancing at the Marinsky Theatre in St Petersburg drowned any others in the audience; what was meant to be a confidential whisper at a reception would go zooming round the room with embarrassing clarity.

He has been described as abrupt, rough, a strict disciplinarian and intimidating—even his children said that he was apt to frighten those who came into contact with him for the first time—but most of this was just an act. As Prince Nicholas said, 'when one knew him better one soon realized what a gentleman he was, how kind and generous . . .', and in private he was a good-humoured, jolly man with a temper which subsided as quickly as it came.

The joys of jousting, tests of strength and playful rompings of Danish Court life did not appeal to the Grand Duke Vladimir. He sought his pleasures in theatres, art galleries, museums, entertaining and the company of pretty women. He enjoyed shooting too, and, as proof of his prowess, there was an enormous stuffed bear at the top of a marble staircase in his palace at St Petersburg.

He was also one of a breed who make today's noted playboys of the western world look like pale, anaemic moths. The Russian grand dukes not only lived it up, they did it in style and in a way which has never been repeated. It was they who discovered and opened up the Riviera to which they fled when St Petersburg was cold and grey, and they rediscovered the beauties of Venice, taking over whole floors of the only hotel which had plumbing and electricity and filling it with a huge entourage and a regiment of servants. They had their laundry done in London and Paris; in mid-winter their flowers came from the South of France. They lived with a gusto and enjoyment which only a combination of immense wealth and lively minds can produce. They were great patrons of art in all its forms, and filled their houses with treasures from all over Europe.

The Grand Duke Vladimir was President of the Imperial Fine Arts Academy and knew more than most about painting and other forms of art; he was a gourmet (his wine cellar and table was reputedly the best in St Petersburg) and he was probably the finest historian in Russia if not the whole of Europe. His knowledge of history was due in part to his phenomenal memory for facts and dates. It should also be mentioned that he had the reputation of being an anglophobe, and his dislike of the English was possibly the result of the disagreements over protocol between Queen Victoria and his only sister Marie, the Duchess of Edinburgh, who was also, incidentally, his wife's closest friend.

The Grand Duke married a German Princess (the daughter of Grand Duke Frederick Franz II of Mecklenburg–Schwerin by his first marriage to Princess Augusta of Reuss), who was christened Maria. When she became the Russian Grand Duke's wife she took the name of Marie Pavlovna, and she was given the family nickname of 'Miechen'.

The Mecklenburg family (there were two branches with their respective capitals at Schwerin and Strelitz) was very much in demand for royal marriages. They could trace their descent back to the tenth century and earlier to a Slavonic tribe known as the Wends. The Grand Duchess's half-brother, for example, was Prince Henry of the Netherlands, who married Queen Wilhelmina of the Netherlands and was the father of Queen Juliana: her niece, Alexandrine, became Queen of Denmark.

The German courts were known as the 'marriage bed' or 'breeding-ground' of Europe and even 'the German Stud Farm'. There were two reasons why important royal houses used members of these ruling states for mating purposes. In the first place, they were usually of impeccable birth and breeding and anyone rash enough to take part in a morganatic marriage was normally disinherited, if not disowned. (So important was it that, as Mr James Pope Hennessey records in his biography of Queen Mary, there were those who tut-tutted as they looked at her and spoke of 'Poor May and her tainted Württemberg blood' because one of her Teck ancestors had married a mere Countess. The Battenbergs, who also stemmed from a morganatic marriage, were similarly suspect.) And in the second place, they were all Lutherans. Although the simple Protestant service was very different from the elaborate Russian Orthodox ritual, the basic dogma, in particular the Holy Communion, had a certain similarity. In the normal way the Germans had no difficulty in changing their religion. French, Spanish and Italian princesses were never chosen to be Romanov brides because, as Roman Catholics, they were forbidden to embrace another faith. Even in the more relaxed atmosphere of today, Roman Catholics and members of the Greek or Russian Orthodox Faith cannot celebrate Communion together.

The Grand Duchess Marie Pavlovna was one of the rare few who did not embrace the Russian Orthodox faith when she married. She was an unsophisticated young girl and had been strictly brought up in the secluded, restricted and rather stuffy atmosphere of the small North German Duchy when she fell in love with the handsome Grand Duke, and in 1872 when she was eighteen and he was twenty-three they became engaged. But it was only then that she realized that she would be expected to change her faith and to everybody's surprise and consternation, she flatly refused to do this.

For two miserable years she resisted pressure from her father, her irritated future father-in-law Tsar Alexander II, and her fiancé, when they tried to make her change her mind. In the end it was the Tsar who cracked; he was still annoyed by her obstinacy but he recognized the courage with which she clung to her convictions in spite of her intense love for his son and the obvious merits of such a match.

Some say that he relented because he thought that such a strong-minded girl would make an excellent wife for the rather flirtatious Grand Duke. And as the third son neither the Grand Duke Vladimir nor his descendants were likely to succeed to the Russian throne. If this had been so, such leniency would have been impossible for a Tsar had to be born of parents who were of the Orthodox faith.

They were married in August 1874, and the marriage transformed the girl who had once been unsophisticated and shy. Through the years the Grand Duchess Vladimir turned into an elegant, wordly and witty woman and a noted hostess.

The Grand Duchess had four sons and one daughter. The eldest son died in childhood; the other sons were called Kirill, Boris and Andrei. The youngest child and the apple of her father's eye, was the pretty brown-eyed, dark-haired daughter Helen.

Everyone who knew the Grand Duchess Helen when she was young says that she was outstandingly beautiful. In the Russian court, which was crammed with lovely women, she was known as 'la belle Hélène' after the heroine of Offenbach's opera based on the life of Helen of Troy. Prince Felix Youssupov, who was in love with her for a long time, said that her beauty fascinated him. 'She had the loveliest eyes imaginable,' he said. 'Everyone fell under their charm.' She also had a passionate and tempestuous nature. 'A princess,' it was said more than once, 'in need of love.'

As a child, since she was the smallest in the family and the only girl, she had rather a tough time with her three brothers, but whether they rode ponies, skated, tobogganed, or played tennis she did her best to keep up with them. After seeing a performance of *Othello* they nearly smothered her to death with pillows; and when the four of them were once sent for a treatment of mud baths in Finland to recover from some skin ailment, they tied a rope around her and hoisted her to the top of a flag pole.

They all travelled abroad a good deal and when they were in Russia shuttled between the Vladimir Palace in St Petersburg and the Grand Duke's summer house at Tsarskoe Selo. They also went to the Imperial palaces at Peterhoff and Gatchina where they stayed with the Tsar Alexander III whom, like Prince Nicholas, they knew as 'Uncle Sasha', and their 'Aunt Minnie' (Princess Dagmar), the Empress Marie Feodorovna.

In 1894, when the Grand Duchess Helen was twelve years old, Tsar Alexander III died and his eldest son became Tsar Nicholas II. In the same year the fateful union between the Tsar and Queen Victoria's granddaughter Princess Alix of Hesse, afterwards known as Alexandra Feodorovna, also took place. Prince Nicholas was in Russia then and again he met the Grand Duchess Helen.

Four years later, the Grand Duchess Helen became engaged to Prince Max of Baden. But it was a short-lived engagement for Prince Max broke it off a few months later. The Grand Duchess Helen was sixteen at the time and was, naturally, very upset to be treated in such a fashion. However, at sixteen, hearts mend easily, and for the next few years she had a very gay time.

In 1902 the Grand Duchess Helen was twenty, and she had grown into a strikingly good-looking young woman. She had huge black eyes and a mass of dark curly hair, and she radiated vivacity and love of life, so much so that somebody once described her as a 'burning beauty'. It was at this time that Prince Nicholas reappeared in her life, although they had often met each other in those intervening years.

Prince Nicholas and the Grand Duchess Helen became engaged on 13 June 1902, and two months later, on 29 August at 4.30 p.m. in the afternoon on a pleasant, sunny day, they were married in the church attached to the Great Chatherine Palace at Tsarskoe Selo.

Russian Imperial weddings were always magnificently spectacular and the correspondent of the *New York Herald*, who watched the procession of gorgeous bridal carriages leaving the Grand Duke Vladimir's house described it ecstatically as 'like a line of living gold' as it made its way up the avenue leading to the Palace. And the report went on to say that, 'after reaching the main entrance, the Emperor and Empress, members of the Imperial family, the King and Queen of the Hellenes, the grand dukes, grand duchesses, princes and princesses entered the palace. Once inside, the Grand Duchess Helen was escorted by members of the family to private apartments where, in keeping with historical tradition in the case of a grand duchess, a crown sparkling with great diamonds was placed upon her head . . .'

Strict custom in fact governed all the Imperial weddings. They were by tradition all similar to the wedding day of Catherine the Great. So the bridal dress and train, hair style, jewels, some of the wedding presents—and even the nightclothes worn by the newly-married couple on their wedding night—always followed the same set pattern.

The Grand Duchess Helen, like her predecessors of the last one hundred and fifty years, wore false ringlets and a shining, shimmering, silver dress trimmed with huge solitaire diamond buttons. Then she was ritually and formally arrayed in a red velvet mantle with a forty-yard train edged with ermine, and a mass of glittering jewellery—including diamond ear-rings, bracelets, necklace and ornate bride's crown, all bequeathed for the purpose by the Empress Catherine II. She looked 'wondrously lovely' but it was all so heavy that it was almost impossible for her to walk.

When the celebrations were over, Prince Nicholas and his bride went away for nearly three months' honeymoon. It began at one of the Imperial Estates, about forty miles from St Petersburg. And later he took his wife to Denmark, a visit which was not quite the success he had hoped; even the Grand Duchess Helen, now known as Princess Nicholas, found it rather provincial and boring after the gaiety of St Petersburg, and did not get on all that well with her husband's Danish relations.

Yet one thing is certain, during the first few months they were together the two people found in each other the qualities they needed. The charm of Prince Nicholas, his kindness, his gaiety and his understanding, completely captured the affection of his bride.

After their stay in Denmark, Prince and Princess Nicholas returned briefly to Russia before leaving for Greece. At their departure, Prince Nicholas stood nervously surveying the crowd of relatives and friends standing on the platform at St Petersburg railway station to wave goodbye. His trepidation was understandable. It was only then that it dawned on him for the first time exactly what he was letting his new wife in for; he realized that he was taking her away from a life of luxury and ostentation at the most splendid court in Europe to Athens which, at its best, was crude and primitive by comparison.

True, they had been promised a new house in Athens as a wedding present from the Tsar, but until that was built the only home he could provide was an apartment in the dusty, draughty Royal Palace of Greece.

What would the Grand Duke Vladimir's daughter think of unfashionable Athens? It had no society to speak of, and a remarkable lack of any form of culture other than that which had existed two thousand years before. To the end of his life Prince Nicholas never forgot his feelings as he watched that sophisticated and fashionable gathering on the railway station. 'How conscience-stricken I felt, taking my wife away from her old home,' he said, 'life was so simple with us at Athens, where luxury was unknown and comforts often missing. . . .'

His fears were not helped by the last part of their journey across the Black Sea and through the Dardanelles in the Greek royal yacht. It was a trip which was always unpredictable and the Black Sea is notorious for the violence of its sudden storms; but this one was the worst he had ever experienced. 'The sea was indescribable, the cold terrible and nothing could warm us,' he said, and it was a frail and pea-green couple who landed at Piraeus to be greeted by King George, Queen Olga, and the rest of the Royal Family in full dress for the occasion, with the Mayor of Athens, resplendent in his uniform, ready with a huge bouquet of white roses to welcome the new bride.

There was delighted applause from the crowd waiting on the beflagged quay when she appeared on the deck of the yacht. With the unerring instinct for wearing the right clothes on the right occasion, which she had inherited from her mother, Prin-

cess Nicholas, like her mother-in-law, made her first appearance
in Greece dressed from head to foot in the national colours of
blue and white.

Nor need Prince Nicholas have worried about her feelings.
She loved Athens and Athens loved her. In later years when he
thought about what might have been her reaction to the discomforts of her new home, he said 'fortunately there are charac-
ters fine and unselfish enough to understand that if you balance
all these things against love, love outweighs them all'. But
Princess Nicholas also loved the warmth and sunshine of
Greece, its clear, pure air, its strange beauty, the illusion that
one could almost touch the Parthenon from the top floor of the
Palace, the mass of violets, oleanders and wild cyclamen in the
Palace Gardens, and the noise of owls hooting there at night.
But most of all she liked the people—a feeling heartily reci-
procated by a nation which has always appreciated the sight of
a lovely woman and has no inhibitions about showing it. Within
weeks of her arrival she was being as much admired and spoilt
as she had ever been in her old home. And her glowing beauty
developed a new radiance for she was already expecting her first
child.

4 | *Birth of Princess Marina*

The first of Prince and Princess Nicholas's three children, Princess Olga, was born on 11 June 1903 at Tatoi. She had blonde hair and blue eyes, which later changed to grey. Her entire layette was bought in Paris by her maternal grandmother, for the Grand Duchess Vladimir believed in starting her granddaughters off in the way she intended they would go on. She did the same for Princess Elizabeth and of course for Princess Marina.

The following year Princess Elizabeth was born at Tatoi, on 24 May, she was as dark as her sister was fair and had such a mass of thick, curly, brown hair that she was given the pet name of 'Woolly', which she kept all her life.

The two princesses had an English nanny to look after them—a Norland-trained nurse called Kate Fox. This was the era when the English nanny was as invincible as the British Raj, and Norland girls could be found in the nurseries of the majority of the European royal houses. Miss Fox was to remain in the service of Prince Nicholas and his family for over half a century.

At the end of 1905 the family moved into the house which the Tsar had promised as a wedding gift. It was known as the Nicholas Palace and caused a great stir in Athens at the time because it was easily the most confortable, elegant and modern building in the city, with hot and cold running water, several bathrooms, central heating, and furnished 'more like a museum than a private house'. Perhaps one of the most striking items of furniture was an antique Russian settle of elaborately-carved black wood, with red velvet cushions, which stood in the hall at the top of a flight of marble steps. Indeed the whole house was filled with beautiful things. The grounds were not extensive but contained—and still do—a fountain, a rockery and bushes of

pink and white oleander. It was built on what is now the broad
Avenue Queen Sophie at the side of the Royal Palace. The first-
floor drawing-room had a balcony which overlooked the Royal
Gardens where Prince Nicholas's children were pushed in a
pram, walked through to visit their grandparents, or played with
some selected companions.

Princess Nicholas ran the household; a situation which suited
her husband as he was busy with his regimental duties. But
he took a very active part in the furnishings and the general
arrangement of the house and put into operation some personal
quirks and fancies—such as insisting that the male servants
cut off their fine, flowing moustaches and had a more sophisticated, clean-shaven appearance—an unpopular order which he
confessed afterwards nearly caused a mutiny.

Both Prince and Princess Nicholas were frequently in and out
of the nurseries, bathing their children, playing with them and
taking more trouble than was usual among, for example, the
British aristocracy, who were normally content with a brief
glimpse of well-scrubbed children at tea-time. But this was not
the way of Greek Royalty brought up in the traditions of
the Danish Royal Palace. In Athens as in Denmark there
were constant family get-togethers. On Sundays everybody went
to the Royal Palace, on Tuesdays they gathered at the Nicholas
Palace, and there were numerous other visits, as well as plenty
of trips abroad when Prince and Princess Nicholas took their
children with them.

On 13 December 1906, Princess Marina, Prince Nicholas's
youngest and last daughter, was born. Her birth must have
seemed a mixed blessing at the time as Princess Nicholas was so
ill afterwards that there was a strong possibility that she might
not recover. 'I lived through months of terrible anguish,'
Prince Nicholas recalled, and referring to his youngest child,
said 'she was a very dear baby. She nearly cost her mother her
life.' The anguish was made more acute by the recollection of
what had happened to his sister Alexandra, who died while
giving birth to a son named Dmitri. Since her death the Greek
Royal family always treated childbirth with more than usual
consideration and care.

Because she had a bad cold, Miss Fox was not in attendance
when Princess Marina was born and her sister Jessie, also a

Norland nurse and specially brought over for the occasion as
second nurse, took charge, while Kate Fox waited outside with
Princess Olga and Princess Elizabeth until the baby was born.
There was also an added complication: the new baby's left foot
was slightly twisted to one side. Five years later Princess Marina
had an operation to put it straight—an operation which was
simpler than it might have been due to the fact that during
those years Miss Fox had massaged the baby's foot twice a
day. Afterwards the Princess's left leg was always just a little
bit thinner, shorter and weaker than the other leg and it was
always necessary for her to wear different-sized shoes. And
Princess Nicholas was so ill that for two years she had to go
away for long periods of treatment at a health spa and it was
months before she could take up any of her public duties again.

One of her first brief appearances was at Princess Marina's
christening in January, an affair of pomp and ceremony even in
Greece. It took place in the church inside the Royal Palace
and the baby was taken there by coach flanked by outriders and
escorted by Evzones all in full-dress uniforms. At the ceremony
itself Princess Marina was carried by an elderly Greek Mistress of the Robes, who had performed the same service for her
sisters, her father and all her uncles and aunts.

All Princess Marina's godparents were relations; and so
carefully selected that the choice was guaranteed to please and
include every branch of the huge family circle into which she
had been born. Among the godfathers she had her grandfather,
King George of the Hellenes; her great uncle King Edward VII
and two of her uncles—Prince Andrew of Greece (later to be
Prince Philip's father) and the Grand Duke Boris Vladimirovitch, her mother's favourite brother.

One of her godmothers was the former Princess Victoria
Melita of Edinburgh, once married to the Tsarina's brother,
Grand Duke Ernst of Hesse. After a divorce—an unusual event
in those days—she had married Princess Marina's uncle, Grand
Duke Kirill. Another godmother was Princess Mary of Teck,
then the Princess of Wales, later to be Queen Mary. As a
christening gift she presented her god-daughter with a silver
mug and porringer.

The three princesses had an almost identical upbringing. As
was customary they were suckled by peasant foster mothers

before being weaned on to cow's milk provided by the Tatoi farm. In addition Miss Fox dosed them with camomile tea. She sponged the three children with cold sea water, made them do physical exercises, and, when they were a little older, tied them all to a tree trunk by a long cord and let them play almost naked in the sun. The last was a practice which horrified their doting grandparents, King George and Queen Olga. 'My poor father was in despair and predicted that their complexions would be ruined for ever when he saw these children become as brown as berries,' said Prince Nicholas, 'but English hygiene proved satisfactory.' And he approved too of the English nurse's disciplinary methods. She was a great believer in the maxim 'spare the rod and spoil the child' and the misdemeanours of Princess Marina and her sisters were frequently corrected with a slap. Prince Nicholas himself sometimes dealt out punishment, using a rolled-up copy of *The Times* which, he asserted, was 'admirably suited to make them feel, yet not hurt'. He used it, he said, over and over again, particularly on Princess Marina 'as she was so naughty'.

Not that Nurse Fox was entirely happy with everything she did for her charges. She would have much preferred to bring them up in what she considered to be a more civilized country. 'I often wish we were in England or that the cooking was done in English fashion,' she moaned. 'It is impossible even when there are many cooks to get just what one wants for the babies; the style of cooking and the times of meals are so at variance with English ideas. . . .' In fact, Prince Nicholas's family, following the custom of King George, had lunch at eleven o'clock in the morning and dinner at three o'clock in the afternoon, a custom which was certainly unusual, and Miss Fox was not the only one who complained.

In spite of the Greek Royal family's modest way of living, any of the children's outings were conducted with some ceremony. A toot on the bugle and a smart 'present arms' was performed by the picturesque Evzone sentries on guard outside all the royal residences, and this took place whether it was the King who emerged or one of Prince Nicholas's three daughters pushed in a perambulator by Miss Fox.

As soon as they were old enough they were taught to acknowledge the salutations they received whether they came from palace sentries or people waving from the pavement. It was training which they did not always appreciate and sometimes tried to avoid. One of them—there is a difference of opinion as to whether it was Princess Marina or her sister Elizabeth—made a doll do the bowing for her for quite a time before she was stopped. Often they accompanied their parents on drives to historical monuments or to Tatoi to visit their grandparents. Even when they were very young Prince Nicholas, who had gained a great deal of his own knowledge from Walter Schliemann, the celebrated German archaeologist of some repute, told them the history of the many ancient ruins scattered around Athens and continued to do so throughout their childhood and adolescence.

Most afternoons they went out in an open carriage and were driven with as much style as any senior member of the family; a coachman in front, with a footman beside dressed in the blue and white livery designed by their grandfather. Sometimes they jogged along the six miles of rough road to play on the wide sands of Phaleron, then still only a village. And often they called on their numerous cousins, particularly the two nearest their age—Prince Andrew's daughters Theodora and Margarita, who were not only close relations but their dearest friends and still lived in an apartment in the Royal Palace so it was just a question of crossing the road to go and see them.

One would have thought that Princess Andrew, the former Princess Alice of Battenberg and later of course the mother of Prince Philip, would have had a lot in common with Princess Nicholas. They were both much the same age, had married within less than a year of each other, were far from home, had each had the struggle of learning a new and complicated language and also had children—all girls at that time—of roughly similar ages. But in fact none of King George's daughters-in-law ever really got along well together and Princess Nicholas and Princess Andrew were no exception. Their characters and interests were worlds apart and as much in contrast as their looks; one brunette, one blonde—and both beautiful. Princess Nicholas was sophisticated and worldly with a forceful, lively personality, and, as Queen Olga cared little for entertaining, it was Prince and Princess Nicholas—in the elegant first-floor salon of their house—who provided the focal point for society in the Greek capital.

Very much in the style of the Grand Duchess Vladimir, Princess Nicholas held court in her drawing-room and was hostess to any persons of notability who visited Athens, whether royalty, politicians, artists, historians, singers, or actors. And she ran any charities or organizations in which she was interested with the same superb efficiency as her mother.

Princess Andrew was shy, retiring, self-effacing, and not nearly so good at coping with her charities and official duties— she often gave up in despair when some complicated arrangement became too much for her. She had an additional handicap which, if she had let it, could have been an insuperable barrier. For she was very deaf indeed. Back in 1891 the Empress Frederick wrote about her: 'One can hardly take one's eyes off little Alice's face, it is so interesting and picturesque. If she remains so, she will be one of the prettiest girls in Europe.' But five years later, when the English princess was eleven years old, the Empress, speaking of a visit by 'Victoria Battenberg here with her three children' (the other two were later Earl Mountbatten and Queen Louise of Sweden) commented, 'Alice is so handsome and one cannot really call her deaf, she is only not very quick at hearing, that is all. . . .'

The deafness increased—a tragic handicap in such a lovely young girl but one which Princess Andrew virtually overcame through determination and concentration. She became so adept at lip-reading that she could eventually speak and understand English, German, French and Greek. It is a tribute to her skill that if any of her Greek or Russian relations were carrying on an indiscreet conversation, which Princess Andrew could easily follow from the other side of a crowded room, they would automatically cover their mouths. And when the cinema became popular she would amuse friends by describing what silent screen actors were really saying, often in direct contradiction to the sub-titles.

But the rivalry between mothers did not disturb Princess Marina and her sisters and under the benign and tactful supervision of King George and Queen Olga, no rift was at all apparent. The children of the two families were bosom friends, their fathers were devoted to each other and they were all of them often photographed together with every appearance of mutual amity.

Apart from playing with their relations and friends, Princess Marina and her sisters were on the whole a self-sufficient unit, adoring each other and their parents with an equal enthusiasm which was never to waver. Because there was less than a year between their ages, the two older girls were more like twins and did everything together. The fact that Princess Marina, inevitably known as 'Baby', was several years younger than her sisters though the difference was negligible when they were grown up, meant that as a child she spent most of her time trying to catch up with her elders. However much Miss Fox bossed and bullied the other two—at times she was downright unfair to Princess Olga—she was always a good deal less officious with her youngest 'charge' and it says much for the eldest sister's temperament that the disparity of her treatment never caused her to be jealous of her young sister nor lessened the care with which in years to come she treated her former mentor. And to be truthful it is doubtful whether the brusqueness of Miss Fox's manner meant that she cared any the less for any of them.

All three princesses were remarkably good-looking, a fact which ensured them a great deal of attention from the time they were very young. 'My three beauties,' Miss Fox called them in public; though it did not stop her complaining occasionally, in private, that Princess Marina at three was 'too fat to please me' and to add, 'She is on the whole a very good baby, but likes her own way and does not hesitate to scream hoping to get it.'

It was a trait that did not always suit Prince Nicholas. 'Why does she always cry when she comes to see me?' he once complained after he had been vainly waving his handkerchief in his daughter's face to stop some lusty yelling. 'I think she does not see enough of Your Highness,' was the tart answer from the doughty Norland nurse, which was a little unfair, for as has been said, he saw a great deal more of his children than most upper-class parents of the time. He played with them almost daily, bounced them on his knee, threw them, carried them on his back and spent hours drawing pictures for their amusement.

The princesses grew up to become extremely devout. Their religious instruction started early and was given to them by one of Queen Olga's ladies-in-waiting; and personally supervised by the Queen herself. They could have had no better mentor.

Queen Olga not only knew the New Testament 'from end to end', as Prince Nicholas said, but she tried to mould her whole life and actions on the teaching of Christ. At one time, when she first went to Greece, Queen Olga sponsored an attempt to have the language of the Bible translated into simple Greek which anyone could understand. There was political intervention and the project was dropped, but where her own family was concerned there was nobody to interfere. She was very particular that prayers were said according to strict orthodox rule and that the whole family should attend services held in her private chapel in the palace.

During Holy Week and Easter—a religious festival which in the Orthodox Church has much more significance than Christmas—they attended two services each day; one in public in the newly-built Athens Cathedral, and the other in Queen Olga's chapel. Only the King would sometimes be missing. Unknown to most of his people he had his own Protestant chapel in the Royal Palace and although he attended the Orthodox services in his official capacity, basically he never changed his faith.

Athens can be extremely hot at the height of summer and cold in winter, and Prince and Princess Nicholas and their daughters spent a lot of their time away from Greece, and for months on end they would be in England, France, Germany or Russia.

Princess Marina's first recorded journey to Britain was in the summer of 1910 shortly after the death of her godfather, King Edward VII, when she was nearly four years old.

The visits followed a fairly routine pattern. For Prince and Princess Nicholas it meant a stay in Buckingham Palace or Windsor, the inevitable shooting parties at Sandringham, and visits to various country estates belonging to those friends the Prince had first met as a very young man.

For their three daughters the initial visit to Buckingham Palace would be followed by three or four months at resorts on the South coast always accompanied by Miss Fox. Sometimes they stayed at some flats run by the Norland Institute at Bognor and on other occasions they went to Westgate-on-Sea near Margate.

Like all the other children they played on the sand, searched

D

for shells and shrimps, rode on donkeys, listened to banjo players—prototypes of the black-and-white minstrels—and happily ate an enormous amount of ice-cream, chocolate and pink sticks of lettered rock. It was a pleasant, uneventful existence, with much more freedom than was possible in Greece; and broken up only by trips to London, visits from their parents and less welcome incidents, such as the time when Princess Olga accidentally hit her sister Marina on the head with an iron spade and, as usual, bore the brunt of Miss Fox's wrath and was banished to bed.

There were also trips to London, and short stays in Buckingham Palace, chiefly notable for the pampering the three young princesses received from their relations, especially from the spinster Princess Victoria, Queen Alexandra's eldest daughter. Princess Marina's godmother, no longer the Princess of Wales but Queen Mary, seems to have paid a great deal more attention to them than she ever did to any of her own children.

Queen Mary read them stories about British history and had something of the Grand Duke Vladimir's encyclopaedic knowledge of dates. She also had a wide knowledge of the tangled kinships of European royalty. Her interest was so great that she would frequently annotate books of memoirs and biographies in her library, adding bits of information which she thought should have been included. She probably hoped, even then, that one of the three Greek princesses might be chosen in the future as a bride for one of her sons.

'Last Friday we motored with my princesses to Buckingham Palace,' wrote Miss Fox to her father during one holiday at Westgate. 'We went straight in by the Privy Purse door . . . and went upstairs in the lift. Then we were ushered into the dining-room where there was a family lunch.' King George V, Queen Mary and Queen Alexandra were there and, as she noted, either 'talked a good deal' or 'spoke to me very kindly' and a rather self-conscious Miss Fox commented, 'I had to dress my babies with all the royalties looking on . . .'

But her attitude towards the monarchy was not quite as humble as might appear. Once, when all of them were staying in London, Queen Alexandra was alarmed when she first went to visit her great nieces at bedtime and found that Princess Marina slept alone without a nursemaid in attendance.

But she got no concessions from their nurse. 'Your Majesty, baby is used to it. She sleeps better by herself,' said Miss Fox firmly, and with that the Dowager Queen had to be content. Knowing that her methods were backed by the Norland Institute, approved wholeheartedly by Prince and Princess Nicholas, and accepted by her charges, Miss Fox developed an almost autocratic arrogance towards anyone who attempted to interfere with her dominance of the nursery. It was only in Russia, where they knew a lot more about autocracy than she did, that she finally met her match in the person of the children's grandmother, the Grand Duchess Vladimir.

Princess Marina and her two sisters went to Russia once and sometimes twice a year. It took them a week to get there from Greece and generally they travelled by boat to the Crimea and finished their journey in the luxurious imperial train which had considerably more comfort than their Greek grandfather's palace.

The first time Princess Marina went to Russia it was winter and they all stayed at the Vladimir Palace in St Petersburg. Like the Marble Palace it was built on the quay of the wide and impressive River Neva, and separated from the Tsar's Winter Palace by one other building and the Hermitage museum which was also used for theatrical productions and parties. A bronze, imperial, double-headed eagle was above the entrance of the imposing brown-stone exterior of the Vladimir Palace built at the time of the Grand Duke Vladimir's marriage, and in Florentine style, with graceful arched windows. Inside, the rooms were filled with antique furniture from France and Italy, the walls were encrusted with gold and hung with Gobelin tapestries, and from the ceilings massive chandeliers were suspended.

On the top floor Princess Marina and her sisters took over the nursery suite which had once been occupied by their mother and their Russian uncles. It overlooked the Neva, which in winter was either covered with thick ice or had great ice floes on the surface, and opposite their windows was Krestovsky Island where they could see the great gloomy fortress and tall spire of the Cathedral of Saint Peter and Saint Paul in which their great grandfather Tsar Alexander II lay buried.

'Everything is exquisite,' Miss Fox wrote home. 'My nurseries consist of eight beautifully furnished rooms; dining-room, two saloon ante-rooms, night nursery, dressing-room, bathroom and so on. . . . There must be a regular army of servants here; it is a huge place. The King's palace in Athens is supposed to be big, but it is nothing like this. We are such a distance from the Grand Duchess's rooms that when I take the children along to their mother I have to wait for them. It is too far to go again to fetch them. . . .' Like all the other Imperial residences it was beautifully heated in winter. The double- and triple-glazed windows were kept firmly closed and the warm air was scented with fresh flowers, the pungent perfume of incense and the all-pervading delicious aroma of Russian leather. On the first night the princesses were there, Miss Fox precipitated some trouble when, in defiance of the bitter weather and true to 'English hygiene', she unfastened all the carefully-sealed windows in their bedrooms and left them open. The Grand Duchess Vladimir's comments on the blast of freezing cold air through the carefully stoked tropical temperature of her beautiful palace were apparently devastating; and she personally went to the nursery and shut the windows herself.

It says much for Miss Fox's obstinacy that before very long they were open again, but she would have been much wiser to have left them shut; it was an act of defiance which did nothing to endear her to the stately Russian Grand Duchess who was not accustomed to having her orders disobeyed and had already had more than enough of 'English stiffness' from the Tsarina, with whom she did not get on at all well. But perhaps more than anything else the Grand Duchess was appalled and angered by the spankings the three princesses received. 'That dreadful woman knocks them about,' she complained to her friends.

Both the Grand Duke and the Grand Duchess loved their three small grand-daughters. The Grand Duke always frightened them a bit at first because of his loud voice, but the children soon became used to this for he was very gentle with them. Once, on one of those early visits to St Petersburg Princess Marina disgraced herself by howling when she was being shown off to some guests and was sent into the next room to cry on her own. The crying stopped so abruptly that Princess Nicholas went in to see what had happened only to find her father cuddling his grand-daughter on his knee. And the Grand Duchess fussed over them and petted them and played games like lotto and did jigsaws with them. She often handed out 'surprises' from a special cupboard which she kept stocked with small gifts, and showered them with other presents such as dresses, dolls, prams, bicycles, a pony and carriage and jewellery suitable for their ages, such as silver muff-chains, watches, strings of pearls and diamond and turquoise pendants.

Princess Marina and her sisters also loved looking at their grandmother's own jewellery—a fantastic glittering array of gems which, like the Tsarina and the other grand duchesses, she kept arranged in glass cases in her dressing-room, rather like a jeweller's display. Even the American-born Duchess of Marlborough—mother of the 10th Duke and a Vanderbilt—was impressed when she saw them once when she visited what she called that 'majestic personality' the Grand Duchess. 'There were endless parures of diamonds, emeralds, rubies and pearls,' she said afterwards, 'to say nothing of semi-precious stones such as turquoises, tourmalines, cat's eyes and aquamarines.' But of all her jewels those in which the Grand Duchess Vladimir was pictured most frequently and apparently wore more than any others, were a long waist-length necklace of pearls and diamonds and a matching tiara composed of diamond circlets, each one hung with a huge pear-shaped pearl.

Apart from enjoying the company of her grand-daughters, the Grand Duchess invariably preferred to have young people round her. The princesses' other grandmother, Queen Olga, had rather elderly ladies-in-waiting, but the Grand Duchess Vladimir liked her feminine entourage to be young and good-looking. Somebody once said that to be chosen as one of her maids of honour was the equivalent of winning a beauty competition. But they had to behave themselves. A stickler for what she considered to be her duty, whatever the circumstances and however inconvenient, the Grand Duchess Marie Pavlovna expected everyone else around her to have the same sense of dedication, and she was not in the least amused when they lapsed from her own high standards. Once, she appointed the seventeen-year-old daughter of the American-born Baroness de Hoehne to be one of her maids of honour to the 'joy and pride', it is recorded, of the de Hoehne family. The young girl—named Halla, and the grand-daughter of a former United States Minister in Russia—used the excuse of her grandmother's death in Estonia to go off and meet a young man with whom she was in love.

Heavily veiled, and in her innocence hoping to be unrecognized, she accompanied him to the Aquarium, a fashionable café-concert in St Petersburg with fish-tanks full of live trout, and where respectable unmarried girls were not expected to go. But her presence was noticed and reported back to the Grand Duchess who, when the young girl returned to duty a day or two later, asked icily: 'Do you consider the Aquarium a suitable place for the celebration of your grandmother's funeral?'; and refused to allow the love-lorn truant to remain as a member of her Court—though the story had a happy ending because the dismissed maid of honour married her young man shortly afterwards.

Princess Marina and her sisters liked Christmas in Russia with the excitement of the snow and ice, tobogganing, playing snowballs, taking journeys by heated sleigh, and all the trappings of imperial wealth, such as helping to distribute presents to the hundreds of servants. Sometimes, because of the freakish difference between the Gregorian and Julian calendar, they had the added advantage of two Christmases; one in Greece or Russia and the other, thirteen days later, with the Duchess of Edinburgh (sister of the Grand Duke Vladimir) at Coburg. But though they enjoyed staying at St Petersburg and meeting their grandmother's eminent guests they preferred the freedom of their summer house in Tsarskoe Selo. Here, in the pretty village of some two thousand inhabitants surrounded by forests, everything was much more informal. The Grand Duke's big villa was bright and chintzy; they often had meals in a tent in the garden and there were mostly family gatherings or visits from intimate friends. They could also play in the Great Park which surrounded the big Catherine Palace in which their mother was married.

Here, as in Athens, there were not only their uncles to entertain them but a vast amount of young relations to keep them company. They often saw the Tsar and Tsarina and their children. Every Sunday and frequently during the week they went to tea either at the Alexander Palace at Tsarskoe or at Peterhoff. This was a palace on the Gulf of Finland about thirty miles the other side of St Petersburg, with grounds full of intricate fountains which were open to the public on certain days of the week. It has still very much the same popularity for Soviet tourists.

The four grand duchesses—Olga, Tatiana, Marie and Anastasia—played games with them and so did the Tsarevitch: all of them were as spirited and lively as any of the traditional Romanovs. They all shared an interest in painting, dancing, and watching a toy theatre for which servants changed the scenes and switched on various coloured lights. They also spent hours sliding down a wooden chute and sometimes ate bon-bons or drank tea with a slice of lemon or a spoonful of jam in the glass. Often they were watched by the Tsarina or the Tsar's sister, Grand Duchess Olga Alexandrovna. And always there was a burly Russian sailor to look after the Tsarevitch. By this time they all knew that they had to be careful when playing with their cousin Alexis and that a bump or fall could cause painful internal bleeding which was extremely difficult to stop. And understandably the Tsarina became increasingly more morbid and neurotic; for it was through her that he had inherited the haemophilia from which he suffered.

When Princess Marina was two years old, the Grand Duke Vladimir died suddenly at 6 p.m. on 17 February 1909. He was sixty-two. He had not been well for a few weeks but nobody had expected him to die, and not even his wife was with him at the time. 'He was a charming host and a man of enlightened views,' *The Times* reported. And the Grand Duke also left a fortune estimated at millions of pounds.

Prince and Princess Nicholas and their family were in Greece when they heard the sad news and they were not able to reach St Petersburg in time for the funeral. Instead, they comforted the distraught Grand Duchess who was an 'inconsolable widow', and eventually took her on a tour of Italy to try and assuage her grief. On her return she accepted no social engagements for a year, and took over all the Grand Duke's former committees, patronages and interests as far as she could.

Although the Grand Duchess Vladimir was now a widow, her personality was as forceful and dominant as ever. She was one of the great ladies, third in the Russian hierarchy, ranking after the Tsarina and the Dowager Empress and a much stronger character than either of them. Indeed, at this time, due to the

Tsar and Tsarina's dislike of Court life and the continued
absence of the Dowager Tsarina, Grand Duchess Vladimir
virtually took over as First Lady of Russia, certainly from a
social point of view she did. She held a little court of her own
in her palaces in St Petersburg and Tsarskoe Selo and was admirably fitted to play the part of hostess and to do the honours
of the Court.

Meanwhile, three years passed by without any major mis-
haps until, in the autumn of 1912, the peace of the Greek
Royal Family was shattered by the outbreak of the first Balkan
war.

Princess Marina and her sisters were sent away for the duration of the war, and, accompanied by Miss Fox, they went to
Russia and to Paris with the Grand Duchess Vladimir. In
Paris the Grand Duchess ensconced her grand-daughters in the
old Hotel Continental overlooking the Tuileries Gardens. It
was full of palms and fountains and had at that time the reputation of being the grandest and most luxurious hotel in the
French capital. She took the children driving in the Bois de
Boulogne, showed them off to her French friends, showered
them with toys, presents and chic new dresses and sent them
off in blue reefer coats and patterned bonnets to look at Punch
and Judy shows—which they seemed to like best of all.

Part of the time Princess Marina, accompanied by Miss Fox,
went off to Harax in the Crimea to stay with her Aunt Marie,
the Grand Duchess George (daughter of King George I of
Greece), and during the visit was driven over to the Tsar's
estate at Livadia. It was the first time that she had been apart
from her sisters and it is possible that the reason for her absence
was the ever-increasing friction between her grandmother and
her nurse. For, in spite of the fact that the Grand Duchess gave
Miss Fox some splendid presents, such as a diamond bracelet
emblazoned with her initials, the two strong-minded women
had never got along well. And, in fact, although Miss Fox
did not know it at the time, the Grand Duchess's feelings were
so aroused by 'that dreadful woman' that she delivered an
ultimatum to her daughter Helen and threatened to cut off
her massive income from the Apanages unless Miss Fox was
dismissed for inefficiency. The Grand Duchess's influence with

the Tsar was indeed strong enough to convince Princess Nicholas that this was no empty threat. Meanwhile in Greece Prince Nicholas was fighting in the army and Princess Nicholas, together with Queen Olga and other feminine members of the Royal Family, worked in the hospitals and organized ambulance trains. By March 1913, the war was nearing its end, and it was decided that it was at last safe for the three princesses to re-join their parents who were at that time living in Salonika which had been recaptured by the Greeks and where Prince Nicholas had been appointed as the Military Governor. King George of Greece was there as well, living in a temporary 'palace' on the shores of the Gulf of Thermai. He was delighted with the victories which had been achieved by the Greek Army. His Silver Jubilee—the 50th anniversary of his reign—was due in October. At the same time he planned to abdicate in favour of Crown Prince Constantine. And he was looking forward to seeing his three granddaughters again. Arrangements were made for them to meet their mother in Vienna and travel back on the train with her.

It was a journey which never took place.

5 | *The First World War – Greece*

On 18 March 1913, in Salonika, two and a half months before the end of the first Balkan war, King George I of the Hellenes was assassinated. He was aged sixty-eight. In Athens he had been used to taking long walks unaccompanied by a bodyguard, and he thought it would be safe to do so in Salonika. On that fateful afternoon he went out at about three o'clock accompanied only by his equerry. They walked through the busy, crowded streets in the direction of the White Tower, an ancient and conspicuous building near the harbour. On their way the King and his companion passed a small, rather squalid café and as they went by a ragged man emerged, watched them as they disappeared in the distance and sat on a stone seat eating dried figs and dates, and smoking cigarettes, until they returned nearly two hours later. As the two men repassed him he took a revolver out of his pocket and shot King George in the back. The King died almost immediately. There was no reason at all for the assassination—the man, a Greek, was feeble-minded and said afterwards that he did it because he was 'driven to desperation by sickness and want'.

Prince Nicholas, who had lunched with his father that very day, had the melancholy task of telegraphing the news to his family and other relations. Queen Alexandra, it was reported, was 'prostrate' at the news of the murder of her brother Willy, and Queen Mary recorded in her diary: 'In the evening we received the shocking news that poor dear Uncle Willy of Greece had been assassinated at Salonika—G. [King George V] was terribly upset—We heard by telephone from Marlborough House that poor Mama was in a great state of mind at the death of her favourite brother. It is a great tragedy.' And Princess Nicholas, who had got as far as Belgrade on her way to pick up her daughters, was recalled.

'He has died a hero of his people, and the whole nation will mourn his loss,' said *The Times*.

After the death of King George the whole Royal Family returned to Athens, except Princess Marina who was considered too young to attend her grandmother's funeral. She spent the interim waiting time in Russia—but without Miss Fox who had been with the family for ten years. The Grand Duchess Vladimir would not accept her back in St Petersburg. 'Letting you go, Foxie,' wrote Prince Nicholas to his children's former nurse, 'is one of the hardest things we have ever done'; and in her testimonial Princess Nicholas said, 'Unfortunately circumstances obliged us to part with her for reasons quite outside her own or our will and to our mutual regret. . . .'

The King was buried at Tatoi on a pine-covered hill about half a mile from the house where he and Queen Olga had often stood to admire the panoramic view of the Plain of Attica. It was a situation where it was quiet and cool on the hottest day, always filled with the sweet scent of resin from the trees, abounding with bright butterflies and in the early autumn carpeted with a mass of mauve and purple wild cyclamen. He was to be joined there eventually by many members of his family and it was to become what must surely be the most peaceful, simple and beautiful royal burial ground in the world.

King Constantine was a very different monarch from his father, more headstrong, yet more conscientious—he carefully read every State paper he signed (King George reputedly never read any)—and he had a strong personal magnetism which inspired great devotion in his people. It took an assassination to make the Hellenic people value the true worth of King George I; his son could do it by his personality. But this also created enemies. In his will King George had given his heir some advice: 'Be courageous but patient,' he had written, 'for you are reigning over a Southern people, whose temper and irritability may take fire rapidly and who at any moment may say and do things which will probably be forgotten the following day.' It was sound advice which the impulsive new King of the Hellenes sometimes forgot. However, the most important difference as far as his future was concerned was his attitude towards a

Cretan-born politician named Eleftherios Venizelos, whom his
father had liked and trusted and King Constantine did not.

Venizelos had first clashed with the Royal Family when he
virtually forced King Constantine's brother, Prince George, to
resign from his position as High Commissioner for Crete in
1906. In 1909, Venizelos was invited to Athens by a powerful
Military League which had just successfully headed a revolt, and
for a time forced the Greek princes to give up their military
ranks. A General Election was held in 1910 and the Venizelist
party gained a majority, and King George, who was a reasonable
man, appointed Venizelos as his Prime Minister.

King Constantine, however, never really forgave Venizelos
for his attitude towards his brothers and himself. But for the
first few months of his reign he and Venizelos got on tolerably
well together. As far as the people of Greece were concerned,
King Constantine's attractive personality and good looks
ensured his popularity. His picture was hung in virtually every
household; a song was composed in his honour called 'Son of the
Eagle', which was played every time he appeared and became in
a way his symbol and signature tune; and he was godfather to
every sixth child born that year. 'Although we were in mourning for my father,' said Prince Nicholas, 'the glorious moments
in which we were living helped us considerably to bear our sorrow.' But he was honest enough to admit afterwards that 'It
was perhaps the only happy year of King Constantine's short
reign.'

Princess Marina returned from Russia and she and her family
fell back into a regular and pleasant routine. On Sundays after
Mass they lunched with Queen Olga. On Tuesdays, as before,
Princess Nicholas was hostess to the Royal Family, and on
Thursdays everybody dined with King Constantine and his wife,
Queen Sophie, at the Palace. Not the old Royal Palace—which
apart from all its other drawbacks had been gutted and damaged
by fire—but the smaller more convenient palace on the other
side of the Royal Gardens which King Constantine had built for
himself when he was Crown Prince.

The first Easter after King Constantine's succession was one
the sisters remembered. This was because it was full of noise—
the booming of guns, the peal of hundreds of bells, the crack
of rifles, long processions, flags and myrtle garlands, which

all contrasted with the solemn lighting of Pascal candles and of thousands of smaller candles in the Cathedral. It was always the most sacred festival in the Greek Orthodox Church.

Princess Marina and her sisters also coloured hard-boiled eggs and, like the Northern English custom, knocked them against each other to see whose egg cracked first. And they received presents of china, jewelled and enamelled eggs.

Life in Greece gradually returned to normal, and the three princesses, now aged seven, nine and ten, resumed their education. If their parents were away there were written reports on their progress awaiting their return, and Princess Marina often did a lot of vain pleading in an effort to get her numerous noughts turned into nines by the addition of a tail.

They already spoke good English (which they had learned from Miss Fox) and Greek. Now they were taught French by a new and rather strict governess, German by a visiting teacher, and polished up their Greek which had lapsed a bit in the months they had been away. In addition they were given piano lessons and they joined up with friends to do physical exercises, then very fashionable, under the eye of a mountainous Swedish lady gymnast.

They were very keen on bicycling, and were also taught riding by an English groom. Princess Marina and Princess Elizabeth both enjoyed riding and became very experienced and accomplished horsewomen. Their parents took great interest in their education and in their other pursuits. Prince Nicholas taught them all to draw and paint, and in the evening before bedtime Princess Nicholas read to them in either English or French. She had a beautiful speaking voice and those night-time reading sessions, which she kept up until they were adults, was a pleasure which they always remembered. And always there was an emphasis on good manners. However high-spirited the children were Princess Nicholas insisted that these were essential. As Prince Nicholas said later, 'We endeavoured to bring them up on the simple principles of our own home life, and to be unpretentious and full of consideration for others.' It was a maxim which in the future Princess Marina—and her sisters—were to carry out regarding the upbringing of their own children.

Sometimes, with a group of friends, the princesses went to

one of the Greek islands, such as Spetsai, for holidays. Princess Nicholas, in the grand manner of the Russians, took over rooms on the top floor of a hotel and organized informal picnics at which the three princesses were allowed to gnaw chicken legs. Often the three girls would go to more remote parts of the island riding on donkeys and led by their mother, who enjoyed these outings as much as her daughters and still managed to look dignified even when sitting on a saddle, holding a parasol. For weeks on end during these carefree holidays the three girls led a tomboyish existence. They swam, sailed boats, climbed trees and rode their bicycles.

Their parents also rented a villa for the summer at Kiphissia, a suburb midway between Athens and Tatoi in the foothills of Mount Pentelikon, which has provided marble for Greece for five thousand years yet still has no more than a scar in its side to show for it. Because of its position Kiphissia is cool at night even in the hottest months and is still a refuge for well-to-do Athenians.

The house which Prince Nicholas leased eventually became a deserted ruin, but at that time it was bright and comfortable, gay with potted geraniums on the terrace and a magnificent view from the sloping garden, full of figs and orange trees, in which the three princesses often had lessons. At the side of the villa, on the flattest part of the grounds and hidden from the road, there was the inevitable lawn tennis court and Princess Marina used to watch her parents play with their friends and seemed quite unconcerned that she rarely joined in herself because of her weak leg. In fact nobody ever took any notice of it at all; Princess Nicholas ignored her daughter's handicap, never mentioned it and always behaved as if it did not exist, with the confident expectation that everyone else would do the same. It was an attitude which was largely successful and, as time went by and she grew older, Princess Marina's limp became less and less apparent until it was no more than a slight awkwardness in her walk. Eventually, as well as being able to ride, swim, dance, skate and ski, she could also play a reasonably hard game of tennis.

But there were other distractions at Kiphissia besides tennis. They also kept pets—a rabbit, a beautiful white Persian cat called 'Pussy', and a grey mongrel dog (which really belonged to

Princess Nicholas) which Princess Marina had found straying in the streets and named 'Kiffy' after the place where it was discovered. Already the three Greek princesses had met most of the close companions whose friendship they would retain for the rest of their lives. Nearly all Princess Marina's women friends first knew her in her childhood or had some connection with her family.

Meanwhile, events in Greece were conspiring against them. The assassination of the Archduke Franz Ferdinand at Sarajevo marked the beginning of the First World War.

It is not necessary to delve into the complicated labyrinth of explosive Greek politics: there had been crisis after crisis ever since the beginning of the reign of King Otho. Now the antagonism between King Constantine and Venizelos flared anew. Their vital clash arose over the question of Greece's entry into the war. The King wanted the country to remain neutral; Venizelos wished to go in on the side of the Allies. Britain and France, two of the three powers which put the dynasty on the throne in the first place, were highly indignant at the King's refusal to plunge his country into war again—and they suspected that his German-born wife (the Empress Frederick's daughter Sophie) was the cause of his reluctance.

At the beginning of September 1916 Allied warships blockaded the Piraeus. The situation deteriorated and the following month an ultimatum was given to King Constantine. Early in December, apparently under the impression it had been accepted, Allied troops, under the command of a French general, marched into Athens and were met by such strong resistance they had to retreat. That afternoon French warships bombarded the city for three hours.

This attack caught members of the Royal Family in some awkward situations. Some shells burst near the Palace and most of the occupants, including the King and Queen, took refuge in the cellars.

Princess Andrew, who had gone off to a needlework shop she ran in aid of charity, drove home among whizzing bullets to look after her children and found that one shot had broken their nursery window and embedded itself in the opposite wall. Prince Christopher, who had been having tea with Prince and

Princess Nicholas, set out for the Royal Palace when the shooting began, and had some trouble starting his car. 'For several
agonized minutes the chauffeur and I, two perspiring and
desperate men, turned the handle frantically, while the firing in
the streets grew worse every minute and the crack of rifles was
answered by the boom of guns at sea,' he said afterwards. It
was a predicament made more uncomfortable by the fact that
some Venizelists were taking aim at him from a house on a
corner opposite. 'Mercifully, there were some poor shots in
Athens then,' he commented.

And Princess Marina, Princess Olga and Princess Elizabeth,
who found the shelling a rather exciting experience, watched
happily all that was going on from their top-floor nursery window and were extremely disappointed when their horrified
mother found them doing it and forced them to go down into the
cellar until the bombardment was over.

After the incident there were several days of shooting and
rioting before order was restored. Six months later King
Constantine was deposed. Britain and France were not prepared
to abolish the Greek monarchy altogether—and among suggestions as to who should succeed to the throne came one from the
British ambassador in France that 'Prince Nicholas, who
married the daughter of the Grand Duke Vladimir, might be an
acceptable substitute'. In June 1917 King Constantine was
asked to abdicate. But in fact he refused to do this. Instead he
decided to go into exile, together with his eldest son, Crown
Prince George, and proposed that his second son, Alexander,
aged twenty-three, should reign temporarily in his place.

The Allies accepted this plan and Alexander took the oath of
allegiance with tears in his eyes in a small, secret, sad ceremony
which took place one afternoon in the palace ballroom watched
by Prince Nicholas and Prince Andrew. It was made all the
more weird by the wailing which came from thousands of
people gathered round the building in increasing numbers as
news spread that King Constantine was leaving the country.
'One by one they took up the cry . . . that age-old lament in a
minor key with which Greeks proclaim death or disaster,' said
Prince Christopher. None of them ever forgot it.

Royalist crowds stayed surrounding the palace railings all
night; a warm, beautiful night with the air scented by the

fragrance of jasmine, roses and orange blossom. And they refused to let any member of the Royal Family leave. 'We were
literally besieged,' said Prince Nicholas and he recalled that they
all spent hours pacing up and down the passages, full of gloom
and scarcely saying a word to one another. And eventually some
of them had a little sleep, three and four to a room or draped
uncomfortably on sofas and armchairs. At six o'clock in the
morning the palace was still surrounded, and when Prince
Nicholas with his wife and Prince and Princess Andrew tried
to sneak home by the back gate they were prevented from leaving. When he explained they wanted to bath and change they
were told that they could have a wash where they were.

A proclamation announcing the change of monarchy only
increased the size of the crowds and some people became so
worked up emotionally that, according to Prince Christopher,
'the lamentations turned to hysteria and there were cries that
it would be better to kill the deposed King than let him leave,
which caused an alarmed representative of the Allies to insist
that the King should depart from Athens immediately. It was
an order easier to give than carry out, but it was eventually
accomplished that afternoon by decoy cars drawing most of the
attention to the back entrance while the Royal party scuttled
out of the front in an undignified scramble into the Royal
gardens opposite. They clutched each other tightly while people
tore at their clothes or flung themselves on the ground at their
feet. 'All of us, especially the ladies, were somewhat roughly
handled,' said Prince Nicholas, 'we . . . fought our way through
the gate'; and Queen Sophie, lagging behind, was picked up
under the arms by two of her stalwart brothers-in-law and taken
across the road so quickly that her feet hardly touched the
ground.

Once across the gardens the King and Queen and their
children, of whom the youngest Katharine was aged four, were
bundled into waiting cars and set off for Tatoi in such haste that
the Crown Prince, their eldest son George, was still lying on the
floor of one of them with his legs waving out of an open door.
Then unexpectedly there was a shower of unusual summer rain
which helped to disperse the shouting and wailing crowds.

The next day King Constantine made his farewells in a more
regal manner. All through the morning and afternoon a steady

E

stream of visitors drove out to Tatoi to wish him goodbye.
Afterwards the whole family gathered at King George's plain
white marble tomb on the hilltop. 'We stood there, a sad and
silent group round the simple grave, and never did we pray so
fervently,' said Prince Nicholas.

Twenty-four hours later King Constantine left in the Royal
yacht from the flower-strewn pier of what was then the small
fishing port of Oropos on the East Coast and sailed, via the
Corinth Canal, to Italy on his way to Switzerland. In Athens
afterwards those of the Royal Family who were left behind
lived in an atmosphere of suspicion. The new King's household
was selected for him, many royalists were arrested, photographs
of King Constantine were confiscated—and it was made a
punishable offence to sing 'Son of the Eagle'.

Then Prince Nicholas and his family were also asked to leave
Athens, and so was Prince Andrew. The two days before they
departed Princess Marina and her sisters lived among a constant
crowd of visitors. 'From early morning till late at night on those
two days our house was filled with friends, mere acquaintances
and even strangers who came to say goodbye,' reported their
father and, as he said, it was a demonstration of affection and
love which touched them more deeply than any 'manifestation
of loyalty and attachment in the days of happiness'.

Just before they left, on the evening of 4 July, King Alexander
came to see them off. As they drove away all their servants
clustered in the doorway of the Nicholas Palace and in front of
them the young King stood in the garden waving goodbye,
'feeling perhaps more wretched and unhappy than we who were
forced to abandon the home and house we loved so dearly', as
Prince Nicholas commented later.

After the King's departure, Venizelos returned to Athens
with his government, but it was not until the spring of 1918 that
his army was fit to go into action. In the final assault of the
Allies in September the Greeks were at last able to make a
belated contribution to it. In November the First World War
came to an end.

6 | *The First World War—Russia*

In Petrograd (St Petersburg changed its name at the beginning of the war) and Tsarskoe Selo Princess Marina's feminine relations went to war in their traditional way. The Tsarina and her four daughters took a course in nursing, Queen Olga, who was still in Russia at the time, worked in hospitals, and the Grand Duchess Vladimir, like her daughter-in-law, Grand Duchess Kirill, organized ambulance trains to bring wounded soldiers away from the front, while Russia, with its seemingly inexhaustible manpower, slowly gathered itself together to fight a war for which it was ill-prepared and ill-equipped.

Transport services and industries were inefficient and all authority was centralized in a bureaucracy which, even in normal times, was unwieldy and incapable of administering so huge a territory. There was no co-ordination between government departments: each minister was directly responsible to the Tsar alone—and was under no obligation to inform his colleagues what he was up to. Even the President of the Duma (the Russian Parliament) had no right to control ministerial actions and there was no collective responsibility for the organization of the country's rich natural resources. So the Russians, always magnificent fighters, went to the front in their thousands and—after a few initial victories—were slaughtered in their thousands; often through lack of munitions which were rusting away in railway sidings at Petrograd. As the British Ambassador said later, 'The fighting spirit of the Russian Army was almost broken, while its loyal devotion to the Tsar was cooling fast.'

In an effort to inspire the morale of his fighting men the Tsar was often away visiting troops or staying at the Army

Headquarters at Mogilev, and these frequent wartime separations involved him and his wife in some steady correspondence. The Tsarina in particular was a prolific writer, and daily wrote long letters to her husband saying how much she loved and missed him. She also detailed never-ending lists of the ailments she suffered in his absence and a great many complaints about Princess Marina's maternal grandmother the Grand Duchess Vladimir. The painfully shy but strong-minded Tsarina very much resented the grand duchess's success as a hostess and was envious of her assurance and self-possession. And the antagonism was mutual. The formidable grand duchess not only disliked the Tsarina's 'English stiffness' but any mistakes made by the charming weak-willed Tsar she blamed on the Tsarina. Quite often the grand duchess's assumption was correct.

There was plenty about their children's activities in the letters which the Tsarina wrote to the Tsar; and it is a pity she could not restrict herself to domestic affairs. But, misguidedly, with tremendous energy, misspelling words in her eagerness to write them and with patriotic fervour, she set out to control the Tsar, win the war and virtually govern the country.

Some of her suggestions, seen in the light of later events, were wise enough. Left to herself she may have been of some assistance to her poor, harassed, over-burdened husband. But behind so many of her insistent demands was the voice of Gregory Rasputin—the man who appeared to be able to ease her son's suffering and whom she felt was 'guided by God'. And no one was more aware of this than the wiser, older and more experienced Grand Duchess Vladimir who, however, never made the mistake, as so many did, of openly criticizing Rasputin. Having lost one son herself, she understood the Tsarina's dependence on him as a healer. But the rest she found it impossible to approve.

Rasputin had first been introduced to the Russian Court in 1905. Since that time his influence over the Tsarina and his power in the Court had increased to alarming proportions. Eventually, in 1916, a small group of men of the highest social position decided to rid the Russian empire of Rasputin.

Three people were specifically involved in the conspiracy to get rid of the notorious 'Man of God' for ever. They were Prince Felix Youssupov, who had once been in love with Princess

Marina's mother, a Duma deputy named Purishkevitch, and the Grand Duke Dmitri Pavlovitch, a lively, good looking young man, aged twenty-four, who was doubly related to Princess Marina. His mother, who had died at his birth, was Prince Nicholas's sister Alexandra. His father, Grand Duke Paul Alexandrovitch, was a younger brother of Grand Duke Vladimir. The date selected for the murder was 16 December (O.S.) as Prince Youssupov, the self-appointed executioner, was to leave for the Crimea the following day to spend Christmas with his wife, Princess Irene (the daughter of the Tsar's elder sister, Grand Duchess Xenia). It was on the pretext that he was to meet her for the first time that Rasputin was invited to the big Youssupov Palace on the Moika Canal that night.

Princess Irene knew what was about to take place. One of her brothers, Prince Dmitri Alexandrovitch, motored over from his own near-by estate to wait with her on that fatal night until they should hear the news from the capital that the murder had taken place. He stayed until two o'clock the next morning and then, assuming that there had been a hitch or that nothing had happened, he drove back home.

As everyone was to find out much later there *had* been a hitch which was both serious and unforeseen; for Gregory Rasputin took an uncommonly long time to die. He was fed cyanide in cakes and wine, he was shot in the heart and in the back, and he was beaten, all of which took roughly four hours. Yet he was still alive when his body was dumped in the River Neva through a hole in the ice some time between six and seven o'clock the following morning in the pitch darkness of the long northern winter night.

The police report of Rasputin's death, of 17 December (O.S.), has a familiar ring of officialese, but it was jerky, at times almost incoherent and, as the Grand Duchess Vladimir said, 'very difficult to read'. It begins: 'Today at about 2.30 in the morning, the policeman who stands on guard at the house of the Home Office situated on the Morskaia heard a detonation from the palace of Prince Youssupov situated on the opposite side of the Moika. As this post is a special one and the policeman on duty is forbidden to leave it, he went into the Home Office premises and communicated by telephone with the police sergeant on duty at the adjoining station. . . .'

The chief police officer, Colonel Rogov, took the matter in hand and sent a deputy to the palace to find out what had happened. Youssupov's butler told him that a reception was taking place and that one of the guests, who had been having a little target practice, had missed the target and hit a window instead. As proof, the deputy was shown a broken pane of glass.

No sooner had the deputy left the Youssupov Palace than a detective belonging to the Okhrana (Secret Police)—who had been detailed to look after Rasputin—reported to his own chief about a mysterious motor car and four men whom he suspected were 'robbers', who had sneaked in through a side door of the palace.

This incident was reported to Rogov, who sent his deputy, accompanied by several officers, back again to the Youssupov household. This time the butler said that some 'highly placed guests' had just arrived.

At least twice more the harassed police were called out to the Youssupov Palace that night. The report, not unnaturally, becomes a little confused in the course of relating the story. It mentions more shots, police whistles, and a chase along the canal side after a fast car with no lights and no number plate and with two struggling women of the *demi-monde* inside. And then comes a more sinister paragraph: 'The servants, assisted by the chauffeur, in the presence of an officer wearing a long fur cloak, carried out what looked like a human body and placed it in the car. The chauffeur jumped in, and, putting on full speed, made off along the canal side. . . .'

By the end of the day the news was all over Petrograd. And there was a brief announcement in the evening paper: 'Today, at six o'clock in the morning, at one of the aristocratic residences in the centre of the capital, after a party, the life of Gregory Rasputin ended suddenly.'

That night Grand Duke Dmitri went to the theatre with his cousin Grand Duke Boris, Princess Marina's uncle. The next day, by order of the Tsarina, Grand Duke Dmitri was placed under house arrest, an instruction which was confirmed by the Tsar, who had been summoned hastily from his headquarters. When he arrived at Tsarskoe Selo he received a visit from Grand Duke Paul asking for his son to be released. The Tsar hedged when confronted personally, as was his usual custom, and would not give an answer straight away, but the following morning he sent a letter to his uncle: 'I cannot waive the house arrest until the affair is terminated. I pray God that Dmitri will come out of this all right. . . .'

Frightened by the furore which had been caused by the killing, all the conspirators, including Grand Duke Dmitri, panicked and denied all knowledge of the murder. Even when his nephews, Boris and Andrei, went to see him and assured him that whether he was guilty or not they would stand up for him, Grand Duke Dmitri, though touched and thankful for the visit, solemnly swore that he had not even seen Rasputin. He told them he had 'left at three o'clock in the morning with two ladies, and in the courtyard of the Youssupov Palace a dog rushed at me which I shot'. He then took his companions off to the Caravanya (a gypsy café) and had gone home. He knew nothing more, he said.

Later he was not quite so untruthful when his father asked him about the affair, but he swore a sacred oath on a portrait of his mother that, as Grand Duke Andrei recorded, 'his hands were not stained with the blood of this man'. There is not much doubt that at the time Grand Duke Andrei believed that his statement was true. But it was Grand Duke Dmitri, the 'officer wearing a long fur cloak', assisted by Youssupov's valet, who dumped Rasputin, still alive, in the waters of the icy River Neva and finally killed him.

But by the end of the week the Tsar knew most of the details about that night's work. Purishkevitch was ignored, Prince Youssupov was banished to his country estate, and it was Grand Duke Dmitri, the Tsar's favourite cousin, who bore the brunt of the blame.

On the Russian Christmas Eve, exactly a week after the murder, a telephone call told Grand Duke Andrei that his uncle was to be sent to Persia for service with the Russian troops. Shortly afterwards there was a family meeting. The Grand Duchess Vladimir, Grand Duke Kirill and his wife, and two other members of the family, held a midnight conference to decide whether it was better to attempt to prevent Grand Duke Dmitri's banishment or take action later. But there was really no time to do anything; at two o'clock on Christmas morning, 'calm but pale' and 'very downcast', Grand Duke Dmitri, accompanied by two army officers, set off by train on his long trip to Kasvin on the Persian border. It was a long, miserable and uncomfortable journey. Nobody remembered to take any money or food and for two days they had nothing to eat. On top of this, the strain of the past week's events took its toll of the young Grand Duke. A few hours after leaving Petrograd he had 'something in the nature of a nervous breakdown' and was very ill for some time afterwards.

Eventually, in an effort to help Grand Duke Dmitri, the Imperial Family combined to take action, and, at the Grand Duchess Vladimir's suggestion, decided to send a petition to the Tsar. As the British Ambassador at the time, Sir George Buchanan, reported to King George V later: 'It was couched in the most respectful terms. After referring to Grand Duke Dmitri's youth and delicate health and to the affection which the Tsar had always shown him, it beseeched His Majesty to modify his decision and allow His Imperial Highness to be moved from Persia to his estate near Moscow, as to keep him in the Persian district where he is now would be equivalent to a sentence of death on one whose lungs were weak.' At a meeting held in the Vladimir Palace on a Thursday in January 1917, sixteen members of the Imperial Family, headed by Queen Olga of Greece, who was of course not only Princess Marina's grandmother but Grand Duke Dmitri's as well, approved and signed a document which was handed to the Tsar that night. The others who signed included Princess Marina's maternal grandmother the Grand Duchess Vladimir, her three uncles Kirill, Boris and Andrei and the Grand Duchess Kirill, who was also her godmother. The petition was returned a few days later with a note written by the Tsar across the top, 'Nobody has the right to commit murder.' He had added significantly, 'I know the conscience of many gives them no peace as it is not only Dmitri Pavlovitch who is implicated,' and he ended curtly, 'I am astonished that you should address yourselves to me.'

The furious Grand Duchess Vladimir sent a copy of the letter —and its notation—to Grand Duke Dmitri and, abandoning all caution, she had no hesitation in showing the original document to anyone who wished to see it.

Said Alexander Mossolov, the Court Chancellor, 'The dissolution of the family could not have been more complete.'

The Grand Duke Kirill

The Grand Duke Boris

The Grand Duke Andrei

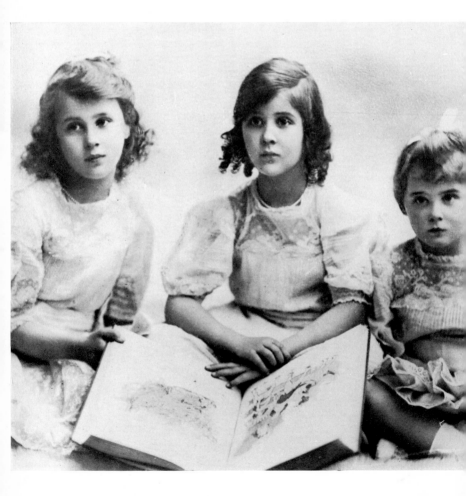

The Princesses Olga, Elizabeth and Marina

Olga, Princess Paul of
Yugoslavia in 1938

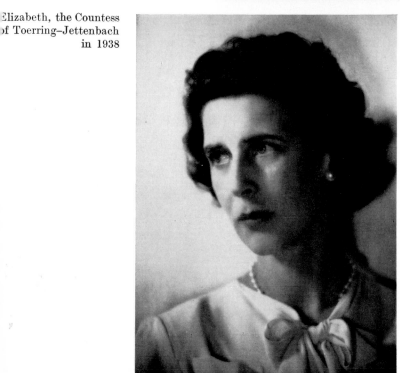

Elizabeth, the Countess
of Toerring–Jettenbach
in 1938

Engagement group 1934. *From left to right*: Mrs Ralli (a close friend of Princess Marina), Prince Christopher, Princess Nicholas, Prince Nicholas, Prince Paul of Yugoslavia, Equerry. *Seated in front*: Princess Marina and Prince George

The Royal Palace at Athens   The Nicholas Palace

Outside the Imperial Family, the situation in Petrograd and the unrest among the Russian people continued to get worse. Grand Duke Andrei left the capital for Kislovodsk, a Caucasian spa. 'I am glad to get out of Petrograd,' he recorded in his diary. 'It appears there are no honourable men left. Everybody slanders each other and above all they slander Russia. They lie in the Duma, ministers lie, newspapers lie. In a word, everybody is lying, without conscience or scruple, and in these filthy lies it is very difficult to live and so harmful for our country.' Even Grand Duke Dmitri, having received a hint from his father that the Tsar might agree to let him return some time in March, did not want to come back to Russia. For one thing, he found the warm Persian climate 'certainly better than Petrograd or even Moscow'; for another he thought that the less asked of the Emperor on his behalf the better. And there was one final objection—the political side of the matter. 'While here I am far removed from gossip and dirty rumours and insinuations,' he declared. He considered that it would be better for him to return later, when he could do so without attracting attention.

Outwardly the Grand Duchess Vladimir lived her life as usual —she gave a dinner party for young people in honour of her great-nephew Carol, the Crown Prince of Rumania, and a reception for several members of a British mission who were in Petrograd attending an Allied Conference. Except for the Tsar, she was the only member of the Imperial Family who entertained them, and they went back and reported that they heard 'quite open discussion, even in the highest circles of Petrograd society, as to the probability of the Tsar and Tsarina being assassinated'. 'Indeed, in some quarters the highest hope entertained in regard to the Allied Conference was that it might produce some arrangement which would, on one pretext or another, remove Nicholas and his wife from Russia,' said Lloyd George.

And in the Imperial Palace at Tsarskoe Selo there was at last a realization that the rift between the Tsar and his relations had widened too far and that there must be some attempt to restore peace. The first move was made by the elderly and respected Court Minister Count Fredericks, who, although normally loath to take any part in a discussion with the Tsar which might cause trouble, was sufficiently upset by all that had happened to bring up what was bound to be a touchy subject.

Afterwards, he reported what had taken place to his colleague Alexander Mossolov. 'I took the opportunity to say how sorry I was to see the Imperial Family completely disunited, and added that a reconciliation was essential in the interests of the dynasty and the country. We had a very long conversation in which the Tsarina took a most active part. It was agreed that a way out must be found by hook or by crook. I ventured to say that the first thing that was needed was a reconciliation between Her Majesty and Grand Duchess Vladimir. The rest would be a much simpler matter and would settle itself.'

The Grand Duchess Vladimir and the Tsarina had never got on well together, now the situation was much worse. Yet even at this critical hour the feud between the two proud women was not to be settled easily, although the Tsarina agreed that it was necessary. Times were too difficult to let family dissensions continue, she said, and she was ready for a reconciliation with the Grand Duchess—but only on three conditions: that the Grand Duchess must make the first step towards such a reconciliation; that she must recognize that there had been mistakes on both sides; and that she must help to restore the solidarity of the Imperial Family.

The poor, faithful old Count, worn out and suffering from high blood pressure, arranged an audience with the Grand Duchess Vladimir, but half an hour beforehand he begged Mossolov to go in his place. 'I am supposed to be going to see her on my own initiative, without mentioning the conversation I have had with Their Majesties, to do my best to persuade her to accept the Tsarina's three conditions. But I am too ill to tackle this difficult task.'

The Grand Duchess was not upset that Mossolov went to see her instead of the Count. 'You were quite right to leave the Count at his home,' she said. 'An important conversation might have brought on in my presence the thing I most fear— a fit of apoplexy,' and she settled down to an hour's discussion on the topic of her relations with the Tsarina.

'The Grand Duchess Vladimir realized at the outset that a reconciliation was indispensable in the interests of the dynasty and of the whole country,' reported Mossolov afterwards. But the Tsarina's first condition proved too much for her to agree to. When Mossolov told her that it was absolutely vital that she should take the first step, the Grand Duchess replied, 'If that is so, I am not ready even to discuss the subject with you. It is impossible.' Eventually, however, she agreed to a compromise. 'I will go to Tsarskoe Selo if Count Fredericks comes to invite me in Her Majesty's name,' she said.

'That was her last word,' said Mossolov afterwards and went back to report to the ailing count who decided that when he was well enough he would go to see the Grand Duchess himself and tell her that he hoped the Tsarina would shortly be inviting her to Tsarskoe Seloe. What happened after that is not clear. Presumably the Tsarina refused the request. 'I learned later that it had been impossible for this invitation to be conveyed to the Grand Duchess,' said Mossolov. But in any case it was already too late.

On 17 February 1917, the anniversary of the Grand Duke Vladimir's death, his widow went to the fortress of Saint Peter and Saint Paul for a service in his memory. Shortly afterwards, two weeks before she was due to join Grand Duke Andrei at Kislovodsk, the French Ambassador gave a dinner party for her. 'I badly need sun and a rest; the emotions of recent times have worn me out,' she told him. 'I can't tell you how down-hearted I feel. Everything seems black wherever I look. I am expecting the most dire catastrophes. And yet God can't mean Russia to perish.'

On the evening of 4 March, she left Petrograd by train for the Caucasus. The next day the Russian Revolution began—a hap-hazard, disorganized, untidy affair, which erupted so suddenly that for several days nobody knew quite what was happening.

As news of the Revolution spread across Europe Royal telegrams sped out of various embassies like demented pigeons. From Switzerland, where Prince Nicholas and his family were in exile, came a telegram inquiring where the Grand Duchess Vladimir was; from Rumania, Queen Marie wanted information about her sister, the Grand Duchess Kirill, whom, she heard mistakenly, had been captured; and from England, Queen Alexandra inquired about her sister.

And it was typical of the thoughtfulness of Princess Marina's paternal grandmother that Queen Olga in Petrograd, oblivious to the fact that her own position might be hazardous, sent a message *out* of Russia asking about the welfare of her daughter Marie who was in England.

On 15 March Tsar Nicholas II abdicated in favour of his younger brother Michael, who refused to accept the Russian throne. For a time the Tsar and his family were imprisoned in the Alexander Palace at Tsarskoe Seloe. Five months later, apparently for their safety, they were moved to Tobolsk in Siberia. They lived in what had once been the governor's residence and enjoyed comparative freedom and comfort. They stayed at Tobolsk until April 1918, when false rumours that monarchists were planning their escape caused their removal to a house in Ekaterinburg, where they lived under more rigorous conditions. There were further restrictions, they were treated with less civility than before and for the first time their personal baggage was searched. The Tsar accepted it all with customary impassiveness but the Tsarina 'seized every opportunity to protest against conditions imposed on her by the regulations and insulted the guards as well as the officials representing the Regional Soviet', says an extract from a report written by one of the officials on duty at the house. If she had known how the Tsarina behaved during her last days the Grand Duchess Vladimir would have been proud of her.

When the Tsarina's sister Victoria—the Marchioness of Milford Haven—heard that the Tsar had left for Ekaterinburg, she wrote a letter to Arthur Balfour, then Foreign Secretary, asking if it would be possible for at least three of the Tsar's children to be brought to England and placed in her custody. 'I quite realize that the boy is a political asset which no party in Russia would allow to be taken out of its hands, but the girls (except perhaps the eldest) can be of no value or importance,' she said. 'I and my husband would willingly keep them here in quiet obscurity.' She received a reply saying that the difficulties in the way of such a proposal were 'almost insuperable'.

On 16/17 July 1918 around midnight (ten o'clock Petrograd time, twelve o'clock Ekaterinburg time) in a basement room with a curved ceiling and striped wallpaper, Tsar Nicholas II, aged fifty; the Tsarina Alexandra Feodorovna, forty-six; the Tsarevitch Alexis, nearly fourteen; the Grand Duchesses Olga, twenty-two; Tatiana, twenty-one; Marie, nineteen; and Anastasia, seventeen, were executed. Their bodies were taken ten miles away from the town to a secluded, abandoned and overgrown iron-mine known locally as 'the four brothers' after some pine trees which once grew there and the stumps of which still remained. Here the corpses were dissolved in acid, burnt on a huge bonfire and the remains thrown down a disused shaft. On 25 July, Ekaterinburg, now called Sverdlovsk after the member of the Soviet Central Executive ultimately responsible for the decision to kill the Tsar, was relieved by a reconnaissance party of the White Siberian Army and troops from the newly-formed state of Czecho-Slovakia.

Ten days after the murders the outside world learnt what had happened. From the British Legation in Moscow a cable was sent saying: 'Ex Tsar of Russia Nicholas was shot on the night of 16 July by orders of the Ekaterinburg local Soviet in view of the approaching danger of his capture by the Czechs. The Central Executive Moscow has approved this action.' It was sent on 17 July but was not received in London until the 27th. And it was Prince Max of Baden, now Chancellor of Germany and negotiating the Armistice, who told the British Minister in Berne, saying that it was 'a military execution'.

And when Prince and Princess Nicholas heard about the death of the Tsar and his family it filled them with 'unspeakable horror'. Princess Marina and her sisters mourned their former companions and playmates and wept bitterly. For their mother Princess Nicholas, the Grand Duchess Helen, the Russian Revolution spelt utter tragedy. The Tsar was a first cousin of both herself and Prince Nicholas—and altogether she lost eighteen of her closest relations.

7 | *The Russian Uncles*

Among those of Princess Marina's relations who did escape the worst consequences of the Revolution were her three uncles the Grand Dukes Kirill, Boris and Andrei. In Petrograd circles the three sons of the Grand Duke Vladimir were known collectively as the Vladimirovitchi, but it was a derisory term and whenever it was mentioned there would be some disapproving tongue-clicking. The three Grand Dukes have been described as wild, degenerate, intemperate, immoral and extravagant—descriptions which were not always deserved.

Grand Duke Kirill, the oldest and perhaps the handsomest of the three brothers, though fond of enjoying himself like the rest of the Romanovs, was comparatively sedate. His main 'crime' was the fact that he had fallen deeply and irretrievably in love with his cousin regardless of the fact that she was a married woman. (This was Victoria Melita, daughter of Alfred, Duke of Edinburgh and Marie of Russia, who was Grand Duke Vladimir's sister. She was also the hated sister-in-law of the Tsarina, for she had first married the Tsarina's brother, Grand Duke Ernst of Hesse. They were divorced in 1901.

On Sunday, 8 October 1905, Grand Duke Kirill had achieved his heart's desire and married the divorced Grand Duchess of Hesse. The ceremony took place in the private chapel of the house which belonged to the Duchess of Edinburgh in Tegernsee, about forty miles south of Munich. Only eight people were present to witness the ceremony. It was a wedding which caused a monumental family row.

Grand Duke Kirill went back to Tsarskoe Seloe soon after the wedding although, according to the Tsar, he had been told that the marriage must result in his banishment from Russia, the loss of his title of Grand Duke, the withdrawal of his military rank and the loss of all his revenue from the Apanages. He went alone, leaving his new bride in Coburg, and the purpose of his visit was to personally inform the Tsar that the marriage had taken place.

Princess Marina and her family were in Russia at the time and, unwittingly, it was Prince Nicholas who first informed the Tsar of the wedding and also told him that Grand Duke Kirill was back in Russia. The Russian Emperor was exceedingly angry when he heard this news though, strangely enough, it was the fact that the Grand Duke had flouted his wishes by returning which displeased him most.

The Tsar took immediate action. Count Fredericks, the faithful Court Minister, was dispatched to Grand Duke Vladimir's house at Tsarskoe Selo and had the unenviable task of telling him that his son must leave Russia within forty-eight hours and be deprived of all his military ranks, his income and his title.

When Count Fredericks was announced, Grand Duke Vladimir and his family were playing bridge after having had dinner. 'I knew this late visit was ill-omened and I also knew its meaning,' Grand Duke Kirill said later, 'but I did not anticipate the stringency of the measures which had been taken against me. They came as a great blow to all of us. . . . We were dumbfounded by the severity of the decision . . . the Tsar had at no time indicated or even vaguely hinted at such a drastic step but had, on the contrary, whenever I had mentioned this matter to him, expressed his sincere hope that things could be straightened out. . . .'

The next day the angry Grand Duke Vladimir stormed over to see the Tsar and protest against the severe measures taken against his son—an interview which the Tsar described as 'strong and disagreeable'. Finding the Tsar adamant in his decision the Grand Duke tore off his medals, and resigned his position as Commander-in-Chief of the Army. Prince Nicholas too wrote and asked the Tsar for clemency. Shortly afterwards Grand Duke Kirill's title was restored but that was all. He had to leave Russia and it was not until 1909, shortly before the death of Grand Duke Vladimir, that the Tsar forgave Princess Marina's uncle and he was allowed to return, together with his wife and family. They had two daughters, the youngest of whom was to be one of Princess Marina's bridesmaids.

When the Revolution took place in 1917 Grand Duke Kirill was among the first to go to the Duma and officially recognize the new Provisional Government. He marched there at the head of a detachment of Navy Guards which he commanded. A red revolutionary emblem was in his buttonhole and the men carried a red flag.

After the Bolsheviks came to power in the October Revolution the Grand Duke and his wife and daughters escaped to Finland. It was there that his third child, a son named Vladimir, was born and it is he who is now one of the present claimants to the Russian throne. After living in Finland for a time Grand Duke Kirill and his family went to live in Coburg and then France.

Grand Duke Boris was the one who was mainly responsible for the rakish reputation of the three brothers. He was a noisy, boisterous extrovert who did everything to excess; whether it was drinking, gambling or making love. But everybody liked him in spite of all his faults.

'He was gay, irresponsible, wild and sentimental by turns, rich, over-prodigal, carefree, full of fun and nonsense . . .,' wrote his cousin Queen Marie of Rumania in her memoirs. She was the Grand Duchess Kirill's sister, and he used to visit her quite often. 'Being a grand duke,' she said, 'he could not easily be set aside and had to be received with every honour.' But she knew that the staider characters at the Rumanian Court were always full of apprehension whenever he appeared on the scene, especially as he flirted openly with his pretty cousin who was their prospective Queen. 'The "Old Palace" anxiously watched the development of our association,' recalled Queen Marie; 'when Boris was let loose amongst us anything might be expected, as he lived according to his whims; loving fun and excitement, he looked for it everywhere. . . .'

But in spite of his high spirits the Grand Duke, like all the Romanovs, had that strange, mercurial temperament which came directly from his Tartar ancestors. Even Queen Marie, who herself had Romanov blood in her, noticed it clearly in her cousin. 'He had about him that touch of the imponderable . . . something unaccountable, unfathomable, which made him a stimulating but also a somewhat disquieting companion,' she wrote. 'In most Russians there is that strange something, a mixture of saint and sinner, and one can never know which side will suddenly predominate.' But she did not have much doubt which side predominated in her cousin's character and declared that 'There was . . . little of the saint about Boris!'

He has been described as 'a splendid figure of a man, as assured and autocratic as the Tsar was shy and retiring'. He was also kind, brave and popular. 'It is pleasant to hear from all sides such praise of Boris and of how he is loved, not only by his regiment but by others as well,' wrote the Tsar in September 1915.

But none of this counted for much less than six months later when his alliance with the Tsar's eldest daughter, Olga, was proposed by Grand Duchess Vladimir. The proposal was indignantly refused by the Tsarina, who considered the idea an outrage. (The matter, of course, did not improve the already strained relations between the two Imperial ladies.)

The Tsarina was still simmering about it after the Tsar had returned to his headquarters in February 1916. 'The oftener I think about Boris the more I realize what an awful set his wife would be dragged into,' she wrote. 'His and Miechen's [Grand Duchess Vladimir] friends, rich French people, Russian bankers, "the society" . . . and all such types—intrigues without end—fast manners and conversations and Ducky [Grand Duchess Kirill] not a suitable sister-in-law at all—and then Boris's mad past . . .' As her pen flew over the paper she warmed to her subject. 'Well why do I write about this, when you know as well as I do how disastrous it would be to give over to a well-used, half-worn-out, blasé young man a pure, fresh young girl eighteen years his junior. She would have to live in a house in which many a woman has "shared" his life—only a "woman" who knows the world and can judge and choose with eyes open, ought to be his wife and she would know how to hold him and make a good husband out of him. But an inexperienced young girl would suffer terribly to have her husband fourth, fifth hand or more.'

There was, however, yet one further reason why the suggested marriage was unwelcome. The Grand Duchess Olga, who had already twelve months beforehand refused to marry Prince Carol of Rumania, was in love with somebody else: her second

F

cousin, Grand Duke Dmitri Pavlovitch. But, of course, in late 1916 the favourite cousin of the Tsar was banished from Russia for his part in Rasputin's murder—a banishment which, though cruel at the time, turned out to be the best thing that happened to him for he was in Persia when the Revolution began and was thus one of the few who escaped.

In the end, Grand Duke Boris Vladimirovitch, after a succession of mistresses, met someone named Zina Rashevskaya, the former wife of a Russian officer, shortly before the start of the Revolution. And at last he fell deeply in love. He set her up in a separate establishment and kept her apart from his mother and her friends.

Grand Duke Boris and Grand Duke Andrei had a lucky escape from the Bolsheviks. According to Grand Duke Alexander Michaelovitch, 'The Bolshevik commander entrusted with their execution happened to be a former struggling artist who had spent most of his life in Paris trying in vain to find purchasers for his paintings. A year before the war, the Grand Duke Boris ran across an exhibit of very artistically-painted cushions, while strolling in the Latin Quarter. He fancied their originality. He bought quite a few of them. That was all. The Bolshevik commander could not see himself shooting the man who had appreciated his art! He put the Grand Dukes Boris and Andrei in a car bearing the insignia of the Communist Party and brought them into the zone occupied by the White Army.'

From there, some time later, Grand Duke Boris and his mistress also escaped and went to live in France.

The youngest brother, Grand Duke Andrei, credited with being the brightest and most intelligent of them all, also fell unsuitably and passionately in love with a woman who was, in one sense, disastrous for him—Mathilde Kchessinska, the most famous, powerful and temperamental of the prima ballerinas in the Russian Imperial Ballet.

At one time, when she was eighteen, she had been the mistress of the Tsar and though he never saw her alone again after his marriage, he retained enough affection for her to be an all-powerful ally whenever she wished him to intervene in the stormy politics which went on back-stage at the Russian Ballet. It is said that Tsar Alexander III himself suggested Mathilde

Kchessinska as a suitable mentor for his heir; and she enjoyed the friendship of a whole covey of important and influential men, including one of the Grand Dukes of Mecklenburg–Schwerin, the young man who was later to be King Christian X of Denmark, and an assortment of grand dukes, among them all three of Princess Marina's uncles. She said that even the Grand Duke Vladimir himself told her that at times he regretted that he was no longer young and called her his 'little darling'.

The Grand Dukes Kirill and Boris first introduced their young brother to the prima ballerina as far back as 1897, when they took him along to a dinner party she was giving. As a result of that first encounter her attraction was so great that Grand Duke Andrei fell hopelessly in love with her and thereafter showed her the devotion and faithfulness for which the Romanovs, once they had given their affection, were noted. Never again did he show the slightest interest in any other woman.

In 1897 he was twenty and she was nearing thirty, but age difference meant nothing to him and little to her; and in fact she out-lived everyone. At the time of Princess Marina's death, Kchessinska, in her nineties, was still living in Paris.

In the summer of 1901, on 22 July, after attending his mother's annual birthday picnic, Grand Duke Andrei spent the night with Mathilde Kchessinska for the first time; a date which they celebrated every year afterwards as a special anniversary. That autumn she became pregnant and handed over her ballet roles to a newcomer named Anna Pavlova. The following June, 1902, their son was born.

The baby was named Vladimir, with the consent of the Grand Duke, who produced a cross and chain as a christening present and paid a visit to Kchessinska when she was convalescing after the birth. She recovered so well that, two months later, she danced at a gala performance given at Peterhoff, part of the celebrations for the marriage of Princess Marina's parents.

The Grand Duke Vladimir must have viewed the association with mixed feelings. This was not the first nor the last time that a baby had been born into a royal family out of wedlock. There could be no question of marriage, not even a morganatic one, and at that stage, with so young a man as the Grand Duke Andrei, his family presumed that he would eventually make a suitable match at a later date. In the meantime it was both right and proper that, as a Grand Duke and a gentleman, he should fulfil his obligations and become responsible for the welfare of both his child and his mistress.

The Grand Duchess Vladimir must also have been perfectly aware of what was going on and there is evidence that she objected strongly to this liaison. But she was a broad-minded woman, particularly where her sons were concerned, but there were limits—and she knew where to draw them. Never by the flicker of an eyelash did she ever indicate publicly that she knew of Kchessinska's existence other than as a talented dancer at the Marinsky Theatre.

Grand Duke Andrei managed to escape from Russia. So did his mistress and his son. They all went to live in France.

Thus Grand Duke Vladimir's whole family, including Grand Duchess Vladimir, was preserved and some of his grandchildren live today.

8 | *The Two Grandmothers*

It will be remembered that the Grand Duchess Vladimir had gone to Kislovodsk, a noted Caucasian spa, the day before the Revolution began. Kislovodsk is more than a thousand miles from Moscow, and is a lovely place and very warm; the surrounding slopes and valleys are full of orchards with grapes, figs, oranges, apricots, plums, peaches, pomegranates and sweet pears. In the woods and forests grapes grow wild. The one disadvantage is the bitter and unpleasant taste of the curative waters said to give relief to dozens of ailments ranging from rheumatism to indigestion.

When the Grand Duchess Vladimir was there the town possessed many ornate and splendid houses and was the haunt of rich oil men from Baku and wealthy Ural mine-owners. She rented one of the houses herself, which she shared with her son Andrei and some of her suite. She would have preferred to go as usual to her favourite spa at Contrexéville in France but the Grand Duchess settled down in March, 1917, to enjoy a peaceful and restful holiday, calm her jangled nerves and improve her health.

It was not until some days after her arrival that the Grand Duchess heard 'that somehow power has passed to other hands'. On 15 March, 'like thunder', came the news of the Tsar's abdication. 'In one day the whole past greatness of Russia has disintegrated. Where are we heading?' wrote Grand Duke Andrei in his diary that night.

The Grand Duchess and her son decided to stay where they were until things should become more settled. Soon they had no option other than to do just that. By the end of March the Grand Duchess was under house arrest, apparently as the result of an indiscreet letter written to Grand Duke Boris which had been opened by a censor. The arrest took place at 2.30 in the morning when a deputation of the local revolutionary 'Town Committee' burst into her bedroom and read out the warrant; she showed no sign of nerves at the time but the incident distressed her so much that it was some while before she recovered from the shock.

Vainly she petitioned the Head of the Provisional Government protesting against her imprisonment, backed up by Grand Duke Andrei, who also asked if something could be done to prevent the appearance of 'scurrilous articles blackening the name of my mother'.

In June the Grand Duchess was released and was able to go where she chose. She stayed on in Kislovodsk. Life there was amazingly normal, for the place was scarcely touched by the Revolution, and more and more of her friends left Petrograd and joined her.

Eventually, Grand Duke Boris, together with his mistress, joined his mother and brother. Kchessinska was already there. The Grand Duchess continued, however, to ignore the existence of her sons' mistresses and never acknowledged them by a word or a look: socially they were invisible. And the two Grand Dukes performed marvels in a Jekyll-and-Hyde manner: they managed successfully in turn to be both dutiful sons and devoted lovers.

On a smaller scale the Grand Duchess Vladimir entertained in much the same way as she had in Petrograd, although she had to be careful of her health. She regularly took baths in the 'sour water'; and sometimes her once-pretty legs were swollen so much she had to rest them for days at a time. But her spirits and her humour were, for most of the time, undaunted. Once she was godmother at a christening. The rules of the Orthodox church do not permit the inter-marriage of a child's godparents and, smiling as she said it, the Grand Duchess was quick to point out to the nineteen-year-old boy who was one of the godfathers, 'You realize of course that now you and I can never be husband and wife.' And she was cheered by the news that she had another grandchild—the boy, named Vladimir after his grandfather, born on 30 August 1917 to the Grand Duchess Kirill in Finland.

But the Grand Duchess Vladimir had no information whatever of her daughter Helen or of her three Greek grand-daughters. She did not even know that they were no longer in Greece
but passing away their exile in Switzerland, safe from harm,
while all around them events were taking place which would
change their whole future.

In September 1917 once again the Grand Duchess's privacy
was rudely interrupted. In the early hours of the morning she
had another visit from revolutionaries who remained until six
o'clock searching the house.

Twice after that there were night alarms and she and her two
sons and her entourage had to retreat up to the mountain foothills. On the first foray the revolutionaries made there was so
little warning that she only had time to put on a dressing-gown.
On the second occasion she and her sons had to leave Kislovodsk
for three months. The two Grand Dukes were continually on the
move but the Grand Duchess and many of her friends lived in a
small village belonging to a Cossack tribe and they paid for the
generous peasant hospitality with jewels or I.O.U.s—pieces of
paper signed with the great names of Petrograd which promised
sums of money to be repayable at a future date. She and her
friends used them like five-pound notes. 'When the revolution
is over,' they said, 'we will give you the money, and more.'
For they found it impossible to believe that the situation could
be permanent.

At the end of 1919 the Grand Duchess Vladimir was advised
by the General commanding the last resisting Cossack troops in
the Caucasus that she must leave Kislovodsk permanently.
Typically she managed to do it with both style and dignity in
spite of the almost impossible conditions.

The local railway line had been destroyed so to reach the
nearest railway station about fifty miles away, where a special
train had been put at her disposal, she left the spa in an open
carriage drawn by two horses driven by a Cossack, and those
who watched her go have never forgotten what she looked like
then.

She sat bolt upright in the carriage and a young Maid of
Honour sat opposite her. The Grand Duchess wore discreet and
sensible travelling clothes and with her was a box containing the
jewels she had taken to Kislovodsk. 'If they kill me they can

have them; but not otherwise,' she told her closest friends. And she never turned her head as the horses clip-clopped away followed by the carriages of her staff, and a procession of other refugees who left with her.

When she reached Novorossisk on the coast of the Black Sea, the town itself was full of other eminent refugees on their way out of Russia including the Tsar's sister Grand Duchess Olga Alexandrovna, who, although she had loved Princess Marina and her sisters, was one of those who had never liked the Grand Duchess Vladimir.

But in such times old emnities fade. 'I went to see her,' reported Grand Duchess Olga later. 'I was amazed to learn that she had reached the town in her own train, manned by her own staff, and still had her ladies with her. For all the dangers and privations she still appeared every inch a Grand Duchess. There had never been much love between Aunt Miechen and my own family but I felt proud of her. Disregarding peril and hardship she stubbornly kept to all the trimmings of bygone splendour and glory. And somehow she carried it off. When generals found themselves lucky to find a horse and cart to bring them to safety, Aunt Miechen made a long journey in her own train. It was battered all right but it was hers. For the first time in my life it was a pleasure to kiss her.'

The Grand Duchess Vladimir, like the rest of her family, went to France, travelling by way of Greece, where she spent a few hours visiting the empty Nicholas Palace and picking five violets out of the garden—one for each of them—which she sent to Princess Marina and her family, together with a prayer that they would all see their homes again soon.

She would have been nearly destitute but an English friend recovered the bulk of her jewellery which had been left in a secret safe in the Vladimir Palace. Some of the pieces, such as her tiaras, including the pearl and diamond one she liked best, were taken to bits, wrapped in newspaper and placed with the rest of her jewels in two battered leather gladstone bags. These were smuggled out of Russia to England and eventually returned to her.

Princess Marina's other grandmother, Queen Olga of Greece, who had remained in Russia when the war began and was still there during the Revolution, divided her time between the Marble Palace in Petrograd and her country home at Pavlovsk, where sentries were posted. No harm had come to her but there had been one nasty moment when a detachment of Soviet soldiers and sailors were sent to the palace, when Queen Olga was asleep, to find out whether a store of arms was hidden there or not—a rumour had been going round that there was. Some sailors were just about to enter Queen Olga's bedroom door when a maid, who had been in her service for fifty years, stopped them. She recognized one or two of the sailors as belonging to the Russian ships which Queen Olga had visited when they had stopped in Greece. The maid told them that they should be ashamed of their ingratitude and she loosed upon them such a flood of abuse that the whole party slunk guiltily away. The raid was postponed for several days.

It was only when Queen Olga heard that her eldest son King Constantine, in exile in Switzerland, had become seriously ill that the Queen decided to leave Russia. Her departure was arranged by the Danish minister in Petrograd and she even managed to get most of her jewellery to safety before she left. It was smuggled out by a Greek student who called at the palace with a box of books which was opened and searched on his arrival but not when he left. Of course, when he left the Queen's jewels were inside the box in place of the books. The jewels were later delivered to the Danish Legation and forwarded to Copenhagen.

At the beginning of July 1918, two years before the Grand Duchess Vladimir's departure from Russia, Queen Olga arrived in Switzerland, where she was met by her family whom she had not seen for four years.

9 | *Greek Refugees*

The reunion between Queen Olga and her family was a joyful one. 'For us poor exiles, to meet our mother . . . was like shipwrecked passengers meeting on a desert island,' said Prince Nicholas. He and the rest of the Greek Royal Family, who had been in Switzerland since they left Greece so hurriedly in July 1917, were to remain there for nearly four years moving between St Moritz, Zurich, Lucerne and Lausanne, leading a roving, nomadic existence surrounded by an atmosphere of hostility and intrigue. For a while Prince Nicholas rented a studio and took up painting in earnest, often keeping at it for six hours a day. Time hung heavily on his hands and it helped him to forget and also earned him money. He did enough sketches and water colours to hold a modest exhibition, and was delighted to sell some for a 'decent price'.

Quite often Princess Marina went with him to his studio and on his sketching expeditions and he bought her an easel and some paints and encouraged her to paint, which sometimes she did. All three sisters were proficient at drawing but she perhaps was the most talented. A succession of part-time governesses were employed to continue their formal education, though there were plenty of other distractions: ski-ing, tobogganing and skating in the winter; tennis, swimming, rowing and sunbathing in the summer.

'No rigid code of etiquette oppressed their youthful spirits,' commented their uncle Prince Christopher. 'Their discipline was of the mildest and in the intervals between lessons they ran wild.'

But behind all the cheerfulness of their daily lives there was a great deal happening. 'We had soon to discover,' said Prince

Nicholas, 'that here in the calm and peacefulnes of this neutral country, we were still marked down as dangerous, political intriguers who had to be closely watched, and shunned by everyone belonging to the Entente nations.'

Queen Olga found King Constantine very ill indeed with pleurisy, but a second operation in St Moritz, soon after she arrived, seemed to bring about an improvement. Meanwhile, in Greece the young and lonely King Alexander battled with the affairs of state as best he could. And he consoled his loneliness with the company of a childhood playmate, the 'exquisitely beautiful' daughter of his father's A.D.C. named Aspasia Manos, whom he married in a secret ceremony asking neither the consent of his father nor the head of the Greek Orthodox Church. The morganatic marriage caused a storm of protest when it became known, but was eventually recognized as legal. The baby daughter born to them and called Alexandra was given the title of Princess, though the King's wife was known as plain Madame Manos.

In the early summer of 1920 the Grand Duchess Vladimir· made her way from France to Switzerland to rejoin her daughter and her grandchildren whom she had not seen for six years. The three girls were now aged seventeen, sixteen and thirteen. To Princess Marina, who had been not quite seven years old when she had last seen her grandmother, the Grand Duchess seemed at first to be almost a stranger. But not for long. The indomitable Grand Duchess, tired and ill after all that she had experienced, but with her courage and humour still intact, and her hope that she would one day return to Russia undimmed, entered with great zest into all that her three grand-daughters were doing—even to taking a keen interest in a weekly western film serial they were allowed to watch—and making great plans for their future. In a very short while they returned to the same loving relationship they had had with her before.

In July the Grand Duchess Vladimir left her family and returned to France to Contrexéville, a French spa, which she was convinced would restore her health. They never saw her again. Two months later at dawn on 6 September 1920, at the age of sixty-six, the grandest Grand Duchess of them all, died at the French spa. Her three sons, Kirill, Boris and Andrei and her daughter Helen were all with her—but not Prince Nicholas.

Politics again stepped in. 'I was denied the privilege of going to her death bed, as I was refused a passport to France,' he said bitterly afterwards. And nor were Princess Marina and her sisters allowed to leave.

The Grand Duchess is buried in Contrexéville in a chapel which she had had built not far from the hotel where she used to stay; and one of the streets in the town is still called the Avenue Grande Duchesse Vladimir. In her will she left her pearls and diamonds, including her favourite tiara, to Princess Nicholas, her emeralds to Grand Duke Boris and the rest of her jewels divided between Grand Dukes Kirill and Andrei.

Not long afterwards Grand Duke Boris married Zina Rashevskaya; Grand Duke Andrei married Mathilde Kchessinska; and from Switzerland Miss Fox received a telegram asking her to spend a holiday with her former employers, Prince and Princess Nicholas and the girls whom she called her 'three beauties'.

And, if Princess Marina's family had only known it, in Greece that same summer, things as far as they were concerned were changing very much for the better. Early in June, Earl Granville, the British Minister in Athens, wrote to Lord Curzon of Kedleston reminding him that elections were due in November and reported the increasing demand for the restoration of King Constantine as monarch of the Hellenes. 'I have always felt confident that provided the decisions of the Peace Conference were favourable to Greece, Venizelos was safe to secure a majority—and probably a big majority—at the elections,' he said, 'but I confess that during the last few days my confidence has been a good deal shaken; any number of people have told me stories of strong feeling existing in the country against him. . . .'

There was a simple reason for the growing anti-Venizelist feeling: the Greek statesman had been so busy dealing with international matters that to some extent he had lost control of the situation at home and during his frequent absences abroad the internal affairs of Greece were mismanaged by a collection of politicians and officials, many of whom were corrupt and inept. Prolonged mobilization, ever since the Balkan Wars, also caused some revulsion against the government. And, as one member of the British Legation was to say, 'there has always existed among the lower classes, at all events, a considerable affection for King Constantine'. He put the whole situation in a nutshell when he declared that the one desire of the normal Greek was to have both Constantine and Venizelos. But this, of course, could never come about because of the enmity which existed between the two men.

Suddenly in October, one more element was introduced. King Alexander, the unhappy young monarch, was out with his dog one day when it was attacked by a pair of pet monkeys belonging to the keeper of the Tatoi vineyard. Trying to separate the three animals the King was bitten in the arm and leg by one of the monkeys. Blood poisoning set in and on 25 October before his grandmother Queen Olga (the only member of his family allowed to leave Switzerland) could reach him, he died. Once more Greece was without a Sovereign.

Before King Alexander was even dead, there were discussions as to who should succeed him—and King Constantine was not in the running as far as Venizelos or the British Government were concerned. Prince Paul, the King's third son, was asked to accept the throne and refused it because his father and eldest brother had not renounced their rights. And one of the British diplomats in Athens seems to have been influenced by a certain amount of wishful thinking when, on the day of King Alexander's death, he telegraphed to London saying, 'inquiries will be made amongst foreign ruling families; popular sentiment being very strongly in favour of application to English Royal House'. Then he added: 'Queen Olga, widow of King George, arrives today to see her grandson. It is suggested that she may be invited to assume the Regency if he dies.'

The promised elections were held less than a fortnight later and Venizelists won only 120 seats out of the 370 in the Greek Parliament. A message received at eight o'clock on the evening of 15 November informed the British Government that Venizelos was hopelessly beaten and that he had handed in his resignation.

When the election results were announced the politically conscious Greeks went mad with enthusiasm—particularly the gleeful Royalists. In an amnesty prisoners were released and a huge crowd roamed the streets of Athens shouting and firing revolvers in the air in the old traditional manner and were so excited and good humoured that many of them congregated in

front of the British Legation cheering for England. But inside
the Legation British diplomats were in a mood of troubled per-
plexity, wondering what attitude they should take towards
this new and unexpected turn of events. The whole thing was
brought to a head by the projected return of Prince Nicholas
and Prince Andrew and their respective families, and the vexed
problem of whether the British Minister should call on them and
write his name formally in their visitors' book. In support of
this he said, 'Nobody outside Greece can realize the complete
change of popular opinion which has taken place . . . and the
almost insane enthusiasm at this moment for Constantine'. He
also expressed his 'deep regret' for his mistaken assessment of
the probable results of the General Election. 'My only consolation,' he said, 'is that I am in good company.' He wrote to
England for advice and received a curt reply from Britain:
'You should refrain from seeing or communicating with the
Princes or writing names, and avoid taking any action whatsoever which would imply eventual recognition of the ex-King. . . .'

During the interim Princess Marina's grandmother, the
gentle warm-hearted Queen Olga who had never in her life
dabbled in politics, became, as predicted, the Regent of Greece.

In Switzerland Princess Marina and her sisters were blissfully
getting ready to go home again after those three and a half
futile years of exile. They never forgot the 'incredulous joy and
emotion' the day they began their journey back to Greece and
their excitement when they found the Nicholas Palace just as
they had left it. 'It was like a dream come true,' they said years
later. Every public appearance made by them—or any other
members of the family, who returned one by one, during November—was greeted with ecstatic displays of welcome from
the cheering crowds—who sometimes, swayed by almost embarrassing fervour, would try to carry them shoulder-high
through the Athens streets. Pictures of King Constantine reappeared miraculously in shops and houses, and 'Son of the
Eagle' was played with energy and increasing regularity.

On 5 December 1920 a plebiscite was held all over Greece
at King Constantine's request to decide whether he should be
recalled. More than a million votes were polled and less than
eleven thousand were against his return.

On 19 December, a day when there was a violent snowstorm,

King Constantine returned to his capital where he was formally greeted by his delighted mother. And the Greek people turned up in thousands to welcome back the King. That night an enormous, illuminated crown shone over Athens from the heights of the Parthenon, a local brewer distributed free beer and flags flew from almost every building. But not on the British Legation. Lord Granville had been instructed not to enter into any official or ceremonial relations with King Constantine or his Court, and not to attend any official function of the present Greek Government. He was also told that flags should not be flown. It was an embarrassing position for him to be in, and one which was not relieved for many months.

For a short time Princess Marina and her sisters had a happy time in Greece. They were overjoyed to be back in the country of their birth, and to see all their old friends again. There was the additional pleasure of three family events, including two big weddings which took place in 1921. One was the marriage of their cousin Helen (King Constantine's eldest daughter) to Crown Prince Carol of Rumania, to whom they were also related, another was the marriage, in Bucharest, of Crown Prince George to Princess Elizabeth, sister of Crown Prince Carol.

On 10 June 1921 there was an addition to the Royal Family. At 'Mon Repos' in Corfu, a boy later named Philip was born to Princess Andrew. He is now, of course, married to Queen Elizabeth II.

But perhaps the happiest person was Kate Fox who had rejoined the family immediately after their arrival in Greece after a separation of eight years. Princess Marina hardly remembered her, but it did not take Miss Fox long to resume her former relationship with the three princesses and in spite of the fact that she was obviously no longer needed as a nanny she busied herself looking after their welfare and ordered them about as she had been accustomed to do for so long after their birth.

Before King Constantine had been back on his throne for three months Greece was mobilizing for yet another war against the Turks, this time to establish sovereignty in Asia Minor. The wheels had been set in motion by Venizelos and King Constantine could do little to prevent the war, although it was entirely against his wishes. The Greek people, excited by the prospect of increasing their territory, and the Greek Army, convinced of victory, clamoured to go to battle and the King's objections were over-ruled. But without the backing of Britain and France—withdrawn mainly because of their antipathy to the monarch—Greece did not stand much chance. The war lasted from January 1921 until September 1922. It ended in total defeat for the Greek Army. As a result of this, Greece lost all the territories she had been given at the post-war Peace Conference; schools were turned into barracks to house the defeated soldiers who limped back into Athens; and a mass of refugees, estimated at more than a million and a half, invaded the capital and were housed in such places as the old Royal Palace. To top it all a vital aqueduct broke, there was a shortage of water and an epidemic of typhoid and typhus.

Athens became a ferment of politics; split right in two by those who supported the King and those who supported Venizelos. Even members of the same family would have bitter conflicts and would not meet or talk to each other. Entertaining was fraught with emotional hazards: if guests of differing opinions were invited to the same house they would either leave or politely ignore one another. Steamers sailing between the islands indulged in a sort of apartheid—royalists sat on one side of the ship and Venizelists on the other.

During the first year of the war Princess Marina and her sisters spent much of the time with Miss Fox at Tatoi. Princess Nicholas worked in hospitals and Prince Nicholas and his brothers were fighting in Asia Minor. Later Prince Nicholas organized shows for war charities in which all three of his daughters took part. But in the spring of 1922 Princess Nicholas, 'much against her will', left Greece with her daughters. And shortly afterwards Queen Olga, whose eyesight was deteriorating, went to Paris for treatment.

10 | *Exile in France*

Miss Fox took Princess Marina off to England for a holiday, whilst Princess Nicholas and her two eldest daughters went to Cannes to stay with Prince Christopher. As a result, Princess Marina missed all the excitement of Princess Olga's engagement to Crown Prince Frederick, heir to the throne of Denmark, which took place there. It was planned that the wedding was to take place in Denmark 'early in the summer'. In spite of the political situation, news of the impending marriage was received enthusiastically even in Greece.

It seemed on the surface a highly suitable match even though their characters differed enormously. Princess Olga, always the quietest of the three sisters, was dignified and stately though she was only twenty; while the tall and strapping Danish Prince was much more of an extrovert.

Twice during the next few months the wedding was postponed, and it was soon apparent that everybody was having second thoughts. Late that summer when all of them, Princess Marina included, were together in Paris, Princess Olga and the Crown Prince had a misunderstanding. The engagement was broken off by mutual consent. At first this caused a great deal of consternation in the Greek family circle. It is not every day that a princess refuses the chance to become a queen. But Princess Olga, although she liked her Danish cousin, did not love him, and she said so. 'Everyone discussed the situation solemnly in the drawing-room after lunch,' said Prince Christopher afterwards. Then fifteen-year-old Princess Marina, who was sitting at the window sketching, shattered them all by butting in and saying loudly and vehemently, 'Why the hell should Olga marry him if she doesn't love him? I wouldn't . . .'

Princess Nicholas, who had been the first to see the advant-
ages of the alliance, was the first to give in. And as nearly everybody was to comment afterwards there was something very
much like an air of relief all round. In Copenhagen, at the end
of September it was announced officially that the engagement
had ended.

Some years later the Crown Prince was happily married to
Princess Ingrid of Sweden and it was she who became Queen of
Denmark. An alliance between Greece and Denmark did not
take place until Princess Anne Marie, the youngest daughter of
King Frederick, married the young man who is now King Con-
stantine II.

While Princess Nicholas and her three daughters were in
Paris that same summer the situation in Greece had now
become so bad that everybody was distracted by much bigger
problems than the foundering of an engagement. The blame
for the rout of the Greek Army was inevitably put on the
King; and disillusioned officers organized a revolt. The Military
League was re-born and the whole country was on the verge of
revolution. Said Prince Nicholas: 'When the retreating officers
turned their swords against their King and Commander-in-
Chief and demanded his abdication he was too stunned to feel
even bitterness or resentment.' On 26 September King Constantine abdicated in favour of Crown Prince George who
became King George II of the Hellenes.

But matters did not end there: the few weeks which remained
between the King's act of abdication and his final departure
from Greece were not only uncomfortable but perilous. Because
of the revolt various ministries in Athens were in a state of indescribable confusion and seven former Ministers were arrested.
But although members of all political parties had taken part in
the upheaval, only the more violent reactionaries were in favour
of executing the deposed monarch. Nevertheless some anti-
royalists were so set on vengeance that the senior French
diplomat in the Greek capital 'animated by humane feeling'
said more than once that it was essential to get the King away
without delay if he was to avoid being assassinated. 'There was
considerable anxiety as to the safety of the Royal Family
which I regret to say was not concealed from them,' emphasized
a special report to the British Government. It came to the

point that Prince Nicholas sent a message to the head of the British Naval Mission asking if a British man-of-war could take the whole family away from Greece as they were 'in imminent danger': a request which, unknown to him, was even backed up by Greek Army colonels.

The government in England were as cautious as ever. 'It is certainly to be hoped that we shall not become involved in the misfortunes of the Greek Royal Family,' said a Foreign Office dispatch to Athens; and it blandly continued, 'On the other hand we would, of course, intervene to avoid actual bloodshed.'

Prince Nicholas, with King Constantine and Queen Sophie and their daughters Irene and Katherine, eventually left just before midnight on 30 October—in an insanitary steamer called the S.S. *Patris*, en route for Palermo in Italy. 'The usual military honours were paid and a considerable number of His Majesty's personal friends were on the pier to say goodbye, which was a painful sight as both men and women were crying,' reported the British Admiral who saw them leave. 'The King's popularity is little appreciated out of this country and although everybody is determined to get rid of him once and for all, as the only means of saving the country, the feelings of the populace remain unchanged.'

But the day after King Constantine embarked his pictures were removed from shop windows and replaced by those of Venizelos. And the organ-grinders in Constitution Square took 'Son of the Eagle' out of their repertoire.

In Paris Princess Marina and the rest of her family were shocked to hear, mistakenly, that Prince Nicholas had been shot. The news came at the end of a nightmare few weeks. Princess Nicholas had caught diphtheria, and, as a result, was asked to leave her hotel room; it was only with the greatest difficulty that a hospital bed had been found for her. It was with enormous relief that, not long afterwards, another telegram arrived to say that not only was Prince Nicholas alive and well but he had arrived safely at Palermo. As soon as their mother was well enough to travel Princess Marina and her sisters set off with her to join their father in Italy.

At first there had been no accommodation ready for King Constantine and his party and they spent a week in what was literally a lousy ship before moving into a hotel in Palermo. 'I was much impressed with the bearing of Their Majesties during the time on board,' said a Royal Naval officer who accompanied them. 'Though obviously very tired and overstrained they showed great dignity and self control and made light of the inconveniences with which they had to put up.' In truth it must have made little difference to the King whatever happened to him for he was a dying man. But apart from King Constantine's failing health there were other members of Princess Marina's family to worry about. Particularly Prince Andrew.

Prince Andrew had been summoned to Athens from Corfu, ostensibly to give evidence at the trial of the seven ministers accused of 'having instigated the Asia Minor campaign', but he had been arrested the minute he set foot in the Greek capital. He was kept in solitary confinement awaiting trial on the same charge and the result, to some people, was a foregone conclusion.

Prince Andrew was not allowed to receive any letters or parcels and the only message he received was one scrawled on cigarette paper and smuggled into him by his valet. It came from his brother Prince Christopher, temporarily back in Athens on a mission to rescue Princess Nicholas's jewellery— which, as well as her own splendid collection, included the valuable gems she had inherited from the Grand Duchess Vladimir.

King George II, who was under constant surveillance, was powerless to intervene on behalf of his imprisoned uncle but strenuous efforts were made elsewhere to free Prince Andrew. In Greece Princess Andrew and various friends did their best. From Paris Queen Olga appealed to the King of Spain, the President of France and the King of England.

But it was mainly due to direct intervention of King George V that Prince Andrew was given his freedom. A British destroyer was sent to fetch him, together with his family, to England. The seven ministers were shot.

The news of this reprieve brightened up the Greek party at Palermo which now included Princess Marina and her family. They were further cheered by a hilarious account of Prince Christopher's adventures. He had tried to make an unostentatious exit from Greece with a vast amount of luggage which included two large suitcases filled with money and securities

which belonged to himself and Prince Nicholas, an insecure
wooden box which contained Princess Nicholas's jewellery and
a basket containing her persian cat, the elderly 'Pussy'.

Prince Christopher had been worried about the box of jewels
because, as he said, the bottom was all but falling out and he had
visions of shedding tiaras and ropes of pearls along the quay at
Piraeus from which he was to leave by rowing-boat to
board a waiting Italian steamer. But it was the suitcases which
burst open, at the same time as the cat began to yowl loudly,
calling a certain amount of unwanted attention to the abscond-
ing Greek Prince and his party.

They all but fell into the rowing-boat while trying to quieten
the cat, scoop up packets of money and retrieve stray socks
scattered along the edge of the harbour. Finally Prince Christopher buffeted a sentry in the stomach in order to climb up the
steamer's gangway and on to 'Italian ground'. It was an episode
which owed more to farce than anything else and he made the
most of it as he told the story.

Even then it had not ended. At Brindisi, where he spent a
night, the poor cat escaped, ran along the corridors of the
hotel where he was staying and took refuge under the bed of an
English maiden lady who had a horror of cats. For a few minutes
pandemonium reigned, but the cat was eventually rescued and
the lady soothed. The train journey to Palermo was also event-
ful. Princess Nicholas had given strict instructions that her
'Pussy' should be well exercised. Every few hours, whenever the
train stopped long enough at a station, Prince Christopher
walked up and down with the jewels under his arm and the cat
on a leash. Again the cat escaped, hid under the carriage seat
and was covered with black soot when finally handed over to
its anxious mistress.

The jewels, which were to be so important to Princess Marina
and her family, were the focal point of this second rescue. But
it was the cat which concerned Princess Nicholas most. 'What
have you done to the poor thing?', she asked her exhausted
brother-in-law. 'What,' he cried, 'has it not done to me?'

This tale even enlivened King Constantine and in a way they
all had something to be thankful for. The climate was warm and
sunny; the Italians were kind. 'It was very different from those
miserable years in Switzerland when the whole of Europe was

against us,' noted Prince Christopher. And referring to Princess
Marina, her sisters and her cousins, he said: 'The younger
members of the family were happy enough.'

Early in January 1923 King Constantine died. Officially his
death was caused by pneumonia: but nearly every member of
his family was convinced that he was killed by a broken heart.
And in December that year Greece became a republic and
Princess Marina's cousin, King George II, joined the ranks of the
exiles. Another new era of banishment started for them all and
some did not live to see the end of it. For Princess Marina, who
was getting on for seventeen, began an existence in a sort of
royal limbo which was to last until she emerged startlingly from
obscurity when she became engaged eleven years later.

In the summer of that year Princess Marina and her sisters
went to London with their mother for the Season and stayed at a
modest hotel in Queen's Gate. Because of the political situation
their presence in England went almost entirely unnoticed.
Princess Marina herself was so little known that on the rare
occasions her name appeared in print it was invariably mis-
spelt, as 'Marita', 'Marie' or 'Marianne'.

During the Season of 1923 Princess Marina's two elder sisters,
Princess Olga, now aged twenty and Princess Elizabeth, nineteen, had a joint 'coming-out' which they greatly enjoyed.
Princess Marina did not officially come out until the following
year but it was obvious even then that Queen Mary already had
high hopes that one of her sons might become engaged to her
goddaughter. The Queen's Lady-in-Waiting, Lady Cynthia
Colville, writing about Princess Marina at that time said she was
'struck by her great charm and good looks'; and added that she
could 'see her now in the King's box at the Royal Tournament in
a most becoming blue chiffon dress'. Significantly Lady Cynthia
also said: 'Many people thought what a happy opportunity this
might be for the Prince of Wales . . . though this did
not materialize.'

It must have been a disappointment for Queen Mary when
neither her eldest son nor Princess Marina displayed much
interest in each other. But no amount of conniving can manu-
facture a romance. As usual it was the unexpected which happened and it was Princess Olga, not Princess Marina, who fell
in love during that English visit: with a tall good-looking

young man whom she met at the races during Ascot Week.

His name was Prince Paul: he was twenty-nine and a cousin of King Alexander King of the Serbs, Croats and Slovenes.

A month after he and Princess Olga met they became engaged: in October 1923 they were married.

At that time Prince Paul was fourth in succession to the throne. His father, Prince Arsene Karageorgevitch of Serbia, was an officer in the Russian Army and a younger brother of King Peter of Serbia who became monarch after the murder of King Alexander Obrenovitch which took place on the day of Princess Olga's birth. His mother was Russian: Princess Aurora Demidoff, a member of a fantastically wealthy family whose fortune came mainly from rich mineral mines in the Urals.

Prince Paul was born in St Petersburg but when he was a year old his parents separated and he was brought up in Switzerland by his uncle Peter, who was a widower with three children of his own. King Peter's second son, Alexander, was to succeed him, first as Prince Regent and then as King.

All members of the Karageorgevitch dynasty were descended from a Serbian chieftain known as Black George, who freed the country from Turkish rule in 1810 and was looked upon by the Serbs as the founder of their liberty. He was a landowner and a pig farmer and a military genius: a tall temperamental man with 'burning eyes and coal black hair' who had his brother hung for rape and killed his stepfather to prevent him being tortured by the Turks. He ruled Serbia for nine years, during which time he organized a constitution and was responsible for the drafting of a legal code, before being assassinated when he was asleep in a cave. He was succeeded by his rival, another Serbian leader, named Obrenovitch.

If Prince Paul inherited any of the disposition of his great grandfather Black George, it was not apparent. From his earliest days he was more interested in art than anything else.

In 1914 he was at Christ Church Oxford and began his undergraduate days in some style arriving with two servants, a Daimler and a chauffeur.

When he left Oxford, he shared a flat in London with a friend and Prince Felix Youssupov also in London then, pronounced him 'a very pleasant fellow, a good musician and excellent company'.

Prince Paul got on very well with his cousin, the King. They had been brought up as brothers and he was therefore not only King Alexander's close relation but probably his most intimate friend. And the Serbian king needed all the friends he could get.

He had succeeded to the throne as Prince Regent ten days before the assassination of Archduke Franz Ferdinand at Sarajevo, and he became King after his father's death in 1921. By this time the country of Yugoslavia had emerged as a result of a manifesto issued in 1918 after the war, which declared that certain independent sovereign states, which included Serbia, Croatia and Slovenia, and several Austro-Hungarian provinces would be combined to form one nation.

It is never easy to combine kingdoms and provinces particularly if the kingdoms and provinces concerned are so different as to be incompatible. In the case of Yugoslavia the new country was composed of an extraordinary mixture of races, religions, political beliefs, cultural traditions and languages. King Alexander had a difficult task in front of him.

In the Serbian capital, Belgrade, Princess Olga married Prince Paul on 2 October 1923. The wedding took place the day after the christening of King Alexander's month-old son and heir, Peter. King George VI and Queen Elizabeth—then the recently married Duke and Duchess of York—were the Serbian equivalent of godparents to the baby. And the Duke of York was the official representative of King George V at the wedding. 'We were quite a large family party and how we all lived in the Palace is a mystery,' he wrote to his father afterwards. 'We were not too comfortable, and there was no hot water.'

It was indeed a family party. King Alexander's wife Queen Marie, known to most of the family as 'Mignon', was another kinswoman of Princess Marina and her sisters as she was the daughter of Queen Marie of Rumania. And another guest was their aunt, the exiled Queen Sophie. 'Aunt Sophie . . . has aged a great deal, poor lady, after all she has been through. She sends you and Mama many messages and is longing to come back to England,' wrote the Duke of York to King George in England.

Princess Olga and her husband spent Christmas that year in Paris with her family and also had a happy reunion with their cousins, the children of Prince Andrew who, like Prince Nicholas, had decided to live in France.

Given a free choice Princess Marina and her parents would probably have settled in England when they were exiled for the second time but it would have been difficult both politically and financially. Because of the rate of exchange it was then considerably cheaper to live in France and Prince and Princess Nicholas were short of money. Almost their only source of regular income was the rent of their house in Athens which from 1925 to 1933 was leased to the Grand Bretagne, Athens' main hotel. Although much of the original furniture was moved into store there was still enough left to make the so-called annexe rather more splendid than the hotel and it was given the new name of 'Le petit palais'.

The large annuity Princess Nicholas had received from the Apanages had of course ceased at the time of the Russian Revolution and it had been necessary to sell some of the Grand Duchess Vladimir's jewels in 1921. There was no public sale. The jewellery was disposed of quietly and discreetly to richer relatives. And it was Queen Mary who bought the Grand Duchess's beautiful pearl and diamond tiara and in her own Will left it to the present Queen. The family's slender resources were supplemented from time to time by the sale of pictures painted by Prince Nicholas, under the name of Nicholas Leprince.

According to some people who knew the family in Paris and saw them occasionally in the South of France during their second exile, they were 'very, very poor'. But 'poor' is a relative term; 'hard up' might be a better description. The hotels they lived in for the first three years were as inexpensive as possible and the apartments they took later were not in the luxury class; but their circumstances, boosted when absolutely necessary by the disposal of another jewel or two, fluctuated like a tide. They had, for example, four servants and sometimes a car and a chauffeur, though the car was a modest one. And if they had only known it there was even more money, not discovered until after her death, which Princess Nicholas had deposited in a Swiss bank during their first exile and had then forgotten all

about. In Paris she very much regretted the loss of her income
from the Apanages. 'When I wanted money before I had only
to ask a secretary for it,' she would sometimes recall with a
sigh.

But both Princess Marina and Princess Elizabeth were always
well dressed. Through a Greek friend they got clothes at discount prices from the noted French couturier Jean Patou;
dresses which were well-worn then remodelled, dyed, and remodelled again.

For a family which for years had lived in the greatest luxury,
they learned very quickly how to practise economy. It was a
lesson Princess Marina absorbed so efficiently that she never
really lost it—which was just as well. Her thrifty ways were to
come in very useful in the future.

Until she became engaged, and the sale of some gems helped
to provide Princess Marina's trousseau, there was only one
other large-scale disposal of the Grand Duchess Vladimir's
jewels during those years in France. With the consent of her
daughters, Princess Nicholas sold enough to rent a château at
St Germain-en-Laye—not for herself or her family but to house
the children of Russian refugees.

Paris was chock-full of émigrés from the Revolution. This
was the period depicted in many a Hollywood film, when every
taxi driver seemed to be a prince, every waiter a count, and
every chambermaid a baroness.

But the necessity of earning a living meant that many
children of refugees were left alone while their parents went to
work. Princess Nicholas was horrified to find that 'children
often too young to speak' were sometimes locked up in attics
all day; and in May 1924 she started a 'Home for Russian
Children' aged from two to ten which was a refuge for more
than fifty such children where they could be looked after, fed,
clothed, taught and housed.

Princess Nicholas was founder and President. A friend from
Russia, Madame Komstadious, was Vice President and Honor-
ary Secretary and eventually took over the organization. A
Russian General did the marketing and his wife superintended
the running of the home. There were Russian nurses, and
Russian priests to look after the children's spiritual welfare.

Twice a year Princess Nicholas, aided by Princess Marina and her sister Elizabeth, arranged some fête, bazaar, ball or similar function to raise money to keep it going and many contributions came from other sources. Some of these came from her own family, like Prince Christopher who at that time had a wealthy wife—or friends such as Mrs Cornelius Vanderbilt and the former Duchess of Marlborough, now Mrs Cornelius Balsan, who had once admired the Grand Duchess Vladimir's gems.

Among the other Russian émigrés in Europe was a large scattering of exiled Romanovs. At this time they were all busily engaged in trying to decide whom they should acknowledge as the next Tsar should Russia ever regain its sovereignty. Even Princess Marina's family circle was not consolidated in its attitude.

The three main contenders for the title of Tsar after the death of Nicholas II were all related in some way to Princess Marina. One was her uncle, Grand Duke Kirill; another was her cousin, Grand Duke Dmitri. The third was another kinsman, Grand Duke Nicholas Nicholaevirch, a grandson of Tsar Nicholas I, who had taken over command of the Russian Army after her grandfather's resignation but was eventually supplanted as Commander-in-Chief by the Tsar. Because of his birth and his former military rank a certain faction of the White Russian émigrés considered his to be the only possible claim.

Grand Duke Kirill, who would normally have been everybody's choice without any hesitation, had three severe handicaps. The first was because Grand Duchess Vladimir had not embraced the Orthodox Faith until after his birth; the fact that she had changed her religion made no difference to the old Romanov law of succession which decreed that to inherit the Russian throne a Tsar must be born of Orthodox parents. Secondly, although Grand Duke Kirill had not married morganatically, his wife was his cousin—another prohibited relationship where the marriage of a Tsar was concerned. Thirdly, there were many who could never forgive him for having marched under a red flag and with a red rosette in his buttonhole to surrender his troops to the Provisional Government at Petrograd after the Tsar's abdication in 1917.

Grand Duke Kirill explained why he did this in his memoirs.

'During the last days of February, the anarchy in the metropo-
lis had become such that the Government issued an appeal to all
troops and their Commanders to show their allegiance to the
Government by marching to the Duma and declaring their
loyalty.' A measure which he said was designed to 're-establish
some kind of order' and get what he called 'the rule of gangster-
ism' checked for good.

It was an order which applied to his men as it did to other
troops and, further, it applied to him as their commander. It
was either that, or he would have had to resign and leave them
leaderless, 'and thus to let them drift on the rocks of revolution
like the rest.'

'My main concern,' he reiterated, 'was to do my utmost to
re-establish order in the capital by every means available, even
if it meant the sacrifice of my personal pride, so that the Tsar
might safely return.' And he might have got away with it had
it not been for that red emblem he had worn; an added piece of
misguided enthusiasm which those who remembered it never
forgot.

The third possibility, the reluctant Grand Duke Dmitri, had
already had more notoriety than he wanted. 'There can be and
never will be any return to the old forms of our country's life,'
he said. 'Only a parliamentary democracy based on the firm
wish of the people can save our fatherland'—and he went on to
make it quite clear that whatever happened he would only
accept the Russian crown in the unlikely event that it was at
the express wish of the whole nation.

He had gone to England from Persia and enlisted in the
British Army. He was appointed an honorary captain and later
became a colonel. When he was discharged after the war his
nerves were so shattered that he rarely went anywhere without
a bodyguard—a great whacking Russian.

So he divided his time between England and France and
managed to remain on good terms with nearly everybody. He
visited Grand Duke Boris in Biarritz, Grand Duke Andrei on
the Riviera, and the Dowager Empress Marie Feodorovna, who
had also escaped from Russia. In Paris he saw a lot of Princess
Marina and her sister Elizabeth and gradually regained his
former good spirits.

But Princess Marina and her family not unnaturally supported the claim of Grand Duke Kirill as the heir-apparent although her uncles Grand Dukes Boris and Andrei preferred to recognize Grand Duke Nicholas. This may have been because they too, disapproved of their elder brother's hasty allegiance to the government which had overthrown the Tsar, but the attitude of Princess Nicholas towards them may have had something to do with it. For she had the same awareness of precedence as the Grand Duchess Vladimir, and refused to acknowledge her morganatic sisters-in-law.

Once when she found herself in a box at the theatre adjacent to Grand Duke Boris and his wife, Princess Nicholas ignored both of them the whole evening. Another time she was extremely angry when she discovered that they had been invited to a ball she had organized in aid of Russian charities and again she was forced to spend the evening pretending that they were not there. The situation was made all the more painful for her as he had been her favourite brother which was why he was Princess Marina's godfather. Yet it must be said that Grand Duke Boris, despite his previous reputation and his unlikely marriage, settled down happily in exile. First at a house at Meudon near Paris, and then at Cannes and he lived stylishly and contentedly 'and in good care' on the proceeds of the Grand Duchess Vladimir's emeralds, with his finances managed ably and shrewdly by his astute wife. According to one of his friends 'Grand Duke Boris never experienced any hardships or need of money until the day of his death'.

Life was not quite so good to Grand Duke Andrei. Mathilde Kchessinska, now known as Princess Krassinska, was never one to economize; though she denied the stories circulating around Paris that she gambled away most of her husband's share of his mother's jewellery in the Casino at Monte Carlo. But it is certainly a fact that she was eventually forced to try and earn some money herself. Not by dancing again—she was now too old for that—but she did set up a studio in Paris where she gave lessons to budding ballerinas and to talented dancers who went to her for further instruction.

While Paris bubbled with the aftermath of Russian politics, Princess Marina at last completed her spasmodic and erratic education with a year at a finishing school run by a Russian refugee called Princess Metchersky who had been at Kislovodsk with her grandmother. She also had professional art lessons and spent a good deal of her spare time helping Princess Nicholas deal with her charity work. And although the family was short of money it was on the whole a very contented one, and, as always, remarkably united and affectionate. Even though they badly missed Princess Olga they spent several summer months at a time in Yugoslavia, and every year—Princess Olga and her husband included—went to England. They were in England in the summer of 1924 when Princess Olga had her first baby, a son named Alexander, born at White Lodge, Richmond. The house had been lent to them by the Duke and Duchess of York who were away on a tour at the time.

Princess Marina's grandmother, Queen Olga, was also in England then, paying a visit to her sister-in-law, Queen Alexandra, at Marlborough House and the Princess and her family went to see her there.

Queen Olga's eyesight had worsened so much that she was almost blind, and Queen Alexandra had become extremely deaf. When Queen Olga was with her grand-daughters she would take them to a window and try to see their faces clearly and sometimes she passed her hands over their features to distinguish them. By this time she was aged seventy-two and still as gentle and loving as she had ever been.

She was now living permanently in Rome where Prince Christopher had bought a villa: and it was there that she died on 19 June 1926.

Even her funeral was marred by 'the canker of politics'. A wreath sent by the Greek Minister in Rome would only be accepted by King George II and Prince Christopher on condition that the ribbons bore an inscription that it was presented 'on behalf of Greece and the Greek people' whom Queen Olga had loved for fifty years and 'for whom she had spent all her strength'. The Greek Minister who had taken along a wreath marked 'Greece, to Her Majesty Queen Olga' took it away again and did not attend the funeral ceremony. Afterwards her coffin was placed in the crypt of the Russian Church in Florence, beside that of King Constantine, to await burial at Tatoi when the Greek monarchy was restored.

After the death of Lenin in 1924, Grand Duke Kirill started a minor furore among the émigrés by issuing a manifesto. The rescue of Russia, he said, should be headed by a supreme authority which was above classes and parties and 'in accordance with this I, the senior member of the Tsarist House and sole legal Heir of the Russian Imperial Throne, take the title of Emperor of all the Russias which without possible doubt is mine.'

In addition he claimed for his son, Prince Vladimir Kirillovitch, the title of Grand Duke, Heir and Tsarevitch. Princess Marina and her family considered the claim legitimate but it was a statement received with some scepticism by English newspapers.

Despite this political talk, Princess Marina and her sister Elizabeth led a quiet and comparatively uneventful life in Paris. When she felt like it she painted and often sat side by side with her father in his studio while both of them gossiped happily as they worked, but he always deplored the fact that she did not take her gift for painting and drawing more seriously. Princess Marina and her sister also took part in several theatrical displays such as tableaux and small plays which were arranged by her father and put on to help raise money for their mother's home for refugee children. Twice a year there was a bazaar at the Ritz to help raise funds and they always served at one of the stalls.

Princess Marina had a great many friends—but they were nearly all children and grandchildren of people who were, or had been, friends of her mother or her grandmother. Many of the great ladies of France, who had been so anxious to entertain them when they had visited the French capital before were not quite so free with invitations. But of course they still spent an enormous amount of time with Prince Andrew's family at St Cloud, and their other Russian and Greek relations.

During this exile in France Princess Marina was a great cinema fan, and she went at least once a week with her sister or her friends. She loved French chocolates and the Parisian habit of eating elaborate cream cakes and ate them with as much delight as she had absorbed ice cream on Bognor sands. She had a childlike capacity for enjoyment, which she never lost the whole of her life, and there were many giggles with her sister Elizabeth and her friends as they travelled across the city by metro or had parties in each other's homes. But

Princess Nicholas brought her daughters up strictly. They were not allowed to go to Montmartre because of the rather odd type of people who could be found there; nor to stay out late at night unless suitably chaperoned to the few balls they attended.

In 1931 the two sisters were asked to take part in an advertising campaign. The year before an employee of a well-known advertising agency, working on the Ponds beauty-products account, came up with the suggestion that the preparations should be endorsed by beautiful society women. The idea was approved and the intended subjects (the more aristocratic and prettier the better) carefully selected. They were not offered a lot of money—fees ranged from £50 to £100—but the standard of the advertisements was high for the photographs were usually taken by skilled and eminent photographers.

The campaign was so successful that it lasted until 1956. In England the first of these newspaper and magazine advertisements appeared in January 1931 and featured Sylvia Ashley, then married to the Earl of Shaftesbury's heir. Others that year included the wife of a noted portrait painter; Lady Eleanor Smith, daughter of the Earl of Birkenhead; and the Marchioness of Carisbrooke, whose husband was a Battenberg.

Two others invited to take part in the series were Princess Marina and Princess Elizabeth. Princess Elizabeth was featured and described in July 1931 'as beautiful as a princess out of a fairy story—with all the graciousness and dignity that is her royal inheritance'. Princess Marina's portrait followed in October, and the caption read, 'The dignity of royal rank rests very graciously on this lovely young princess. For she is charming, gay, versatile—and enchantingly pretty.' It went on to say that 'she is delightfully keen on a number of things— painting, riding, dancing' and 'how stately and royal she looks in Court train and feathers . . . how dignified and gracious at Embassy receptions'. The following year, and again in 1933, the two sisters appeared sometimes alone and sometimes together, when they were described as 'glowing brunette and exquisite blonde'—remarks which, though they appeared to be flattering, were extremely accurate.

Princess Marina was not very domesticated though she could make the ceremonial Easter cakes which are part of the Ortho-

dox celebrations of the festival. 'Life has held few iced cakes for
her except those she made for herself,' her father once said. She
could also sew, but she did not like it much. She preferred to
embroider initials on the corners of handkerchiefs. The work took
her weeks to do because it was so fine and intricate, but in time
she provided every member of the family with a stock of elegant
handkerchiefs each with an elaborate, beautifully-worked
monogram of her own design.

Her cultural activities continued as well. Her father took
her round the châteaux of the Loire, into various buildings in
Paris and several rounds of the Louvre where his amusing and
informative commentaries were often more of a success than the
exhibits. And everything Princess Marina did was entered into
her extensive diaries or described in the innumerable letters she
wrote to her friends and relations.

And of course she did a lot of travelling all over Europe, and
often stayed for months at a time in Yugoslavia.

At the beginning of her married life Princess Olga and her
husband lived in apartments in the palace in the centre of Belgrade; a noisy place with trams rattling outside and traffic
going past the windows but a bustling, exciting city full of
people as fond of arguing about politics as the Greeks and with
a large Russian community. It was a place where the exiled
Greek family felt very much at home.

Eventually both King Alexander and Prince Paul moved,
with their families, out of the old Royal Palace. The King into
a splendid new one, complete with a fully-equipped cinema;
Prince Paul into an elegant house known as 'The White Palace',
which he had had built to his own specifications, on the heights
outside Belgrade, and furnished with antiques.

By this time Princess Olga had given birth to a second son,
called Nicholas, in England in 1928, the same year in which the
Dowager Empress Marie Feodorovna died, aged eighty-two.
And Prince Paul's reputation as a connoisseur had become so
widespread that the noted expert Joseph Duveen said that, as
an art connoisseur, Princess Marina's brother-in-law was 'as
good as anybody'.

But the place the Yugoslavian family liked best was not the
beautifully furnished Belgrade palace but a small, wooden
chalet-type shooting-lodge which Prince Paul owned at Bohinj,

H

near Lake Bled, not far from the Italian border—which was to
have a lasting significance for both Princess Marina and her
sister Elizabeth.

King Alexander, who had a similar lodge a few miles away,
where Prince and Princess Nicholas often stayed when their
eldest daughter had guests, was very fond of Princess Marina
and her sister. She and Princess Elizabeth rode his horses,
amused him, charmed him; and he went to a great deal of
trouble to make them feel welcome. Prince Paul, too, treated the
princesses with more than the usual solicitude of a brother-in-
law and felt that his wife's relations had at last given him a
proper family of his own.

So Princess Marina often accompanied her sister Olga and her
brother-in-law to England. And, naturally, when they were there
they saw a good deal of the British Royal Family. But it was her
godmother, Queen Mary, whom Princess Marina went to see
most often during these visits, and it was in England that she
fell in love with Prince George, Queen Mary's youngest son, and
in Yugoslavia that she became engaged.

2
A New Beginning

1 | *Prince George*

'I shall soon have a regiment not a family,' remarked the future King George V when, nearly two years after the death of Queen Victoria, his fifth child and fourth son, Prince George, was born on 20 December 1902. It is unlikely that the baby would have been called George if the old Queen had still been alive; it was not a name she liked; but he was given it in deference to his grandmother, Queen Alexandra, whose favourite brother was Princess Marina's grandfather, King George I of Greece.

There was one other addition to 'the regiment' a fifth son, named John, an ailing child who was born three years later and died in 1919. He is buried in the little churchyard at Sandringham.

It is said that Prince George showed signs of his enormous charm as soon as he could talk—and as much zest for living as his Greek and Russian cousins. He was given his first lessons in the palace schoolroom by an elderly French lady who had taught Queen Mary before her marriage and was probably responsible for the fact that her pupil eventually spoke French better than any other member of the family. Later he had a tutor and eventually, together with his brother Prince Henry, two years older and known as 'Harry', he went to St Peter's Court, a small preparatory school at Broadstairs which still exists.

He was untidy when he was small. His hair, later so sleekly groomed, stuck up at the back in tufts like an illustration from *Just William*; and not helped by the fact that he twirled his forelock when he was thinking. He was remarkably kind-natured; a trait not normally noticeable among schoolboys. The Marquis of Donegall once recalled that when he was a new

TABLE III

THE BRITISH ROYAL FAMILY

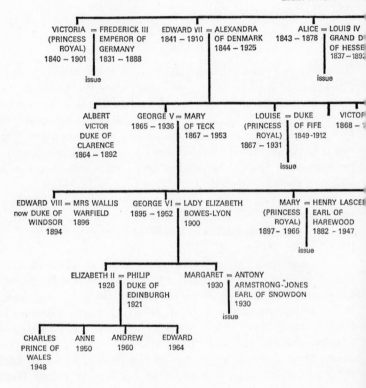

QUEEN VICTORIA 1819–

VICTORIA = FREDERICK III   EDWARD VII = ALEXANDRA   ALICE = LOUIS IV
(PRINCESS | EMPEROR OF   1841 – 1910 | OF DENMARK   1843 – 1878 | GRAND D
ROYAL) | GERMANY   1844 – 1925   OF HESSE
1840 – 1901 | 1831 – 1888   1837 – 1892

issue   issue

ALBERT   GEORGE V = MARY   LOUISE = DUKE   VICTOR
VICTOR   1865 – 1936 | OF TECK   (PRINCESS | OF FIFE   1868 –
DUKE OF   1867 – 1953   ROYAL) | 1849 -1912
CLARENCE   1867 – 1931
1864 – 1892

issue

EDWARD VIII = MRS WALLIS   GEORGE VI = LADY ELIZABETH   MARY = HENRY LASCE
now DUKE OF | WARFIELD   1895 – 1952 | BOWES-LYON   (PRINCESS | EARL OF
WINDSOR   1896   1900   ROYAL) | HAREWOOD
1894   1897 - 1965 | 1882 - 1947

issue

ELIZABETH II = PHILIP   MARGARET = ANTONY
1926 | DUKE OF   1930 | ARMSTRONG-JONES
DUKE OF   EARL OF SNOWDON
EDINBURGH   1930
1921

issue

CHARLES   ANNE   ANDREW   EDWARD
PRINCE OF   1950   1960   1964
WALES
1948

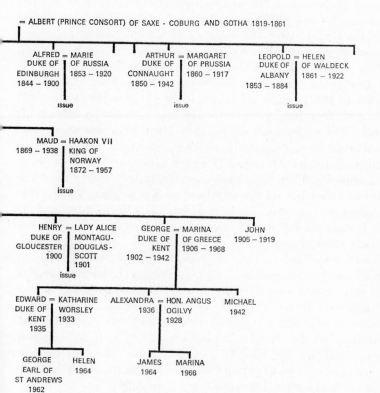

= ALBERT (PRINCE CONSORT) OF SAXE - COBURG AND GOTHA 1819-1861

ALFRED = MARIE
DUKE OF | OF RUSSIA
EDINBURGH | 1853 – 1920
1844 – 1900

issue

ARTHUR = MARGARET
DUKE OF | OF PRUSSIA
CONNAUGHT | 1860 – 1917
1850 – 1942

issue

LEOPOLD = HELEN
DUKE OF | OF WALDECK
ALBANY | 1861 – 1922
1853 – 1884

issue

MAUD = HAAKON VII
1869 – 1938 | KING OF
NORWAY
1872 – 1957

issue

HENRY = LADY ALICE
DUKE OF | MONTAGU-
GLOUCESTER | DOUGLAS-
1900 | SCOTT
1901

issue

GEORGE = MARINA
DUKE OF | OF GREECE
KENT | 1906 – 1968
1902 – 1942

JOHN
1905 – 1919

EDWARD = KATHARINE
DUKE OF | WORSLEY
KENT | 1933
1935

ALEXANDRA = HON. ANGUS
1936 | OGILVY
1928

MICHAEL
1942

GEORGE
EARL OF
ST ANDREWS
1962

HELEN
1964

JAMES
1964

MARINA
1966

boy at the same school it was Prince George who tactfully prevented him from wearing a tie for cricket and generally smoothed the path for newcomers until they were reasonably adjusted to the harsh facts of school life.

Prince George was also reputed to be the naughtiest of the royal princes and he was continually getting into various scrapes. He was irrepressible, although his brothers (particularly Prince Henry, later the Duke of Gloucester) being older and heavier, were apt to bully him, make him fetch and carry, do their errands and act as ball boy when they played tennis.

During the Coronation procession of King George and Queen Mary in 1911, somebody misguidedly put the five eldest royal children together in one state carriage without an attendant, under the supervision of Princess Mary who was then aged fourteen. She and the Prince of Wales sat on one side and Prince Albert (later King George VI), Prince Henry and Prince George sat opposite. They all behaved amazingly well during the drive to the Abbey but on the way back to Buckingham Palace, distracted by the sight of a goat which was a regimental mascot, their decorum fell apart at the seams. Prince Albert and Prince Henry tried to push Prince George under the seat to make more room for themselves, but, as usual, he fought back. In the ensuing scuffle Princess Mary, trying to restore order and prevent all three landing on the floor, lost her coronet. But, like a true daughter of Queen Mary, she never lost her dignity. When the Prince of Wales gave the small crown back to her she replaced it carefully on her head and sat back calmly as if nothing had happened. She was used to such goings-on. There were times when she had a lot to put up with from her brothers, particularly from Prince George who teased her dreadfully.

Prince George had other young companions as well as his brothers. When his aunt, Queen Maud of Norway, was staying at her house near Sandringham, he saw a great deal of her son Prince (afterwards King) Olav, together with Prince Henry and the delicate Prince John. The four of them used to play at soldiers with miniature forts, cannon and lead soldiers—with the tactful rule imposed undoubtedly by King George V, that the 'armies' were not to be called after any known countries, so the 'battles' were between 'Mars' and 'Earth'.

They also dressed up in cocked hats and wooden swords and

The Duchess of Kent in national dress, 1938

The Duchess of Kent in 1939

The Duke of Kent in 1940

The Duke and Duchess
of Kent with their two
children, Prince Edward
and Princess Alexandra

The Duchess of Kent in Wren's uniform
during the Second World War

The Duchess of Kent in 1947 with her family, Princess Alexandra, Prince Michael and Prince Edward

drilled each other. Prince George, after a visit to a military tournament, introduced some variations of his own and made them 'break step' when crossing a bridge; he explained afterwards that this was in case the masonry should become dislodged by the rhythm of their marching feet. At other times they played cowboys and Indians; a traditional version with Buffalo Bill as the hero.

And once, after a bout of whooping cough when Prince George was eleven years old, he went to Norway to stay with his cousin Olav.

Just before his fourteenth birthday Prince George was sent to the Royal Naval College at Osborne and then to Dartmouth. In 1921 he was made a midshipman and appointed to the *Iron Duke,* the Flagship of the Mediterranean Fleet. Unfortunately, during all his years afloat, he was constantly sea-sick. And a bad stomach and insomnia sometimes made him irritable.

He became a sub-lieutenant, and then, in 1926, a lieutenant, and he obtained certificates for navigation, gunnery and torpedo work; and qualified as a French interpreter, serving in this last capacity in the *Nelson* in the Atlantic Fleet. Prince George was the only real linguist in the Royal Family, for he also studied Italian and Spanish, spoke some German and on a visit to Amsterdam astonished Netherlanders by speaking in Dutch.

Prince George was personally very popular in the Navy— mostly because he was pleasant, easy going and never tried to get out of doing unpopular duties. He was given the nickname of 'PG' and was occasionally called 'Babe', and sometimes, to preserve his anonymity, he travelled under the pseudonym of 'Lieutenant Windsor'.

He had a prankish sense of fun. Once in China, some press cameramen, hearing that British Royalty was about, met him as he was about to board his ship and asked if he had seen the 'King of England'. Without hesitation he gestured behind him towards the ship's doctor, a heavily-built man who was being carried in a sedan chair, and left them to sort it out for themselves. He laughed a great deal when the portly doctor's picture appeared in a newspaper later with a caption saying that he was the 'English King'.

He was fond of describing a visit he once made to a naval canteen when he noticed beer on sale at fourpence and sixpence a glass, and when he asked what the difference was he was told 'Twopence, Sir'.

But he was so unknown to the general public that in August 1928 when he was twenty-six years old, he tried to board the liner *Empress of Australia*, en route to join H.M.S. *Durban* stationed off Bermuda, and was stopped twice; first by the police and then by a master-at-arms because he had mislaid his ticket. He was not allowed up the gangway until he had found it. 'No one is allowed on board without a permit,' he was told.

When he was twenty-two years old Prince George was asked to perform one of his first public duties—the inauguration of the Harwich to Belgium train ferry in April 1924. He failed to turn up on time and an agitated official sent a mace-bearer to find out what had happened. The Prince was found sitting in his railway carriage with the blinds down. He had arrived in mufti, changed in the compartment, and then discovered that somebody had forgotten to pack his full-dress naval overcoat. He was waiting, he said, for a messenger to return with another one borrowed from the naval barracks. Prince George was a sub-lieutenant at the time and the coat he was lent bore lieutenant's rings, but 'smiling and unperturbed' he later carried out his official task and was, as was later reported, 'cheered to the echo'; coping with equanimity after a mishap which might have upset plenty more experienced hands.

Apart from his naval service abroad and official duties the Prince also went on three long tours: to Canada in 1927 and South America in 1931 with the Prince of Wales, and in 1934 to South Africa on his own.

Prince George remained in the Royal Navy for ten years but his weak digestion and the seasickness did his health so much harm that on medical advice he retired from active service in March 1929. Afterwards he was attached in turn to the Foreign Office and the Home Office. But for long periods he was so unwell that he could do very few public duties at all, and spent weeks at a time in the country playing golf.

But when he was able to take up his new tasks he was conscientious. At the Foreign Office he did normal routine work and was at times the representative at inter-departmental conferences dealing with international questions, and during his stint at the Home Office he was a factory inspector.

There was nothing desultory in the way which Prince George inspected factories. Again he took the job seriously and gained a remarkable insight into industrial conditions in this country at that time. The scope of his task included welfare, cleanliness, safety standards, lighting, the possibility of contamination by poisonous substances and the working hours of women and what are known officially as 'young persons'. He plodded for miles round noisy, dirty and unattractive works which did nothing for his aching feet but brightened up many a factory worker's day. And what he saw during those visits led him to campaign as much as he could for a five-day working week, which, in the 1930s, was just a dream for most industrial workers.

Off duty, Prince George led a gay, social life. He had grown into a very good-looking young man; tall and slim with a pleasant voice, large dark blue eyes, charming smile, and an aura of shyness. He always looked younger than his age and so full of life that someone commented at this period that he had 'all the eagerness for enjoyment which stamps a naval officer ashore for a bit of leave'. And Edgar Wallace reported that 'There are hundreds of charming creatures throughout the country who have a portrait of Prince George on their bedroom walls and can hardly keep their eyes off it'.

Unlike most other members of his family Prince George did not care much for shooting; and whenever he could instead of going to Sandringham for holidays he preferred the Riviera where he would sunbathe during the day and gamble at the casino or go dancing at night. He was an expert at the tango and once, under an assumed name, won a dancing contest at Cannes.

Queen Mary had an inconvenient habit of expecting her sons to turn up for breakfast at 8.30 whenever they were staying at the Palace, regardless of the time they had gone to bed. Some of the others often looked bleary-eyed and careworn at this early morning confrontation. But not Prince George. He always looked as pink and fresh as if he had just emerged from nine hours' undisturbed rest. In addition nearly every morning he ran about three miles in old tennis shoes, shorts and sweater (or in winter slacks and windcheater), in an effort to keep fit. He continued this after his marriage and would sometimes, if he felt particularly energetic, set off to run from Iver to Windsor

—though some of his more sceptical friends doubted if he ever achieved this.

King George V and Queen Mary were on the whole rather unsympathetic parents; strangely stiff and aloof from their children and with little of the outward love and warmth which characterized the Greek Royal Family. King George, particularly, was a very strict father and his children were afraid of him. But Queen Mary was much more pleasant than she ever looked in her photographs. She refused to smile in front of a camera because she said that when she showed her teeth she 'looked like a horse'. It is no secret that she was especially fond of Prince George. He was the only one of her children who shared her love for antiques and beautiful things: and he was the only one who ever paid her compliments. After he died she once told a friend sadly: 'He often used to say I looked nice. Nobody else ever did.'

Both the King and Queen loathed speed and hated aeroplanes. Neither of them ever flew and once, shortly after the war when Queen Mary paid a private and informal visit to an American airbase near Sandringham, she flatly refused to enter a Flying Fortress even when it was safely on the ground. 'Nasty horrid things,' she called them.

Prince George did not share his parents' views. He enjoyed driving fast cars, such as his six-litre Bentley; he learned to fly, and often borrowed the blue Tiger Moth which belonged to the Prince of Wales; and he seemed to have no physical fear at all. He was quite unperturbed when he was once a passenger in an aeroplane which had a mishap on take-off, spun round and nearly overturned; the incident just amused him. During the last war an enemy plane dived and machine-gunned a car he was driving, and got so near to the target that it hit a wall a few feet away from him—he did not even bother to mention the incident when he got home.

He was considerably better informed and better read than most other members of the Royal Family. In his weekly Turkish bath he always pored over a great pile of newspapers and this habit, combined with his insatiable curiosity, gave him a good general knowledge.

He played the piano by ear and loved sitting for hours going over his large repertoire of the music of the period, by composers such as Gershwin and Cole Porter; and he had a vast collection of gramophone records. He liked more serious music as well and often went to symphony concerts at Queen's Hall.

He read biographies by authors such as Lytton Strachey, who 'treated their subjects like human beings', and Prince George was also very keen on the Russian Ballet. Whenever it appeared in London he went night after night to see it. Indeed, he loved the atmosphere of the world of ballet and theatre, and, like Princess Marina, he was a great cinema fan.

But most important perhaps was the fact that Prince George was far and away the most artistic member of the British Royal Family. He had a flair for colour and design and even before his marriage redecorated his rooms at St James's Palace when he was living there and took an active part in a scheme to standardize the names of colours. One particular blue, for example had eighty names; his suggestion was that it should be called Garter Blue and he sent the ribbon of his own Order—which he had been given when he was twenty-one—to prove his point. Until the advent of Prince Philip, who collects French Impressionist paintings, Prince George was the only one of the family, apart from Queen Mary, to do any serious accumulation of works of art. He began in a small way, buying first editions of contemporary authors, and later, with advice from his mother and friends who were experts in various fields, began to collect pictures and antiques. Eventually he became very knowledgeable about every aspect of the arts, and if he had lived would have undoubtedly taken over formal Royal patronage of the subject.

Those who knew both Prince George and Princess Marina say that they had a great many complementary qualities. And Prince George—good looking, charming, gay, moody and artistic—also had much of the disposition and character of the men in Princess Marina's own family who, until she fell in love, had been her nearest and dearest relations.

2 | *Two Engagements*

After Princess Olga's marriage, Princess Marina and Princess Elizabeth were almost always together and became rather more intimate at this period than at any other because of the absence of their elder sister, whom they both missed, in spite of the fact that they saw her so often, corresponded regularly and were more like sisters than sisters-in-law to Prince Paul.

But neither Princess Marina nor Princess Elizabeth showed signs of getting wed. 'Why don't they marry?' people asked.

In 1930–31, within a period of eight months, all Princess Andrew's daughters—still their closest friends—became engaged and married: Princess Margarita to Prince Gottfried of Hohenlohe-Langenburg, a grandson of the Duke of Edinburgh; Princess Theodora to the Margrave of Baden, a son of the Prince Max who had refused to marry the Grand Duchess Helen; Princess Cecile to George Grand Duke of Hesse, elder son and heir of the Tsarina's brother Ernst by his second marriage; and Princess Sophie, who had been born in 1914 and was only sixteen, to Prince Christopher of Hesse.

Princess Nicholas began to get a little concerned that her youngest daughters, both nearer thirty than twenty, were not married as well. She took them on yet another round of visits to some of their innumerable royal relations in Germany, Italy and Austria, the last in 1933 where she had hopes that one of the Habsburgs would be a suitable husband for Princess Elizabeth.

But the sweet-natured Princess Elizabeth was difficult to please, and it was not until later that year, when they were all back again in Yugoslavia and staying at Prince Paul's timbered shooting-lodge at Bohinj, that at last she fell in love.

One of the other guests at the lodge was Prince Christopher and another was a friend of Prince Paul's—Count Karl Theodor zu Toerring–Jettenbach, more familiarly known as 'Toto' and whom Princess Elizabeth had first met about twelve months before.

Count Toerring was a Bavarian and a member of the Wittelsbach family, as was King Otho, the predecessor of King George I of Greece.

His maternal grandfather, Duke Karl Theodor, was a brilliant oculist who spent much of his time giving free treatment in Munich hospitals and seeing that his three daughters had a scientific education. The eldest, Sophie, a bacteriologist, was Count Toerring's mother; the middle sister, Elizabeth, married King Albert of the Belgians and became the mother of King Leopold III and the grandmother of King Baudouin.

Count Toerring was fair, very English-looking, good company and rather serious and thrifty, in spite of his wealth. He had a large house in Munich, a castle at Winhörring, and a large fortune, much of which came from breweries owned by his family. He and Princess Elizabeth shared common interests in sports, and realized they loved each other one September morning while they were both stalking chamois on a mountainside. Princess Olga and her husband, with Princess Marina, were temporarily away in England at the time. That evening, in the drawing-room of the chalet, he proposed and was accepted. On 10 January 1934, they were married.

'He is the perfect person for Elizabeth,' said Princess Olga. 'There isn't a nicer man anywhere.' And Miss Fox, although she had now retired after being given a silver tea service by her three former 'charges' as a parting gift, was one of the wedding guests and dressed the bride on her wedding day.

Princess Marina was now left alone. But it was not to be for long; shortly after Princess Elizabeth's marriage there were rumours that she too would shortly become engaged. One suitor suggested was said to have been Prince Louis Ferdinand of Prussia—grandson of Kaiser Wilhelm II and great-grandson of the Empress Frederick. The Prince's father, the former Crown Prince of Germany and married to a Mecklenburg himself, was said to be very much in favour of the match. There is a story to the effect that he became extremely agitated during Princess

Marina's visit to the family schloss that year and kept mutter-
ing about his son and saying: 'The silly boy. Here is this beautiful
princess. Why doesn't he say something ? Why doesn't he ask her ?'

But the close affection so necessary, as far as she was concerned, was missing. Eventually, in 1938, Prince Louis became
the husband of Grand Duke Kirill's daughter Kyra.

During September 1933, around the time of Princess Elizabeth's engagement, Princess Marina had come to London with
Prince and Princess Paul, who were accompanying their elder
son, Alexander, then aged nine, to his preparatory school. And
at a luncheon given by that ardent socialite Lady (Emerald)
Cunard she again met the handsome Prince George.

When they had come across each other before neither had given
any special indication of being aware of each other. This time
was different and the spark of interest which flared up between
them at that luncheon party increased when Princess Marina
came back to England once more early the following year, again
with her sister and brother-in-law.

In London they all stayed at Claridges and there were clear
signs of Prince George's increasing interest in the pretty Greek
Princess. They went for walks in Green Park, did some motoring,
theatre-going and dancing together; he took her to Fort Belvedere to see the Prince of Wales and once he waited for some
considerable time for her when she was away from the hotel on a
visit to the hairdressers. But beyond a vague 'I might come over
to Yugoslavia to see you', he said nothing more and she was
left wondering whether he would or not.

In the meantime Princess Marina went off with her mother
to a French spa near Savoie. For the sad truth must be told
that at this stage her fondness for chocolates and sweets had
made her put on so much weight that she was rather plump.
At the spa she energetically swam, played tennis, drank the
waters and went on a rigid diet; at the end of which she had
lost exactly four kilos—just over eight pounds. In August, with
her parents and a friend she was back for what was meant to
be a three-month visit to Yugoslavia and stayed at the shooting-
lodge in Bohinj. To Princess Marina's delight there was an unexpected cable from Prince George that month; and he turned up
shortly afterwards with his equerry in an aeroplane borrowed,
as usual, from the Prince of Wales.

Afterwards Prince George admitted to Princess Marina that he had gone to Yugoslavia on impulse; partly out of curiosity and partly to get to know her better to see if she really was as wonderful as he had first thought—and whether he considered they could live happily together. It took him exactly three days to make up his mind.

Prince Christopher, who had been summoned from Italy by Princess Olga to 'bring luck' to what they all hoped was going to be a happy-ever-after romance, described what happened on the night of the proposal—20 August 1934.

They all spent the evening playing backgammon and then everybody retired tactfully to bed 'until George and Marina were left sitting alone at opposite ends of the sofa'. Said Prince Christopher, 'I had been in my bedroom for about half an hour when I discovered that I had left my cigarette case on the backgammon table. Putting on my dressing-gown I went in search of it. The door of the drawing-room was open; George and Marina were still seated on the sofa, though no longer, I observed with satisfaction, at the opposite ends of it,' and, he added, 'I stole back to bed without my case. . . .'

Thirty minutes later, shortly after midnight, Princess Marina burst out of the room and up the stairs, half laughing, half crying and with an enraptured, radiant face, to tell her sister that she had become engaged to be married.

The next morning, although full of excitement, held the possibility of an awkward situation. Prince George sent off a messenger to his father at Balmoral asking for formal permission to marry, and a telephone call went out to Prince and Princess Nicholas staying in a neighbouring chalet; but nobody else could be told until the King had given his official consent to the betrothal.

Princess Paul took a group snapshot of them all in the sunshine to mark the occasion but when some friends came over, as arranged, for luncheon, the newly-engaged pair were warned to keep away from each other, avoid blissful glances and not on any account to hold hands.

But they were not too successful at hiding their feelings. Rumours of the proposed marriage leaked out and Prince George, answering a telephone query, had to say: 'I'm afraid I

I

can't give any information about an engagement. This is the
butler speaking. . . .'

The news was not official until a week later when, on 28 August, the announcement went out from Balmoral: 'It is with the
greatest pleasure that the King and Queen announce the betrothal of their dearly beloved son, Prince George, to Princess
Marina, daughter of Prince and Princess Nicholas of Greece, to
which union the King has gladly given his consent.'

That started the rush. At this point few people in Britain
had ever heard of Princess Marina, let alone knew what she
looked like, and newspaper offices in Fleet Street were thrown
into something of a panic. For very few photographs of Princess
Marina were available: no snapshots taken at Ascot; no pictures
of her dancing at a debutante's ball; and above all no photograph showing her with Prince George.

Squadrons of reporters and photographers went hurrying off
to Austria where the royal party from Yugoslavia were at the
Salzburg music festival; an expedition which had been arranged
long before Prince George's unscheduled arrival. The pictures
which were sent back to England caused a fantastic stir of
public interest. There was some slight surprise that in one of
the photographs the bride-to-be was depicted outdoors in the
city smoking a cigarette from a long holder, but the main impact was that of tremendous delight that the good-looking
Prince George had chosen such a beautiful girl.

From then onwards they were mobbed wherever they went.
Whether it was in Yugoslavia; in Munich, where they spent a
few days with the Toerrings; or Paris, where Princess Marina
(temporarily parted from Prince George who had gone back to
England) hurriedly chose some new clothes, including the 'pork
pie' pillbox hat which was to become so famous. She was beset
by crowds along the railway route to Boulogne, where with her
parents she boarded the cross-Channel steamer for Folkestone;
and during the journey to London, where the whole populace
seemed to go mad. 'England gave Princess Marina such a burst
of welcome as has not been equalled since the day Alexandra
came across the seas from Denmark seventy-two years ago,' declared the *Daily Express*.

Afterwards Prince Nicholas was lost for words when he
attempted to talk about the reception his daughter received.

'We have had such an extraordinary welcome in England that it is not to be described,' he said. 'We could not begin to describe it. We are really "emotioned" by it, as the French say.'

Princess Marina was even more amazed and astonished, and said, 'I am so overwhelmed. I had not expected this wonderfully generous reception'—but privately put the whole thing down to her beloved Prince George's extreme popularity.

Miss Fox, now white-haired but still pink-cheeked and fresh-faced, came into her own again and was on the quay at Folke-stone to greet her former 'charge'. 'I feel that my heart will burst with pride,' she said, 'that all this should be for my little Marina. Isn't she lovely?' and reported that the Princess had told her: 'I'm so glad you've come; I feel a little dazed.' She also gave a long interview to the *Evening Standard*. 'I loved all my babies,' she recounted, 'but Princess Marina was a darling little thing. I hardly left her side for a moment for her first four years.' Proudly she showed off a precious embroidered linen teacloth with the last Tsar of Russia's signature on one part and Princess Marina's childish scrawl on another. 'I dressed Princess Olga and Princess Elizabeth for their wedding,' she said. 'And I will probably help to dress Princess Marina for hers. She wouldn't like it if I didn't.'

Their youngest son's choice of a bride filled King George V and Queen Mary with delight. The King was proud of Princess Marina's great beauty on which he commented over and over again. He admired her disposition, her good manners and her amusing comments. 'Marina is looking very pretty and charming and will be a great addition to the family,' he wrote. There was also the pleasant knowledge that she was the grand-daughter of his aunt, Queen Olga of whom he had been very fond.

To accentuate his approval not only of his proposed new daughter-in-law but also her parents, King George V appointed Prince Nicholas an honorary Knight Grand Cross of the Order of the Bath and went to great pains to ensure that not only was the insignia ready for immediate presentation to the Prince on the day of his arrival with his daughter for her wedding, but that it should not be gazetted earlier by mistake and spoil the surprise.

Queen Mary herself, almost echoing her husband's words, remarked to him in a letter: 'I am sure that we will like Marina and that she will be a charming addition to the family.' Whilst discussing the engagement with one of her relations, she emphasized that she was very pleased indeed, and added that she was already very fond of the Princess who came from a nice family, had a good background and would, Queen Mary hoped, have what she called a 'settling influence' on Prince George.

There was no doubt about the depth of affection Prince George felt for his fiancée. He talked about her to anyone who would listen. To his relations he spoke about her wit, her beauty and her charm. To a friend he wrote: 'I am very happy and very lucky.' To another friend he said: 'She is the one woman with whom I would be happy to spend the rest of my life. We laugh at the same things, she can beat me at most games, and she doesn't mind how fast I drive when I take her out in the car.'

'Prince George was genuinely in love with Princess Marina, a most beautiful woman I had met earlier at the Fort; and he was also delighted at the prospect of at last having his own home,' recalled the Duchess of Windsor in her memoirs.

In Greece there was apparently only qualified rejoicing. The British Legation reported to the Foreign Office that the news was 'received with interest', and most newspapers published pictures of the engaged pair but printed very little comment.

But the British Foreign Minister, Sir John Simon, received a letter from the Greek Legation in London with an official message of 'sincere congratulations on the occasion of the engagement of H.R.H. Prince George to Princess Marina of Greece'. It was a pleasurable surprise and Sir John, returning his 'cordial thanks', said, 'I beg leave to add that I have informed the King my Sovereign of this agreeable manifestation of the interest shown by the Greek Government in this happy event'.

Meanwhile everybody was busy getting on with the preparations for the wedding. Princess Marina was back in Paris and worrying over the choice of the couturier to make her bridal gown. She was anxious that it should be made by Jean Patou, who had been so kind in the way of 'discount', but Prince George, who took as much interest in her clothes before the wedding as he did afterwards, pointed out that it was essential to have an English dressmaker. A suitable compromise was reached with the choice of Captain Edward Molyneux, a noted English designer working in Paris and whom the Princess had already met socially. Her choice was very simple—the dress was to have long, wide sleeves and the material was to be silver lamé brocade.

The choice of attendants was very easy. 'There are several relations who will be bridesmaids, such as my nieces and cousins; and of course there is Princess Elizabeth, naturally,' Prince Nicholas had declared, shortly after the engagement was announced. Three of the bridesmaids chosen were Princesses Irene and Katharine, the daughters of King Constantine, and Princess Eugenie, whose father was Prince George of Greece. Another three were the Grand Duke Kirill's daughter, Kyra, Princess Juliana of the Netherlands (Princess Marina's cousin and kinswoman) and Lady Iris Mountbatten. And there were two children: Prince George's niece, Princess Elizabeth of York, the present Queen, and Lady Mary Cambridge. The Prince of Wales was best man.

The days were so hectic for Princess Marina that during the period of her engagement, without any effort or any dieting, she lost about fourteen pounds in weight. Never again did she put it back on, however many chocolates she ate.

But the bustle and excitement of this period was interrupted abruptly by an unexpected, shocking and far-reaching event. On 9 October 1934 King Alexander of Yugoslavia, who was on a State visit to France, was assassinated after his arrival at Marseilles.

Princess Olga had planned to go to Paris with her husband to join Princess Marina and do some shopping on her own account for the wedding, but, at the King's request they had postponed the trip until his return to Belgrade. They were jolted out of their pleasant anticipation of sharing in Princess Marina's happiness by a telephone call at six o'clock on the evening of the King's death. 'When the first terrible message was received . . . the whole Palace was stunned . . . it did not seem real at first,' said Princess Olga soon afterwards. And Prince Paul refused even to listen to the distasteful details of the assassination. That it had happened to his cousin and most intimate friend was enough. 'And to think that I all but persuaded him not to go by sea but to travel overland to Paris which would have prevented the fateful visit to Marseilles,' he recalled unhappily.

Prince Paul knew also that for seven years—until the King's eldest son, now King Peter II, came of age—it meant the end of his happy existence as a private citizen for he was now to be one of the three Regents of Yugoslavia whom King Alexander had appointed in his Will to act during his son's minority in the event of his early death.

'My only qualification is that I was always in the closest confidence of the late King,' said Prince Paul shortly after he had taken an oath 'to serve King Peter II loyally, preserve the integrity of the State and the unity of the Yugoslav people, guard the Constitution and seek the good of the nation'. 'I knew his aims and aspirations for our country. I shall do my best to carry them out.'

The funeral of the Yugoslavian King in Belgrade, which Princess Marina attended with her mother and Prince George, and the fact that they had all been so fond of him, put a cloud over Princess Marina's wedding arrangements. But things had gone too far for it to be postponed. The flat in which they lived was chaotic; flowers everywhere, piles of telegrams and letters of congratulations; a miraculous reopening of friendships which had somehow cooled off after the trouble in Greece—and in the middle of it all Princess Marina was also busy helping her mother to organize her bi-annual charity fête in aid of her children's home at St Germain which, wedding or no wedding, still had to be done.

On 20 November, nine days before the wedding, there was a private ceremony at Buckingham Palace. King George V created his youngest surviving son—the only one who had no title other than prince—Duke of Kent, Earl of St Andrews and Baron Downpatrick.

The Dukedom was a title with a long but erratic history. The Earldom of Kent dated back to the Norman Conquest when William I gave it to his half-brother the Bishop of Bayeux. One of his descendants was made a Duke by Queen Anne in 1710; but the title became extinct thirty years later when the first Duke's only heir choked himself to death by chewing an ear of barley. It was revived in 1799 for George III's fourth son, Prince Edward.

This Duke was a very martial man. He had his own private band and ran his household like a barracks. As a military commander he was extremely unpopular as he had Prussian ideas of discipline which he had picked up as a young man in Germany. He was so severe that his troops mutinied and he was forced to resign his commission. But aside from all this he had a passion for musical clocks and bright coloured lights which he used with garish prodigality to illuminate his various abodes—a house in Knightsbridge, another at Ealing and his official residence which was Kensington Palace.

He was fifty-one in 1818 when he married the widowed Princess Victoria of Saxe-Coburg: a year later she bore him the daughter who was to become Queen Victoria. Eight months after that he died, and the title became extinct once more.

A new era in the history of the Dukedom of Kent was about to begin.

3 | *The Wedding*

Nobody who can remember the extraordinary fervour and enthusiasm evoked by Princess Marina's marriage will ever forget that royal wedding: there has never been anything like it—and probably never will be again. Not even the marriage of the Queen, when she was Princess Elizabeth, stirred up quite the same hysterical adulation of a royal event—this was partly because Queen Elizabeth's wedding took place in 1947, a period of utility clothing and rationing and partly because it was never really decided whether it should be a full state occasion or a semi-official affair.

There were several reasons why so much interest was shown in Princess Marina's wedding. To begin with it was the first piece of royal pageantry that the British people had seen for more than ten years. The last had been the wedding of the Duke of York to Lady Elizabeth Bowes Lyon in 1923 which, though it was celebrated in some style, took place in the middle of an economic depression and it was not as elaborate or as joyous as it might have been. And then, the timing of Princess Marina's wedding was right. In Britain, unemployment was down for the first time in a decade; there was disarmament and a National Government; and people were sick of grey and dismal poverty—what they needed was some brightness and an excuse for a party. In the wedding of Princess Marina and Prince George they got it.

'Never in history, we may dare to say, had a marriage been attended by so vast a company of witnesses,' declared the Archbishop of Canterbury who officiated at Princess Marina's wedding. '. . . The whole nation, nay the whole Empire, are the wedding guests.'

He was referring to what he called 'a new and marvellous invention of science' because, for the first time, a royal ceremony was to be broadcast by wireless—'an unparalleled technical feat', and an intrusion which, until then, had been unthinkable. Twelve microphones were dotted about Westminster Abbey and the control room was in the crypt, underneath the tomb of the Unknown Warrior. It was not considered proper to have a commentator in the church and the B.B.C.'s chief announcer, Howard Marshall, had to do the best he could by providing a commentary both before and after the ceremony from the roof of Westminster Hospital. The service was broadcast both at home and abroad and also relayed by loudspeaker to the crowds outside the Abbey.

The tension and excitement which had been building up ever since the news of the engagement and their first glimpse of the beautiful bride began to increase from the day she came back to England from Paris a month before the date set for the wedding—a wedding which, as one of the spectators said afterwards, was to be noted for splendour, simplicity, beauty, perfection, goodwill, and warmth of sentiment. But it was the stranger among them who really provided the spark which set off the whole conflagration of that remarkable wedding—Princess Marina, the girl who had been coming to England all her life and who, if they had realized it, was not really a stranger at all.

The street decorations in London did a great deal to brighten up the dullness of that dreary November. 'The West End has not appeared so gay for many years,' said one reporter; and everybody seemed to join in. At the King's request flags were hung from Government buildings; and in hundreds of shops there were decorated pictures of the engaged couple; streets were festooned with flags, bunting, streamers and garlands of waxed paper and Bond Street was like a long coloured archway hung with crowns, giant wedding bells and masses of white carnations, and a pavement artist took the trouble to write 'Good Luck' in Greek.

Every building seemed aflutter with Union Jacks and the flags of Greece and Denmark, though these in themselves had caused a minor diplomatic flurry before they were hung. As

Greece was still a Republic there were some doubts as to whether the Greek flag could be used for a royal wedding of a Princess who had been deprived of her nationality, but with its usual suavity the Foreign Office found a solution: 'Princess Marina is a Princess of both countries, and if the Danish flag were employed as well as the Greek, the use of the latter should not be open to any political misconstruction.' And just to make sure both the Greek and Danish ministers in London were consulted to confirm that there was no objection from either.

And there was another minor political complication. The Royal Horse Guards' Director of Music was searching for some appropriate music to play to royal guests and he wrote to Athens from the Cavalry Barracks at Windsor asking for a copy of the score of 'Son of the Eagle', which, he wrote, had been very popular during the war. This request for what had virtually been King Constantine's signature tune, gave the British Consulate in Athens a slight attack of hysteria. The Consul replied that he had not succeeded in finding a copy and he warned the Director that if he should get one he should be careful not to play it in any public ceremony connected with the royal wedding without the consent of the Foreign Office. He also pointed out that though it was certainly popular during the war as the rallying song of the Royalist Party it was banned by the Republic, and 'would therefore almost certainly give rise to protests. You will I think do better to limit yourself to the harmless traditional songs and country dances which I sent you . . . they are sure to give great pleasure to members of the Greek Royal Family'.

Appropriately the Greek colony in London gave Princess Marina a rare souvenir wedding plate made for the occasion of her grandfather's marriage—just one of the monumental number of gifts she and Prince George received.

Here again the British public played its part; they not only sent gifts to the couple but well over a hundred thousand people queued up to see the wedding presents which were on display at St James's Palace. Two days before the wedding, the King and Queen gave an official reception for the invited guests and the crowds of sightseers swarmed around adjoining roads in spite of the unpleasant foggy day, and caused a traffic jam which stretched from the Palace to the far side of Westminster Bridge.

For some time it held up Queen Mary and Princess Nicholas who had driven to the palace together.

The gifts were spectacular. There was a sparkling mass of jewellery for the bride: from King George and Queen Mary, her future husband, and from her mother a huge diamond bow which had been given to Princess Nicholas by the Tsar as a wedding present and which she had worn at the Tsarevitch's christening almost exactly thirty years before.

There were scores of pieces of silver and antique furniture, and, amongst others, 45 cigarette boxes, 80 snuffboxes, 70 clocks, 23 decanters, 20 handbags and an assortment of inkstands, candlesticks and matchboxes.

Of course there were some off-beat gifts which enliven all royal weddings, like the elephant tusk nearly ten feet long sent by the Aga Khan; a Glastonbury Holy thorn; one of Nelson's visiting cards and a huge 70 lb Cheshire cheese.

Everything was symbolic of the warmth and affectionate feeling which went out to this good-looking royal couple and in particular to Princess Marina; both from the few who knew her well and the many strangers whom she had enchanted so much in such a brief time.

And every single gift was meticulously inspected and tabulated by the Duke of Kent. With his mother's flair for valuation, he estimated how much each one had cost the donor, until finally, according to the Duchess of Windsor, he caused the Prince of Wales to explode and say to his brother 'Dammit. You're beginning to sound like an auctioneer.'

On the morning of the wedding, Miss Fox, as she had hoped, helped the bride to put on her shimmering silver gown at Buckingham Palace, and was given an aquamarine pendant as a memento. And while this was going on Princess Marina's mother and sisters hovered around and all five of them were in a highly emotional state. A few hundred yards away the nervy bridegroom astonished everybody by slipping out to cash a cheque because, he said, 'it gave me something to do'.

Outside the Palace hawkers sold wedding favours to the massed crowds waiting for a glimpse of the bride. She eventually emerged with her father by her side, 'a vision of loveliness in white and silver, smiling and bowing . . . in a swirl of scarlet jackets, dancing white plumes, flashing swords (her escort of

Life Guards) and accompanied by . . . the plop plop of canter-
ing horses, the pealing of joy bells, and the huzzas of happy
crowds . . .'

Princess Marina's wedding was notable for one other reason.
She had the fastest royal procession on record. Yet almost no
one was aware of the extra speed at the time. The only reference
to it in the newspapers next day was a rather plaintive account
by one of the reporters of *The Times*: 'Almost before one realized
it, a gleaming escort of Life guards had passed; a moment later
the bridal coach had come and gone. All too short after so long a
wait was the glimpse of the Duchess's fluttering veil and the
Duke's waving hand,' he said.

But nobody realized that the procession, instead of pro-
ceeding at walking pace, had been increased to a trot. This was
all on account of a threatened assassination attempt on the
bride's brother-in-law, Prince Paul, the Regent of Yugoslavia.
What was later described as the 'most elaborate protection
scheme ever devised in this country' was put into effect to ensure that the wedding day programme was carried out without
any disturbing incident.

Scotland Yard had received reports beforehand that 'political
fanatics' might attempt some form of violence, not the least of
which was intended to be the killing of Prince Paul, scheduled
to travel in a coach with Princess Marina's parents and King
George II of Greece. To forestall this, detectives made thousands of visits to buildings on the route of the procession check-
ing lists of people who had bought tickets for windows and stands
and inspecting every single house, hotel, public building and
office block and several aliens were asked to leave the country.

The night before the wedding members of the C.I.D. searched
Westminster Abbey using torches to peer into the darkest corners.
They looked into all the chapels and crypts, at the back of tombs
and even checked the waxwork effigies of Nelson and Charles II.
And a fantastic army of policemen, more than eleven thousand
of them, congregated in the middle of London. For the first time
all but a handful of City of London police were transferred into
the Metropolitan area to line Whitehall and Special Branch
men came from outlying divisions to join those from Scotland
Yard. War Department police, normally stationed at Woolwich
Arsenal, were called in and cadets and policewomen were also

on duty, while part-time special constables took over traffic control. There were two lines of police both in front and behind the waiting crowds and picked men were issued with arms and stationed at suspected danger points.

Prince Paul had his own armed bodyguard—two massive, swarthy Yugoslavs, both over six feet tall and dressed in blue ulsters and bowler hats, who stood impassively, hands in pockets, at the door of the Abbey during the ceremony while the Head of Special Branch, more effectively disguised, lurked a few feet away from the unsuspecting Regent. Outside the West Door, concealed under a stand, was another squad of detectives.

These massive precautions were effective. No bombs, gunshots or bloodstains marred Princess Marina's wedding day and the only active demonstrations were those of enthusiasm.

The service in Westminster Abbey was followed by another, held in the chapel of Buckingham Palace, which had temporarily been converted into an Orthodox chapel for the ceremony—the first time it had been used for such an occasion since the marriage of Princess Marina's great-aunt Marie the Duchess of Edinburgh in the time of Queen Victoria.

The reception afterwards was lightened by Prince Christopher repeating to King George and Queen Mary a punning riddle he had heard that morning from one of the Buckingham Palace valets who asked: 'Why will Princess Marina be able to smooth life for Prince George?' and gave the answer: 'Because for twenty-seven years she has been preserved in Greece.' The King delightedly passed it on to several wedding guests and in due course to his own valet; with the result that the original inventor of the joke received a severe reprimand for telling 'dirty stories to visiting royalties'.

And there was a solemn moment when, as they stepped on to the Palace balcony, King George V, looking at the vast crowds shouting, cheering and waving below, as far as the eye could see, took his new daughter-in-law by the arm, pointed to the crowd and said: 'This is all for you.'

Even then she did not believe it.

In Oxford Street fifty thousand people queued up outside Selfridges in a line which stretched from Duke Street to Wigmore Street to be given a piece of wedding cake from a replica of the proper one, which weighed a ton and a half. The crowds were so great that the cake had to be distributed from three different sections of the store. The first were there at mid-day and they were still there at 4 o'clock when Princess Paul's two sons, Nicholas and Alexander, with white heather in their button-holes, arrived to visit Father Christmas.

And in the Red Sea the First Destroyer Flotilla, on their way to exchange ships with the 8th Destroyer Flotilla in China, carried out an unprecedented tribute at sea. The Captain (D) —the senior captain—ordered the nine destroyers to stop and their captains to come on board the Flotilla Leader to celebrate the wedding. Among them was the Duke's cousin, Commander Lord Louis Mountbatten, Captain of the *Daring*. Officers in command of H.M. Ships by tradition do not drink at sea; so there was exactly one bottle of champagne, but it was sufficient to toast the Duke of Kent and his bride. A warm and enthusiastic moment which took place at exactly the same time as the ceremony itself.

Because of the exceptional beauty of the bride and the added impact of the wireless broadcast all the world seemed to love this wedding. In Denmark, for example, there was intense interest and constant references and comparisons with Queen Alexandra. In Belgium, where for weeks beforehand people had been given daily news and pictures of the forthcoming marriage, the interest in the wedding was officially stated as 'quite exceptional'. And even in Republican Greece the barriers went down. All over the country people listened in to that Westminster Abbey broadcast. There were what the British Minister in Athens called 'eulogistic special articles' in Government newspapers. He himself heard the ceremony in the Greek Foreign Minister's private house, and reported afterwards, 'The wife of the Minister of Foreign Affairs and the ladies of several Cabinet Ministers who were present were deeply moved.'

And in America a replica of Princess Marina's wedding dress was already on sale for $30,000—equal to £12,500 today.

But perhaps the most emotional part of the public rejoicing came at the end of the day. At dusk on that dark afternoon thousands crowded round the gates of Buckingham Palace while, in medieval style, a lamplighter went his rounds with a ladder and lighted each gas lamp in the forecourt. Alternately they yelled 'We want Marina. We want Marina,' and sang 'For

He's a Jolly Good Fellow' until the newly-married Duke and Duchess of Kent, pursued by their relations throwing fistfuls of rose petals and silver horseshoes, drove out of Buckingham Palace to Paddington Station, where they were to board a train for Birmingham on their way to Dudley for the first part of their honeymoon.

Again there were crowds all the way and that gaunt grey station was 'scarcely recognizable' with its massed decorations, a great banner across the entrance wishing them 'Good Luck and Happiness' and a huge horseshoe of white chrysanthemums to greet them on the platform; their carriage was festooned with yellow roses inside and a big golden horsehoe outside. And at every station on the route there were crowds, people with no hope of seeing even a glimpse of the royal couple, as the train went by at speeds up to seventy miles an hour.

Suburban platforms were crammed with a mass of fluttering handkerchiefs and waving hats: windows of houses along the track were brightly lit and full of spectators. They lined the roads by the railway lines and there were workers three and four deep outside factories. More than a thousand waited at High Wycombe railway station; at Aynho Junction they were greeted with fireworks, a cascade of white and green flares; and as the train rattled through Banbury at top speed, the royal couple heard a brief crescendo of noise as a throng of people cheered.

If anything the excitement increased. There were three thousand waiting at Leamington, Warwick platforms were packed and onlookers at the beflagged Snow Hill Station in Birmingham knew when the train was near by the noise of the cheering which could be heard from outlying stations as the honeymoon express approached. And when she arrived they gave the new Duchess of Kent (who was wearing a sable coat) a bouquet tied with the blue and white ribbons of Greece.

It still went on for the drive to Himley Hall, near Dudley, where the Castle was floodlit for the occasion and a hundred firework rockets exploded at the entrance of the estate itself, where thousands had been waiting since noon, a last feudal touch; they entered by the light of flickering torches held by estate workers and illuminating the November blackness.

For the beautiful Duchess and her husband the hullaballoo

of that day was over; but all over England people still went on celebrating.

In London there were parties all over the West End. Cinemas and restaurants were packed and trams kept running until the early hours of the morning. At naval ports, ships which had been dressed overall and fired royal salutes earlier that day gave searchlight displays. And in Dover there was a torchlight procession (led by fire engines) which marched to the highest hill in the district. There a vast bonfire was lit which blazed for three hours and was a signal for other bonfires to be lit along the Channel Coast at every one of the Cinque Ports; it ended with firework displays all over the country.

There have been other royal celebrations in Britain since then. There was the Diamond Jubilee the following year. There have been two Coronations and nearly a dozen marriages. But nothing has matched the enthusiasm and the excitement of Princess Marina's wedding day.

Whether or not it will ever happen again, few people can have started married life with what the Archbishop of Canterbury called 'this wealth of good wishes and good will . . . offered to you as a wedding gift'.

It was for a marriage which was to last for less than eight years.

4 | *The First Few Years*

After her marriage to the Duke of Kent, Princess Marina was, for the first time in her whole life, away from the close encircling arms of her own family. Afterwards, when she recalled the hulla-baloo of what even her relations called her 'fairy-like' wedding day she said how strangely detached and aloof she felt through it all, as if she were a spectator. The shouting, the cheering, the crowds, the fuss, amazed and astonished her and gave her a feeling of which she could only describe later as 'thrilled unreality'; only the two religious ceremonies meant anything more. And of course her husband.

Many women fall in love, but few with such deep and consis-tent devotion as the woman who was now the Duchess of Kent. It was a classical, once-in-a-lifetime emotion which had the intensity, ferocity and passion of her Slav ancestors. 'He was her all: he filled her whole life and her whole existence,' said one member of the British Royal Family.

The Duke of Kent was not an easy man to live with. He was often irritable and impatient; sometimes moody and some-times churlish; and he was used to having his own way. He looked like a typical Englishman but possessed none of the re-laxed calmness of temperament which is supposed to be the national characteristic.

Because of her background and the blood which ran in her own veins his wife was the one woman in a thousand who could accept this with complete equanimity. Queen Mary was right: this Danish/Greek Princess of German/Russian descent not only made him a good wife but she provided all the love and affection and stability which he so badly needed. And the likeable, good-looking Duke with his charm, his kindness and his good spirits

K

and even his occasional erratic outbursts of temper, was exactly the right husband for her.

In spite of this the early days of her married life were no easier for the Duchess of Kent than for any other newly-wed and in some ways much worse. The disadvantages of being a member of a royal family are obvious—the continual limelight, the eternal protocol, and other people's expectation that royalty should not only do no wrong but, like Justice, should never be seen doing wrong. Allowances are always made for commoners who join the royal family circle but for the beautiful newcomer this leniency would not apply: she was just as royal as any of them; she should know automatically what to do and how to behave.

But, oddly enough, she needed more help than anybody.

So many people, including Queen Mary, looked upon the new Duchess of Kent as a worldly sophisticated person. She had already experienced much more of life than most, and she had travelled more. She was at home at all the courts in Europe and she looked extremely self-assured.

Yet the exact opposite was the case. For all her outward appearance the Duchess of Kent was amazingly simple and unworldly. For years she had been a roving refugee. Her only settled home during the ten years before her marriage had been a modest flat in Paris which she mostly left every day only to go for lessons of one sort or another. She had had no particular social life and no social duties at all. She had never made a speech, or opened a bazaar, or been part of a 'circle' at a Court ball.

She was too young for any of this when it had been part of her family's life; and when she came of age it existed no longer. On top of everything, she was extremely shy.

Princess Marina knew how to talk with kings and princes; after all they were relations; but in her new role as Duchess of Kent an audience of strangers frightened her to death. What was worse there was no one to teach her how to get used to this; it was something she had to learn by herself. In the up-to-date, modern conception of royalty in England, where they were increasingly expected not only to put in an appearance but to contribute something specific—even if only a few words—she was at a loss.

Not even her regal godmother could do much to help; although Queen Mary was continually 'on show' by her husband's side she rarely made a speech in public in her whole life. Almost the longest public utterance she ever made was when she launched the liner which bore her name. Once she added a sentence or two to an Empire Day broadcast made by King George V; and in 1951, as a great concession and because of her interest in the subject, she agreed to open an exhibition at the Royal School of Needlework. But few people heard what Queen Mary said because a faulty microphone distorted every word; and she never attempted it again.

So when the shy Duchess of Kent was flung into the royal round of public duties—for which, naturally, she was in great demand—it was a great ordeal for her.

In a way the Duchess was made more conscious of her own inadequacy by the example of her sister-in-law the Duchess of York. The non-royal former Lady Elizabeth Bowes-Lyon may have been the first commoner to marry into the British Royal Family without it being a morganatic alliance, but she knew better than anybody how to behave like royalty in public: as the daughter of the 14th Earl of Strathmore she had been doing it all her life.

When she became Duchess of York she stunned everybody in royal circles with amazement and admiration over the way with which she slipped easily and naturally into her public duties without the slightest trace of self-consciousness. Always smiling; always knowing the right thing to say; never ever putting a foot wrong. In private, helped by Queen Mary and an elderly courtier she had to be taught the details of formal regal etiquette and the mysterious formula of precedence but she did her official tasks better than those who were born to it—sometimes it is said to their inner chagrin. And by the time the timid, untried Princess Marina joined the British royal house, the Duchess of York had already had more than ten years' experience of coping with public engagements. Her serene professionalism was so far ahead of everybody else that instead of helping by its example she set a standard that seemed almost impossible to reach.

If the Duchess of Kent had followed her inclination she might have been over-awed and defeated from the beginning; given the whole thing up and retired to concentrate on her home life, her husband and family; and nothing more. But she was the doughty Grand Duchess Vladimir's grand-daughter. Instead she set out determined to conquer her diffidence; with such success that nobody outside her closest family and friends ever knew how she really felt. Though as a result of her pseudo self-assurance sometimes she was misjudged. As Prince Christopher commented, 'Her very shyness and ultra sensitive air of reserve created a false impression of hauteur,' which some of those who met her may have thought was just the result of her royal blood. It would perhaps be more accurate to say that it was a combination of the two.

One of the first public duties she ever undertook in England was, appropriately enough, to open an exhibition of Russian art held in a house in Belgrave Square. It was not a difficult task and any self respecting President of the Women's Institute could have sailed through it without a second's thought and, if necessary, standing on her head. But this ordeal caused the Duchess a sleepless night beforehand. On the appointed opening day it was estimated that more than a dozen members of her family were in the audience to give her support, including old Princess Victoria, the Grand Duchess Xenia (a sister of Tsar Nicholas II, who was living in a cottage at Frogmore on the Windsor estate), and her parents. All the Duchess said were a few formal words; but her relations knew how nervous she was, and afterwards from the front row, say those who were present, came such noisy and prolonged applause that it was as if she had made a brilliant and masterly oration. In a way, for the timorous Duchess, it was just as big an achievement.

The Duchess of Kent did not have far to go home after her initiation into public speaking: she and the Duke had set up their first home at 3, Belgrave Square, less than a mile from Buckingham Palace and once, for a short while, lived in by Queen Victoria's mother, the previous Duchess of Kent. They leased it furnished and took it because it was the right size and in the right location.

To the surprise of his friends and the delight of his parents, the Duke of Kent took to domesticity with the greatest pleasure and delight. Not only did he like being married but he loved having an establishment of his own at last.

The Duke and Duchess of Kent's London house was not large
—there was only one guest room—but it was beautifully decorated and furnished. The Duke spent hours supervising the re-
decoration; and he put a lot of the owner's furniture into store
and replaced it with many of the wedding gifts which he and his
bride had received. He also began to accumulate a considerable
amount of splendid and important antique pieces such as Georgian and Queen Anne furniture; old English and Continental
silver and china; Chinese jade and porcelain; drawings, paintings and lithographs; all of which he arranged with care and
taste. In addition there were a great many valuable and attractive things which the Duchess brought to the household as part
of her dowry.

About a year after the Duke and Duchess of Kent were
married, old Princess Victoria died and left the Duke a country
house called Coppins in the sprawling village of Iver in Bucking-
hamshire about twenty miles from London. It is a nondescript
Victorian mansion which, when it came into the Duke's posses-
sion, was crammed with a mass of antiquated furniture of dubi-
ous origin and surrounded by grounds so choked with trees that
no light seemed to penetrate any of the rooms.

Transforming it into a more suitable and comfortable home
was a task into which the Duke of Kent plunged with enthusiasm. It was essentially a country home and he had it painted in
light pastel colours, added a great deal of pale pickled pine,
which was in vogue at the time, and filled it with pretty, chintzy
furniture. Many of the trees and shrubs were cleared away to
let in air and sunshine, and he did a tremendous amount of the
chopping and felling himself. He also supervised the kitchen
garden and every week fresh flowers and vegetables were sent to
Belgrave Square. But the Duke of Kent never meant Coppins to
be a permanent country seat. He looked at innumerable estates
both in the Home Counties and farther afield during the next
few years, searching for the ideal house in which to settle down.

It was the Duke, not the Duchess, who ran the Kent household; a situation which suited them both perfectly.

Apart from that, the Duchess of Kent was an extraordinarily
docile and submissive wife—far more so than any of her sisters-
in-law. It was an attitude which stemmed partly from her great
love for her husband, which meant that she was eager to do any-

thing he wished; and partly because of her gentle and indolent nature. It was much easier to agree than disagree: and she had neither the inclination nor the training to run a royal establishment.

Every morning at breakfast, the menu book was placed by the side of the Duke's plate, not hers. And though he sometimes consulted his wife about the meals they should eat, the final choice was his. He held consultations with the chef, ordered the wines, dealt with the staff, looked after the table decorations and arranged the seating plan for dinner parties. He also allotted rooms for any visitors, supervised the arrangements for their comfort and looked after all the details of how and where they should be met—just as his wife's grandfather had done.

The Duke of Kent was always concerned that his guests should enjoy themselves and generally invited a mixed assortment of people to dinner whom he thought would complement each other and encourage conversation. It annoyed him when anybody monopolized the attention of one person and he seriously considered having a silver lighthouse made as a table centre, with coloured lights inside which he could control from his own seat. A red light would mean that every man should talk to the lady on his left, on his port side; and when the Duke switched to amber it would indicate that they should begin to terminate their conversation. Then when he moved the light to green all the men would be expected to turn and talk to whoever was on their right, or starboard side. He went so far as to have sketches drawn to his specifications and meant to have it made up eventually.

But even without the lighthouse the parties given by himself and the Duchess were invariably a great success. Queen Mary's Lady of the Bedchamber, the Dowager Countess of Airlie, often accompanied the King and Queen when they dined at Belgrave Square—evenings which she said were noted for brilliant conversation, beautifully arranged rooms and perfectly chosen meals. Once she complimented the Duchess of Kent on the dinner and got the smiling reply 'I am really a very bad hostess. I must confess that I didn't know what we were going to eat tonight until the food appeared. My husband chose the dinner and the wine—and the flowers and everything else. He enjoys doing it, and so I always leave the household affairs to him.'

And she added: 'I let him make all the decisions over furniture and decorations. He has a wonderful sense of colour and design.'

'She recognized the artist in him and the need for expression,' Lady Airlie later commented approvingly, and said that it was not so much the external signs of happiness, like the well-run household, which impressed her as 'the deeper harmony of the two temperaments' of her host and hostess.

Another aspect of his domestic home life which interested the Duke was his wife's wardrobe. 'I always discuss with Marina what dress and jewels I advise her to wear,' he said to a friend. And it was by the clothes she wore that the 'lithe and lovely Duchess of Kent' (as she was called by one fashion writer) made perhaps her strongest impact on the women of Britain.

Many male members of the Royal Family have influenced fashion; most recently George IV as Prince Regent, King Edward VII, and the Duke of Windsor when he was Prince of Wales. But royal ladies have not had nearly so much effect. Queen Alexandra and Queen Mary picked their own individual style of dressing and stuck to it regardless of changing fashions. Queen Mary could go to an informal tea party glistening with huge diamonds, elaborately clad from toque to ankle entirely in pure snowy white, including her parasol, and get away with it; due to her own stately and dignified manner. But it was not the sort of ensemble which could be copied successfully by anyone else. Until Princess Marina came on the scene a trend-setter who was both feminine and royal was non-existent; but few women, royal or otherwise, have had so much influence as she had on fashion.

From the day her picture was first circulated showing her wearing that perky little pillbox hat, to her last public appearance on the centre court at Wimbledon, she was always the epitome of elegance: and she took immense trouble to achieve this. She was always interested in clothes even when she was very young. It was perhaps inevitable with that family tradition: her mother was said to have been by far the best dressed woman in Greece, and her grandmother, the Grand Duchess Vladimir, in her day, the most beautifully gowned Imperial lady in Russia. Princess Marina was to have the same success in England. It would not be too far-fetched to say that she was one of the most elegant women in the world; a position she retained until elegance itself went out of fashion.

To an era of awful clothes—ugly, garish, over-ornamented and often vulgar—she brought a new simplicity and grace.

Her knowledge and what can only be described as her good taste owed as much to natural instinct as it did to tuition or tradition.

She liked plain, simple, classical clothes, mostly with boat-shaped necklines and straight skirts, but their very plainness was deceptive: they were constructed as carefully as the Sydney bridge. She never had less than four fittings for any dress made for her, instead of the mere usual two or three. Couturiers and dressmakers would go on and on, re-shaping, re-cutting, remaking until everything was perfect. Nothing escaped her: seams had to be architecturally exact, hemlines ruler straight, and she paid as much attention to what she wore underneath as to anything which appeared on top. Occasionally if a garment did not reach the high standard she set it would be rejected.

Sometimes there were other reasons why she would refuse to pick a design even if she liked it herself. She would explain that she would not choose it 'because my husband would hate it'. Or she might select a particular colour on the grounds that 'my husband would like it'. Always the Duke took a keen and active interest in her clothes. He said once that it was the way she dressed rather more than the way she looked which first attracted his attention to her.

In the early years of her marriage the Duchess wore a great many shades of blue—variants of that subtle, deep, greeny-turquoise 'Marina blue', again because it was the colour the Duke liked. Her day dresses were nearly always straight and slim and her formal ball gowns luscious and full skirted. For special events and celebrations she could always be relied on to look particularly stunning. At the coronation of King George VI her floor-length gown was straight and uncluttered but worn with the Tsar's vast diamond bow and encrusted with a gorgeous and glittering jewelled pattern of flowers: not composed of real gems such as a dress belonging to the Grand Duchess Vladimir would have been—but equally effective. A gown which was destined for posterity—to go on show in the London Museum; a gleaming and sophisticated contrast alongside Queen Victoria's demure wedding dress.

The prestige of being the Duchess of Kent's dressmaker was enormous, and although she always paid a special price for her clothes—not very much above the wholesale cost—it was well worth while for any couturier to have her patronage. Where she went to choose her wardrobe others flocked to buy. Yet even when she married the Duke of Kent, though they were not immensely rich nobody could call them poor, her years of poverty in Paris had left her with deep-rooted habits which, to those professionals who attend the wealthy, are unmistakable signs of someone who is or has been short of money. There were times when, changing her mind about the colour of a dress, she would have it dyed instead of re-made in a different material; when gowns were out of date she would give instructions for them to be restyled. Nowadays, when duchesses and millionairesses shop at chain stores, nobody would think twice about such elementary thrift but among the big spenders of the 'thirties it was unheard of; in a royal princess unthinkable. Many a time in the dressmaking salons of Mayfair there were astonished upraised eyebrows cast in Princess Marina's direction.

But the result was distinctly worthwhile: always she looked exquisitely lovely and those out-dated words 'smart' and 'chic' were used interminably to describe her, though 'smart' was a word she loathed.

Probably the only criticism the Duchess received about the way she dressed was in May 1935 when in King George V's Silver Jubilee procession she wore a vast dove-grey coloured picture hat trimmed with ostrich plumes, a beautiful piece of millinery which she had difficulty in controlling as it fluttered in the breeze and one which annoyed some of the spectators because the huge brim hid her fine features. The Duchess of Kent was rather upset by the critics because that big hat had a purpose. She was then expecting her first child, with all the attendant discomforts, and she wanted the brim as a screen in case she felt ill.

The baby, the present Duke of Kent, later christened Edward George Nicholas Paul Patrick, was born on 9 October 1935 at the house in Belgrave Square and was at that time fifth in line to the throne.

The Duchess's parents and her sister Elizabeth were there—so was the Home Secretary, whose presence under the same roof was always necessary at a royal birth until King George VI discontinued the practice in 1948.

Princess Nicholas and the Duke were present at the actual birth, which took place just after two o'clock in the morning. Even at that hour there were crowds outside the house. Guns were fired in Hyde Park and at the Tower of London. Someone tied a bow of blue ribbon around a photograph of the new parents and the event stirred up yet another wave of sentiment around the beautiful and popular Duchess.

The Duke of Kent had always liked children and he was immensely thrilled to have one of his own at last. It pleased him enormously whenever anybody said that his son looked like him; and, as one of his friends remarked, 'he spent more time in the nursery than he did in his study'. He passed happy hours filming Prince Edward playing on the lawn at Coppins, and took dozens of photographs. If anybody admired the pictures the Duke invariably replied, 'He's really much nicer than that'. And he put his son's name down for Eton.

The Duke was equally delighted when, nearly fifteen months later, also at Belgrave Square, to the sound of carols played on a cornet outside and the ringing of church bells, the Duchess bore him a daughter on the morning of Christmas Day, 1936. They named her Alexandra Helen Elizabeth Olga and, because of the date, Christabel.

For the birth of both children Miss Fox was in the house; although not officially on duty. She had become so much part and parcel of their family life that it was almost unthinkable that any event of importance should take place without her presence. Princess Paul had followed her mother's example and engaged a Norland nurse for her children; but the Duchess of Kent did not—chiefly because Queen Mary would have disapproved. The idea of having someone in the nursery whose word was law and who was in complete control was an anathema to the Duchess's mother-in-law and the Duke was in agreement. He was very much master in his own house and he wanted to remain so. As usual, the Duchess bowed to their wishes.

Not that it stopped Miss Fox from giving the Belgrave Square nurses the benefit of her own experience and, when Prince Edward and Princess Alexandra were a little older, she entertained them for hours with stories of their mother and their aunts as children, and of her experiences in Greece and Russia. 'If only I were younger and could look after them too . . .' she would sigh, and when the Duchess said that surely she had had her share of babies, the answer would come: 'I know—but it makes it no easier to watch someone else take charge.'

Meanwhile the decorative and popular new Royal Duchess continued to battle bravely with the ever-increasing requests for her attendance at public functions. The furore and interest which she had caused among the population did not lessen: if anything it increased. Hardly a day passed without her photograph appearing in a newspaper, or depicted in a glossy magazine; and whatever she wore she looked so delectable that legions of women clamoured to look just like her—or at least as near as they could.

By 1935 she had become the patroness of organizations such as the Elizabeth Garrett Anderson Hospital, the Women's Hospital Fund and the Central School of Speech and Drama— and continued her patronage of them for the rest of her life. And in 1936, rather appropriately, she took over as President of Alexandra Rose Day, which had once been the province of Queen Alexandra—her own great-aunt and her husband's grand-mother (who had died in 1925, shortly before Queen Olga). There were, of course, also many official duties which she atten-ded with her husband.

As a responsible married man the Duke himself took on more public work than ever and entered into it with his usual zest and interest. He was, for example, particularly concerned over the treatment of mental health and disabled children and involved, because of his naval background, in several nautical organiza-tions, including the Shaftesbury Homes; on the cultural side he patronized various musical and artistic societies. And he was President of the All England Lawn Tennis and Croquet Club.

Because her husband was so often away on his official duties. and in spite of the fact that she dearly loved her children and saw a lot of them, for a long while after she was first married the Duchess of Kent was very lonely. She had many acquaintances: the Duke had proudly showed her off to all his friends in the early days of their engagement and gave parties so that they could meet her. And there is no doubt that the Duchess was just as amused and entertained by them as her husband. Like him, she was also fascinated and enthralled by the many stage and film personalities whom she now had the opportunity of knowing.

But the fact remained that they were his friends not hers. Although she had come to this country so frequently since her childhood she had few companions of her own in English Society. When the Duke of Kent was away she tended to cling to people much older than herself with whom she felt at ease—like the Grand Duchess Xenia or Queen Mary.

On their part, many of the Duke's friends, who did not know the Duchess so intimately as they did her husband, were chary of inviting her out by herself. Others who thought of it were sometimes discouraged by her shyness which they mistook for hauteur. Only Lady Louis Mountbatten would sometimes telephone and suggest a theatre or dinner party—an invitation which was always gratefully accepted.

To keep in touch with her family and friends abroad whom she missed so much, the Duchess of Kent wrote full and frequent letters to them and often put in lengthy telephone calls; sometimes talking for hours at a time. She was also helped by the fact that her husband had a rare and endearing quality. He accepted his wife's friends and relations with the same alacrity as Princess Paul's husband, and felt almost the same affection for them as the Duchess did herself. He never made any attempt to try and dissuade her from having such close contact with her parents and sisters. If anything he encouraged it.

For instance, the Duke of Kent went with the Duchess on long visits to her relations. They often travelled to see the Toerrings in Munich or Winhörring, and went away on holidays with them. By this time Princess Elizabeth had a son, Hans Veit Kaspar Nikolas, born in January, 1935 (when the Duchess was staying with her): and in 1937 a daughter named Helen Marina Elizabeth.

As the wife of Count Toerring, Princess Marina's sister had been delighted to find herself living comparatively near those close friends and relations, Prince Philip's sisters, the four daughters of Prince Andrew. The Duke and Duchess of Kent saw a lot of them too during the trips to Germany.

They also stayed a good deal in Yugoslavia—with Prince and Princess Paul (whose family was eventually increased to three when a daughter, named Elizabeth, was born in Belgrade in April 1936, and with her parents in Paris. The Duke of Kent met and liked his wife's Greek and Russian relations and her special women friends as well. He was happy to entertain them at Belgrave Square whenever any of them were in London and once he went with the Duchess to visit a friend in Poland.

Perhaps the only person close to her whom he did not care for with quite the same feeling as his wife was Miss Fox, who generally timed her visits to Coppins or Belgrave Square to coincide with a period when he was away. But whenever he met her he was friendly and polite and gave her presents such as a gold bracelet, an enamel clock, and another time-piece made of silver.

But the Duke was never too pleased whenever some of the household bills were received. Due to the Duchess's long-distance calls, their telephone accounts, both at Iver and London, were often monumental. 'What is the point of me querying my expenditure and trying to economize when you run up these enormous bills?' he would grumble to his wife; and for a day or so she would try and make her conversations a bit shorter. But it made her so unhappy to feel cut off from her nearest relations that he did not have the heart to do much more about it.

Occasionally the Duchess annoyed him in the same way that Queen Alexandra had infuriated King Edward VII; she sometimes took a long while to get dressed. The Duke, who did not find it easy to be on time himself but had been rigorously brought up with the idea that a member of the British Royal Family should never be late, would pace up and down saying: 'For Heaven's sake, Marina. How long are you going to be?'

And the Duchess, although she was fastidious and tidy like her grandfather King George I, seemed to have a habit of losing such things as ear rings, clips, gloves, handkerchiefs and handbags. When someone once darted to retrieve an object she had dropped the Duke commented: 'You wouldn't be so eager if you had to do it several times a day. . . .'

But on the whole they got on very well together and the Duke of Kent was more content than he had ever been before. He had a beautiful wife and children; he was busy, though perhaps in his own opinion, not quite busy enough; and after his marriage his relations with his father improved almost beyond recognition.

The King on his part always gave a great welcome to his daughter-in-law and even discussed politics with her, which he would not have considered doing with many women. She was not in fact deeply interested in such matters but she had a wide background knowledge of European affairs through having heard them discussed so often at home.

On the less serious side the glamorous young royal couple plunged into much of the gaiety which still marked the early part of the 1930s: going to theatres, films and parties and continuing with their own entertaining. They were both addicted to amusing party games of the same sort which had delighted the Duchess ever since her girlhood: charades, sardines, murder; all sorts of word games such as 'truth and consequences' and others which needed to be written down on paper. There were always plenty of notebooks and pencils scattered around their drawing-rooms where they could be found immediately they were needed. They also played a lot of card games like whist, gin rummy and canasta, though, curiously, never bridge which the Duchess did not even know how to play, in spite of the fact that it was her father who was responsible for first introducing the game to the English Court. And often when they were alone they would bring out the backgammon board or she would listen to him as he played the piano for hours at a time while she read or sketched or did crosswords.

'It does one good to see how happy George and Marina are together,' said Princess Olga.

Their full and pleasant existence was interrupted at intervals by a series of family events which involved them both.

In 1935 another referendum gave Greece a monarchy once more. There was an abortive suggestion—probably unofficial—that the Duke and Duchess of Kent should be King and Queen: a position he would not have accepted in any case. But in November, after eleven years of exile, the Duchess's cousin King George II was back on the throne. A year later the bodies of Queen Olga, King Constantine and Queen Sophie (who had died at Frankfurt in 1932) were removed from the crypt of the Russian Church in Florence where they had lain since their deaths and re-interred in white marble tombs at Tatoi. And the

Duchess of Kent and nearly all the other surviving members of the Greek Royal Family were there for the six days' lying-in-state at Athens Cathedral and the reburial ceremony.

At last for the first time the Duchess was able to show her husband her birthplace and he was enchanted with it. So much so that he said 'although Athens is not home, it is the next best thing'. And he told some Athenians: 'Greece has given me a wife, the full extent of whose influence over me I shall probably never know,' and added: 'Her influence is as incalculable as the Hellenic influence over civilization'. A graceful and charming tribute which the Duchess valued above any other compliment he ever paid her, though he frequently referred in public to 'people who like myself are happily married and have children whom they love'.

The Duke also took more than a casual interest in Greek architecture and pottery as a result of going to that country.

It was at Athens two years later, in February 1938, that sixty-six-year-old Prince Nicholas suddenly became ill and the Duke and Duchess of Kent, who had been ski-ing at St Anton with Count and Countess Toerring, rushed to his bedside. The two sisters were distressed and upset when their train stopped at Belgrade and they were met by Prince Paul who told them that they were too late to get to their father in time to see him before he died: though Princess Nicholas and Princess Olga were by his side until the end.

During his last illness Prince Nicholas was in the Grande Bretagne Hotel, not the Nicholas Palace—which, when the hotel lease expired, was taken over by the Italian Legation, which is still there. But with almost his last breath he said: 'How happy I am to die in my beloved Greece.' And he too was buried at Tatoi. On his tomb and that of Princess Nicholas, when she was eventually buried beside him, is carved the words 'Light and Life'.

Shortly after her husband's death Princess Nicholas settled in Greece permanently. She lived at Psychico, a pleasant Athens suburb in a large villa filled with her own furniture—some of which had once been in the Vladimir Palace in St Petersburg. She was still passionately fond of animals and any stray cat or dog was sure to find a home there.

There were several other bereavements in the Duchess of

Kent's family during the 1930s. Her godmother, the Grand
Duchess Kirill (to her husband's 'boundless and inexpressible
grief'), died in 1936. Less than two years afterwards so did
the Duchess of Kent's uncle. Grand Duke Kirill's death from
gangrene after suffering from arterio-sclerosis resulted in a brief
family reunion. Princess Nicholas and her two brothers Boris
and Andrei, were at his bedside. The Grand Duke died before
he could complete his memoirs and to the end was still battling
to establish beyond all doubt his claim to the Russian Throne.
'Under the Imperial Sceptre Russia will again live in quiet and
peace,' he wrote in a last manifesto which he issued from his
home at St Briac in France barely six months beforehand.

And there was a tragic accident which deeply affected the
Duchess of Kent and her two sisters. In November 1937, their
cousin Cecile, the Grand Duchess of Hesse (the third of Prince
and Princess Andrew's four daughters), her husband and two
children were killed when the aircraft in which they were all
travelling to London for a wedding hit a brickworks chimney as
it took off from Ostend. The crash took place only six weeks
after Princess Cecile's husband had inherited the title as a result
of the death of his father, Grand Duke Ernst of Hesse—the first
husband of Grand Duchess Kirill.

The only surviving member of their family was a fourteen-
month-old baby girl who had been christened Johanna Marina.

The wedding they had all been planning to attend was that
of the Grand Duke's brother, Prince Ludwig, to the daughter
of Sir Auckland (later Lord) Geddes. It still took place privately
with the Duchess of Kent and the other guests in deep mourning
black. Prince Ludwig, now the Grand Duke of Hesse, adopted
the orphaned baby. But there was no happy ending to this
story. She died, of meningitis, in 1939; the whole of that particular branch of the Hesse family were wiped out.

And in Britain on 20 January 1936, in the presence of his
family, including the Duke and Duchess of Kent, King George
V died in his great brass bedstead at Sandringham; two weeks
after having recorded with pride in his diary: 'Saw my Kent
grandson in his bath'; meaning the thirteen-month-old Prince
Edward. The King's death not only caused them all great sad-
ness but precipitated a series of family difficulties which cul-
minated in the abdication of King Edward VIII.

The coronation of King Edward was planned to take place in May 1937. But on 10 December 1936, in order to marry Mrs Wallis Warfield Simpson, he relinquished the Throne in favour of his brother Albert, the Duke of York, who became King George VI.

The night before this renunciation took place the Duke and Duchess of Kent dined at Marlborough House with Queen Mary. It was a painful evening for them all. After dinner the Duke of York arrived with the draft Instrument of Abdication to show his mother and, as he recorded in his diary afterwards, 'broke down and sobbed like a child'. 'It is a terrible blow to us all,' wrote Queen Mary in hers.

Both the Duke and Duchess of Kent knew Mrs Simpson well. They had frequently met her at Fort Belvedere, she had Sunday teas with them at Coppins and dined at Belgrave Square. And it was at the Buckingham Palace reception before their wedding that the Prince of Wales had introduced his future wife to his mother—the only time they ever met. But it was symptomatic of their concern over the situation that during the weeks of crisis which preceded the abdication the Duke of Kent cancelled all his engagements in order to be at his brother's side if needed and it was with deep sorrow that he watched him go out of his life.

So it was the Duke of York, not his elder brother, who was crowned the following May. The first coronation to be held in England for a quarter of a century.

The ceremony probably meant more to the Duchess of Kent than to almost anybody else who was present in Westminster Abbey, with the exception of those who took a principal part in the long, solemn and impressive ritual. Many people who were there enjoyed it as a spectacle. But to the Duchess, with her devout religious convictions and inborn sense of royal autocracy, every word and action was significant. Her devotion and allegiance to the monarch was unquestionable. As head of the Church and State she gave him the same sort of homage and respect as was felt by many towards the old-time Russian Tsars.

And her feelings were exactly the same when in 1953 she attended the coronation of the present Queen.

5 | *The Second World War*

It was with rather mixed feelings—mostly dismay—that the Duchess of Kent received the news in October 1938 that King George VI intended to appoint her husband Governor General of the Commonwealth of Australia, in succession to the sixty-six-year-old Lord Gowrie who had held the office since 1936 and been Military Secretary to the Governor General as far back as 1908.

It was the first time a member of the Royal Family had been suggested for such a position in Australia, apparently because it was considered so remote. There had been some sense of grievance among Australians because Canada had already had two Royal Governors General: Queen Victoria's son-in-law the Duke of Argyll and the Duke of Connaught; and South Africa had also had two: Prince Arthur of Connaught and the Earl of Athlone. Now the situation was to be remedied.

It was intended that the Duke of Kent should take up his new duties in November 1939. 'My wife and I are pleased and proud to go to Australia and looking forward to it very much and I know my children will have the time of their lives,' he said after the appointment had been announced officially. And in a broadcast he remarked that in his public life in Great Britain he had 'tried to gain a real appreciation of this country's problems by personal contact'. In his new job he said, he hoped to do the same and 'when the opportunity offers, meet the worker at his work and the farmer on his farm'. And he endeared himself to the Australians by promising to try and do it 'in a fair dinkum way'.

The news that the Kents were to go away to Australia, 'a momentous announcement', caused a tremendous stir of excite-

ment. Winston Churchill called it a 'master-stroke in Imperial
policy'. The *Sydney Herald* described it as 'a magnificent gesture'. The *Sydney Sun* said: 'It is the greatest compliment the
Throne can pay to the Australian people.' And Melbourne newspapers suggested that a suitable residence for the new Governor
General should be acquired in that city.

The Duke himself, then aged 35, was just as delighted. He was
enormously pleased at the prospect of being entrusted with such
a responsible position as representative of the King—and the
idea of at last having what he considered to be a worthwhile
job. With his noted zeal he immediately started finding out all
he could about the country in which he expected to live for at
least three years.

To be truthful, the thirty-one-year-old Duchess was much
less enthusiastic. Not because she had any particular objection
to Australia but because she dreaded the thought of being
twelve thousand miles away from her mother and sisters. And
social telephone calls from that distance were out of the question.

But gradually she came to share her husband's excitement
and interest. Together they read every book on the Dominion
they could get their hands on; they studied old maps and documents from the Public Record Office, including the original
letters patent constituting the office of Governor General and
the Log of H.M.S. *Sirius* which accompanied the first settlers
who went to the newly discovered Continent. Dozens of astonished Australians visiting England, who never dreamed of
getting anywhere near the Royal Family, found themselves
invited to Coppins for a polite and searching interrogation about
their homeland.

But a great howl of protest was set up by dress designers and
manufacturers at the thought of losing the popular and well-
dressed Duchess. 'It is feared—and openly said—that the
absence of the Duchess from Britain will have an adverse effect
on the whole fashion industry,' said a front-page lead story in the
Sunday Express. 'The Duchess has made fashion history. She
has given London the leadership that belonged to Paris and
fashion houses fear that . . . in her absence London will lose that
lead again.'

'It really is a tragedy,' declared a top-ranking couturier. 'It is difficult to express in words the impetus she has given to dress designing. . . . Fashion memories are short and I'm afraid we may drift back to what we were . . . dull and uninspired.' A fabric designer said sorrowfully: 'The influence of the Duchess on fashions has been one of the most remarkable features of contemporary life. I fear her departure will lessen that influence.' Buyers from London stores said that they were always being asked for clothes similar to those she wore and that the sale of bags, gloves and even handkerchiefs like hers were 'a substantial part of our trade'; while hairdressers lamented that they would miss her as much as anybody, 'because she had shown other women that it is possible to vary the hair style to suit the frock and the occasion . . . a new idea to Englishwomen'.

One fashion house talked of opening a branch in Australia to cope with what they confidently expected would be a rush of orders the moment Australian women clapped eyes on the Duchess; and the newspapers used columns and columns of wordage describing in detail the wardrobe she proposed to take with her. There was even a suggestion from Sydney that she should be persuaded to wear woollen stockings in order to boost the Dominion's most important industry. It was announced that Queen Mary had promised to lend her daughter-in-law £25,000 worth of her jewellery to augment the Duchess's own collection.

Australia itself received more attention and publicity than it had done for years.

Every detail of where the Duke and Duchess would live, pictures of the surrounding countryside, the itinerary of their possible tours, and personal information on a scale almost incredible to believe today, was published in Britain and Australia for months on end. Government House in Canberra, which was to be the Duke's official residence, was renovated, altered, extended and re-furnished. New reception rooms and bedrooms were added and when they were completed photographs were sent to the Duke and Duchess so that they could choose the furniture and decorations.

It was, of course, although few knew it at the time, the Duke who was responsible for what was called the 'revolutionary' pale colour scheme for the Governor General's house and he planned exactly where the new light-coloured furniture—designed in England and manufactured in Australia—was to be arranged. Curtains, hangings and tailored covers without traditional flounces were sent from England. He chose oatmeal-coloured silk tweed curtains, pale blue satin-covered sofas and chairs; and white Grecian rugs, which pleased the Duchess. The Duke also ordered £5,000 worth of household linen, which he paid for himself and included peach-coloured silk sheets edged with satin priced at £50 a pair.

The Duchess was kept busy looking at everything, and also choosing the clothes which she would take with her, most of which came from Molyneux. There were arrangements to make concerning the shipment of the children's toys and Prince Edward's Shetland pony and the Duke, having been given three racehorses (by the Aga Khan, Prince Aly Khan and Lord Derby), decided to take up racing and registered his colours in Australia.

The royal couple arranged to make the first part of the long journey by air stopping off in India to stay with various rulers such as the Nizam of Hyderabad. And after they had left it was intended to put Coppins up for sale.

By July 1939, when nearly all the preparations were complete, there was a pleasant interlude, especially as far as the Duchess was concerned, when Prince Paul, as Regent of Yugoslavia, and Princess Paul paid an official State visit to Britain.

Behind all the fuss and festivities the visit had a serious purpose and was one of three which Prince and Princess Paul made that year. The other two had taken place earlier: one in May to Italy and the other in June to Germany.

King George VI made Prince Paul a Knight of the Garter. Several newspapers pointed out that Prince Paul was Regent of a country which occupied a key position in Europe, that he was in favour of democracy, had been educated in England, and, because of his connection with the Duchess, was sentimentally inclined to Britain. And *The Times* said that Prince Paul and his wife were welcome visitors, and there was no reason to attribute their visit to 'the disquieting political situation' (which in fact, of course, was what it was all about) and pointed out that the Duke and Duchess of Kent would shortly be going to Yugoslavia on a private visit.

It was in August, the following month, that the Duke and Duchess of Kent went out to Yugoslavia. On the way the

Duchess spent a few days in Paris for some final fittings of some of her dresses for Australia and to do some last-minute shopping. Much of their luggage, including the racehorses, was already on its way out to Canberra.

The holiday was meant as a sort of family farewell for the Duchess. Her mother was in Yugoslavia and so was Miss Fox. But the Duke cut his own stay short, disturbed by the ever-increasing talk of the imminent outbreak of war. 'It is best that I go back and make sure of the facts,' he told his wife. He left her with her relations and flew home. A few days later she received a telegram. 'Come at once,' it said.

Less than two weeks after the war began the Duke was back in the Navy and his Australian appointment postponed. Lord Gowrie agreed to carry on; and Mr Robert Menzies, the Prime Minister of Australia, sent a message to the Duke saying that 'when the present troubles were overcome' it was hoped that he would assume the duties of Governor General.

If the Duke of Kent could have followed his own inclination he would have gone back to active service at sea for the duration of the war. He confided to one of his relations that he would dearly have liked to command his own ship and become a normal member of the Royal Navy. But apart from his perpetual sea-sickness there were several reasons why he could not do this. He was a rear-admiral. He had been away from the Service for so long that he was sadly out of date; and he had no recent experience of handling ships.

Instead he went into the Admiralty and did a desk job which irked him so much that soon afterwards he transferred to the R.A.F. and dropped his rank of Air Vice Marshal so that he would not be superior to officers under whom he had to work. Later he was promoted to Air Commodore and became Chief Welfare Officer of the R.A.F. In addition he did a certain amount of work on behalf of Ernest Bevin, then the Minister of Labour, and inspected factories engaged on war production and various civil defence services—the sorts of jobs he had been accustomed to during his spell as one of H.M. Inspectors of Factories formerly under the jurisdiction of the Home Office. He had already resumed this before the war actually began but once he was in uniform he concentrated on making unofficial visits with the minimum of warning. And the emphasis of the visits changed.

As a factory inspector he had toured factories for a specific purpose and dealt mainly with the managerial staff. Now his object was to boost the morale of the workers drafted into jobs which were often unpleasant and sometimes done in extraordinarily uncomfortable and arduous conditions. For example, underground tunnels in the Thames Valley once used for quarrying, were turned into secret gun and aircraft factories. The Duke listened sympathetically when workers told him that they disliked the stuffy atmosphere and working continuously in artificial light. He could not do much about it but at least he made them feel that someone at the top really cared.

One-time furniture workers made the wooden frames of Mosquito aircraft; diamond cutters came over from Holland to work on industrial diamonds for machine tools; people who had rarely attempted rough and monotonous work went into a strange new world. And the Duke of Kent met and talked to as many as he could. He always wanted to know how everything functioned. If someone showed him the intricate mechanism of a bomb he would insist on finding out exactly how it was made. He was fascinated by machinery, and the smaller it was the better. It was very difficult to drag him away from a watch factory at High Wycombe making precision pocket watches for R.A.F. pilots.

On these impromptu visits he never took a chauffeur with him but preferred to drive himself, which he did very fast and very expertly in his Bentley, and at the factory gates he often had to wait for any companions who were accompanying him to catch up. And there was one strict rule he observed. He always insisted on being back at Coppins between four and four thirty to have tea with his children when he would tell them about some of the things he had seen. The only time he was ever late for this domestic ritual was after the trip to the watch factory.

The Duke's work did not prevent him from continuing to take an interest in antiques and the attraction he felt towards clocks was not confined to their works; he had a collection of more than a hundred of all types. Every room at Coppins had at least two or three, all ticking away and giving the correct time.

With the money left him by his father he still bought pictures, porcelain and silver, even in wartime. Three important paintings

by the French artist Claude de Lorrain were purchased for
3,700 guineas in 1940 for example. And he had accumulated a
varied collection of pictures including works of Vandyck, Guardi,
Veronese, Lely, Reynolds and Richard Wilson.

And he became keener than ever on gardening. The house at
Belgrave Square was given up and Coppins was now their only
home and he spent hours there digging, chopping and planting—
a hobby which the Duchess cared for not at all.

But duties came first; and the Duke went all over the country
inspecting R.A.F. bases and was often away for a week or
more at a time.

For her part the Duchess of Kent became Commandant (a
title later changed to Chief Commandant) of the Women's Royal
Naval Service—The Wrens.

At that time the Director of the W.R.N.S. was Vera Laughton
Mathews,, a former sub-editor of a magazine called the *Ladies
Field* and who later became a Dame.

The Duchess of Kent recalled the day 'when my brother-in-
law, the late King, appointed me as your Commandant', nearly
thirty years later at the W.R.N.S. Golden Jubilee Reunion in
1967. She said that her first action as an 'apprehensive fledgling'
had been to ask the doughty Director to go and see her at Buckingham Palace. 'While in theory it was I who had to interview
dear Dame Vera, in the event, there was no doubt whatever
that she interviewed me,' she said.

The Duchess of Kent's sponsorship of the W.R.N.S.—and the
way she looked in her uniform—was like a shot in the arm to the
feminine branch of the Senior Service, who at that time looked
like nothing so much as a collection of orphans in a storm, as
they wore floppy, unattractive hats which were a hangover from
the First World War. When these were changed, at the suggestion
of the First Lord of the Admiralty, then Mr A. V. Alexander,
the Duchess was consulted and took an intense interest in the
proposed new models. Three pretty Wrens paraded in front of
her wearing different versions of the saucy sailor hat which was
eventually adopted. 'They look very nice on you,' she commented, 'but will they suit plainer girls equally well?' She took one
back with her and demonstrated it on her own head to the King
at Buckingham Palace. He said that he preferred her in her
officer's tricorn (also a modified First World War hat but based

The Duchess of Kent and Princess Alexandra in
their car on their way home from a midnight charity
performance in 1959

Princess Marina in 1964

Princess Marina driving to the Commonwealth Prime Ministers' dinner in 1964

Princess Marina inspects Billie Jean King's steel-
framed tennis racket after she had won the Ladies
Singles Final at Wimbledon in July 1968

Three generations wear this beautiful tiara of interlaced diamonds with drop pearls, smuggled out of Russia during the Revolution in 1917

The Grand Duchess Vladimir

Queen Mary

Queen Elizabeth II

on an expensive civilian Reboux model owned by a senior Wren)
but he heartily approved the new style, which was so successful
that a great many women outside the Service copied it as well.
The Duchess also had a hand in other changes of the W.R.N.S.
uniform, such as the tropical kit for girls serving abroad.

She had a certain amount of trouble over her own uniform.
She always looked wonderful but her naval outfit was not always
strictly to Admiralty standards. She was given the rank of
Rear Admiral and turned up for her first visit to W.R.N.S.
Headquarters at Admiralty House in white gloves, which, though
they looked very smart, were not worn officially. She took one
look at Dame Vera and, taking in what she afterwards called
her 'appalling solecism', laughed and said hastily, 'Oh dear, my
gloves are wrong.' The Duchess never did that again but, as she
admitted: 'I rather fear that this was not the last time that—
quite unwittingly—I infringed the dress regulations for officers
as laid down in Admiralty Fleet Orders.' She—and her Lady-in-
Waiting—wore white cap covers outside the permitted time of
May to October; sometimes, mistakenly, she carried a large
civilian handbag; and once or twice she wore earrings and
bangles which were forbidden; and she often wore sheer silk
stockings and sometimes high heels. 'And I must confess,' she
said, 'that it took me a little time in those early days to get used
to calling a kitchen "a galley" and a bedroom "a cabin".'

She had another handicap: she found it difficult to do a
proper salute. The Duchess tried to imitate the regulation Royal
Navy version but somehow her hand always wilted and drooped,
and she ended up with a gesture which, though feminine, graceful and charming, was not in the least bit military. It owed more
to Isadora Duncan than the Admiralty. To try and correct this,
one of the senior W.R.N.S. officers sent her a diagram giving
technical details of the proper salute, including a drawing of a
hand in the right position. This amused her very much and it
made the King laugh too when she showed it to him. But, like
everything else she tackled, eventually she got it right.

She was very conscientious and took her new job extremely
seriously. On one of her first official visits—to a pay section
which was billeted near Windsor and had offices in Eton College—she asked one Wren where her office accommodation was,
and when told there was none at all the Duchess said nothing,

but next day an extra room was allotted almost miraculously. On the debit side during that same visit she omitted to talk to the cooks and stewards of the unit; and added insult to injury by refusing to eat any of the cakes and sandwiches they had prepared. She never forgot such a thing again; in fact sometimes she was almost too conscientious. Once, at a naval dock establishment, she had given a thorough going-over to everything and everybody on the day's programme, when she said during tea, 'Oh, I haven't looked at the officers' sleeping quarters. I must see those'—a remark which caused Wren officers, who were having a party that night, to slip surreptitiously one by one from the room and run to their 'cabins' where they hastily hid crates of beer by pushing them under the beds.

Once she was very curious when she saw that a W.R.N.S. officer had three hats and asked why she had so many. It was explained to her that one was for 'best' and the other two were worn alternately. The thrifty Duchess of Kent was astonished at the extravagance: she had only one.

When the impetus of Wren recruiting died down, despite her extreme nervousness, the Duchess of Kent agreed to broadcast an appeal for volunteers; and pictures of her in uniform appeared in the press the same day. The impact of her radio talk was so great that by first post next morning three thousand applications were received, and they continued to pour in and eventually reached such proportions that somebody at the Admiralty at last said: 'Whatever you do, don't on any account let the Duchess broadcast again.'

She never lost her own interest in the W.R.N.S. and the year before she died she said that it was not only a privilege and an honour to be part of the Service but 'a source of great happiness as well'. It was a sentiment which, as one of her listeners recalled afterwards, was 'spoken from the heart in her beautiful low voice, with that faintest touch of accent to remind us that she was a Greek Princess'.

Tirelessly, the Duchess travelled all over the country visiting naval establishments, talking to thousands and thousands of girls, asking them what they did, where they lived, where they came from, and whether they were happy. And in her more intimate dealings with officers she happily discussed anything from the Stock Exchange to the possibilities of curing smoking by hypnotism—though she eventually cut down her own heavy smoking by the simple practice of snipping cigarettes in half, putting them in a holder and treating each portion as if it were a whole one.

She also found plenty of amusement in incidents which afterwards she retailed joyfully to her family—such as the time when she saw some sinister-looking foreign ratings billeted in an air-raid shelter a few yards away from some W.R.N.S. officers' quarters. She asked one of the Wrens if the girls were ever bothered by them, and got the answer: 'No. Only at night.'

Not once, during all the visits and all the years, did anyone see her give so much as a scowl when, as is almost inevitable even in the best organizations, something went wrong. She rarely missed seeing any published news item of W.R.N.S. activities, and every Wren mentioned in the Honours List received her personal congratulations. The gesture was always appreciated and it was entirely the Duchess's own idea.

There are three solid reminders of her service with the Royal Navy, apart from the memories. Her name is on two buildings: the W.R.N.S. quarters at Portsmouth, named the Duchess of Kent Barracks; and the Princess Marina Block at Lee-on-Solent. And the uniform—which she wore so gracefully, stylishly, and sometimes in such an unorthodox manner—destined for permanent custody in the National Maritime Museum.

The Duchess of Kent, oddly enough, never considered that the uniform suited her. She disliked wearing it and she hated doing anything in the least bit martial, such as saluting or inspecting a parade. Above all else, she was extremely feminine. As far as clothes were concerned, she preferred visiting the Army regiments of which she was Colonel-in-Chief. They did not expect her to turn up in brass buttons or know anything about guns, but were happy to see her in a pretty dress. And if any keen soldier did try to interest her in some complicated weapon or piece of machinery or armament she made no bones about saying that she did not understand it; and was never likely to.

Apart from becoming Commandant of the W.R.N.S. the Duchess of Kent's other war-time duties included a period of hospital work. She was an anonymous V.A.D. in University College Hospital, London, under the pseudonym of 'Nurse K', which naturally became Nurse 'Kay'; and earlier she made splints and did other humdrum tasks at the Cottage Hospital in Iver.

She knitted 'comforts' for troops, and sometimes, when the Duchess was caught in an air raid in London, she took out her needles from a capacious handbag and clicked away until it was all over. And once in Bond Street, when she was on a shopping expedition with Miss Fox, a friend saw them sheltering in a shop passage calmly knitting away while anti-aircraft shells spattered noisily in the road in front of them.

The children were not always with their parents at Iver. Bombs were a constant danger as the house was so near London and Prince Edward and Princess Alexandra were sent away for long periods—to stay near their grandmother Queen Mary who had been evacuated and was living with her niece the Duchess of Beaufort at Badminton; to York Cottage at Sandringham; and sometimes to Windsor where there was a spacious air-raid shelter.

Early on in the war there had been one hilarious evening at Coppins when the Duke was away and the Duchess of Kent together with the two children and a woman friend retreated into an Anderson shelter in the garden at the beginning of an air-raid alert. But when they tried to get out again the friend, who was a bit on the bulky side, became stuck in a narrow doorway; which made the other three double up with laughter. Afterwards a steel 'cage' was built in the children's day nursery and when they were at Iver they continued to play happily there during the most violent raids.

With most of the population the Kent family listened whenever they could to the popular radio show called 'I.T.M.A.'—short for 'It's That Man Again'—which starred comedian Tommy Handley. It also featured a drunken character called 'Colonel Chinstrap', played by Jack Train, who construed almost anything anyone said to him as an invitation to have a drink, and answered in bleary tones 'I don't mind if I do'. It was a catchword which the almost teetotal Duchess of Kent used to repeat consistently together with other phrases such as, 'Cor! That's a bit of orlright!' in a cockney accent. She was generally looking rather like the household help when she said it for the clothes the Duke and Duchess of Kent wore during their off-duty time at Coppins were casual in the extreme. The Duke would dig away in the garden in grey flannel slacks and an open-necked shirt; and it is comforting to know that the beautifully-dressed Duchess was not always as immaculate as she appeared in public and slopped around happily in rope-soled sandals and a simple linen dress—or even baggy trousers, a cotton blouse and a scarf tied turban-fashion round her head.

She made fun of all the discomforts and rationing, went back to riding a bicycle and bought paper patterns from a village shop and had frocks made for herself and Princess Alexandra at a local dressmakers. Considering that for the first time she was cut off from close contact with her family, and her only communication with them was by letters sent through the medium of Lord Mountbatten's sister, Queen Louise of Sweden, the Duchess of Kent was remarkably cheerful. Like many descendants of Queen Victoria, she found that one of the results of war caused an anomalous position between relatives, and a divergence of interests which, although these made no difference as far as personal feelings were concerned, meant that both politically and diplomatically she had to be very careful indeed.

Her sister Elizabeth was married to a German and therefore technically an enemy. It made no difference that Count Toerring had never dabbled in politics; he was a Bavarian and an officer in the German Army. Her four cousins—Prince Philip's sisters— were married to Germans and in the same position, although their husbands were all related in some form or other to the British Royal Family.

The Duchess's sister, Princess Olga, was eventually in an even worse situation because of the part her husband played in the signing of a tripartite pact between Yugoslavia and the Axis.

Like King Leopold of the Belgians, Prince Paul of Yugoslavia will never be forgiven by many people throughout the world for what they considered was the act of a traitor. Yet he was placed in an impossible position—and whatever he did, or even if he had done nothing at all—it would have been considered wrong.

Geographically, Yugoslavia was in a vital position surrounded as it was by Italy, Austria, Hungary, Rumania, Bulgaria and Greece—all of which, except Greece (which this time was firmly on the side of Britain and its Allies), were either pro-Axis or Axis controlled. The Regent was under fantastic pressure from both sides and, as somebody remarked, 'suffered from too many neighbours and too few friends' or, as Winston Churchill put it more picturesquely, 'Prince Paul's attitude looks like that of an unfortunate man in a cage with a tiger, hoping not to provoke him, while dinner time steadily approaches.'

Prince Paul tried to do what King Constantine had done, which was to keep the country neutral, with the object of preserving the status quo until the young King came of age and his own duty was done.

But as Sir John Wheeler Bennet said in his biography of King George VI: 'The unfortunate Prince Paul found himself under fire both from Berlin and from certain of his own advisers for his hesitancy in aligning himself with the Axis.' In November 1940 the Yugoslavian Regent explained his difficulties in a letter to King George, which 'displayed only too clearly his melancholy state of mind'.

'My dear Paul,' replied the King. 'We have been thinking so much of you and Olga since I last wrote to you . . . So much has happened everywhere and the situation in your part of the world has become much more critical in this time. . . .' But not even the British monarch could ensure the supply of much-needed arms for Yugoslavia, though King George assured the Regent that it would only be a matter of time before Britain could do so.

A further plea from King George VI could not change events, although it was clear that he appreciated Prince Paul's dilemma remarkably well. 'Paul must be terribly worried, especially as his Regency comes to an end in five months' time and he naturally does not want to hand over to Peter a country plunged into war,' he wrote in his diary in March 1941.

With German troops massing on the Yugoslav border and Italy attacking Greece, Hitler urged the signing of the tripartite pact with the Axis which basically guaranteed Yugoslavia freedom from attack if the country would allow German war material to pass through its territory to Greece. It was either that or war against Germany.

The decision whether to sign it or not caused an almighty row in the Yugoslavian Government. One member of the Serbian opposition went so far as to say to Prince Paul: 'If you accept the pact we shall accuse you of being pro-German. If you go to war we shall accuse you of dragging us into the war

because of your wife.' Another wrote later that it was obvious
where Prince Paul's sympathies lay: 'He had gone to school in
England, the friends of his Oxford years were now important
figures in British politics, his sister-in-law was a member of the
British Royal House, his wife a Greek Princess.' Paul himself
said: 'I have a conscience too, and a sense of tremendous responsibility towards our people. I cannot lead them to slaughter
and that is what we must expect if we precipitate a war with
Germany.' When German invasion seemed inevitable and he
was urged by the American Ambassador in Belgrade to preserve
Yugoslavia's integrity and retain its reputation abroad by refusing to countenance the signing of the pact, Prince Paul
replied in a voice which was 'sad and tired', 'You big nations
are hard. You talk of our honour but you are far away.' And he
was so depressed and pessimistic by the terrible quandary in
which he was placed that at least twice he said he wished he were
dead. He had finally been told that Yugoslavia could not count
on British military support in case of war.

By a vote of fourteen to three, on 20 March, the Yugoslavian
Cabinet decided to sign the pact after an ultimatum from Hitler.
The Commander of the Yugoslavian Air Force on hearing of this
decision warned Prince Paul that if the pact was signed his
officers would mutiny and overthrow the Regency: and Churchill
instructed the British Minister in Belgrade: 'Do not let any gap
grow up between you and Prince Paul or Ministers. Continue to
pester, nag and bite. Demand audiences. Don't take NO for an
answer. . . . This is no time for reproaches or dignified farewells.
Meanwhile, at the same time, do not neglect any alternative to
which we may have to resort if we find the present Government
have gone beyond recall. . . .' 'Direct action,' explained Mr Churchill in his memoirs, 'had been discussed for some months
among a small circle of officers, and a revolutionary stroke had
been carefully planned.' In addition the British Foreign Secretary, Mr Anthony Eden, had telegraphed to the British Minister
in Belgrade: 'In considering the chances of a successful *coup
d'état* you should bear in mind that rather than allow Yugoslavia
to slip by stages into German orbit, we are prepared to risk
precipitating German attack. . . .'

The pact was signed on 26 March. The same night Prince Paul
left Belgrade for Slovenia to rest. At four o'clock the following

morning his aide received a telephone call at a small station to be told there was trouble in Belgrade, then the line went dead. Three hours later when he reached Zagreb the revolution was over. In Belgrade Princess Paul together with her three children found the palace surrounded by armed guards and at nine o'clock that morning the voice of King Peter came over the radio announcing, 'I have decided to take Royal power into my hands'—a statement which surprised the young King as much as it did Princess Paul for he was sitting with her at the time. The broadcast was made by a young officer impersonating him.

That evening Prince Paul abdicated and with his family left Yugoslavia by train leaving the King technically in charge, with a new government.

In the streets of Belgrade Serbian crowds sang, cheered and shouted, 'Rather war than the pact: rather death than slavery.' And in England news of the revolution, said Winston Churchill, 'naturally gave us great satisfaction'.

Just over a week later the Luftwaffe bombed the Yugoslavian capital for three days killing seventeen thousand people, and on 14 April German troops marched through the streets while King Peter escaped first to Greece and then eventually to Britain when he flew in an R.A.F. Sunderland flying boat to Poole Harbour where he was met by the Duke of Kent.

When the Duchess of Kent's sister and her family reached Athens they received at first a slightly chilly welcome, even from Princess Nicholas with whom they stayed at her Psychico villa. But the Greek Royal Family, whose country stood to lose everything through the German occupation of Yugoslavia, did at least understand and sympathize with Prince Paul's predicament. However, nearly all of them had to leave Greece shortly afterwards because of the German invasion. Prince Paul and his family retreated to Cairo. Two weeks after their arrival in Egypt Prince and Princess Paul and their children were flown to Kenya where Prince Paul was interned as a British political prisoner.

The only members of the Royal Family left in Greece, where they stayed throughout the German occupation, were Princess Nicholas and Princess Andrew. One remained in her villa; the other lived in an apartment off Kolonaki Square not far from the old Royal Palace. And at long last, drawn together by their mutual situation, their old antagonism was forgotten and they were friendlier than they had ever been before.

As a result of the German take-over the Commander of the German troops asked for permission to call on the Duchess of Kent's mother as he wished to take over her house as a hospital. When he arrived she was in her drawing-room, sitting upright in a chair, waiting dignified and unsmiling while he approached her. He clicked his heels, bowed and kissed her hand; then Princess Nicholas showed him her rooms. All she asked for, she said, was permission to continue to do her charity work and freedom to visit her husband's tomb and the other family graves at Tatoi. Her house was not requisitioned and her request was granted.

During the trying time which Princess Paul went through in Yugoslavia, her two sisters the Duchess of Kent and Countess Toerring were leading much less complicated lives.

Countess Toerring spent most of the war living quietly at the castle at Winhörring—though she had managed to spend the Christmas of 1940 in Yugoslavia—the last Christmas any of them were to spend there.

In England the Duchess of Kent was not only peaceful but blissful. Particularly in the summer of 1942.

In spite of the war, the past three years had probably been the happiest of her married life. She and her husband were closer together and more in love than they had ever been; especially during the previous twelve months when, for part of the time, she was expecting their third child.

The Duke of Kent, of course, was away a good deal, but when he was at home they had spent idyllic days together, playing with their children, gardening at Coppins, going to Badminton to visit Queen Mary and taking her shopping in Bath for antiques; and having small parties for their most intimate friends. Quite often they went to see Queen Mary with Prince Edward and Princess Alexandra, who were a noisy, vociferous, turbulent and unruly pair when they were young, with such abounding energy that at times they made their more elderly relations wince, though apparently Queen Mary, who was Princess Alexandra's godmother as well as the Duchess's, bore her young goddaughter's exuberance 'with amused forbearance'. Even

M

at the age of five Princess Alexandra showed signs of her future beauty.

On 4 July 1942, American Independence Day, the Duchess's second son Michael George Charles Franklin was born, and christened early in August. They called him Franklin after the United States President who was his godfather, and Charles after Prince Nicholas's relative and one-time rival, now the King of Norway, and also a godfather.

'I am so delighted about it all. My wife is doing very well and my son is *very* sweet,' the Duke wrote to another friend and Queen Mary, who had spent the day with the Kents nine days after Prince Michael's christening, admired her son's 'interesting things' and noted in her diary: 'he looked so happy with his lovely wife and the dear baby'.

And it was indicative of the blissful relationship between the Duke and Duchess that it was the Duke himself who telephoned the news of the birth to Miss Fox and invited her down to see the new addition to the family.

But the Duke of Kent was restless and dissatisfied with the part he was playing in the war. Inspecting factories, shipyards and bomb damage was not his idea of fighting and he did not hesitate to say so. 'It's not very exciting to spend an awful lot of time looking at ablutions,' he said. But he found it difficult to break the system which, half a century beforehand, had expected princes to fight in battles, and now preferred them to keep away.

To mollify him, in 1941 he was sent on a comparatively 'dangerous' mission across the Atlantic to report on the results of the Commonwealth Air Training Plan—a scheme for training aircrews overseas—and he finished it off by visiting aircraft factories in America and staying a few days with President Roosevelt. The welcome and informal treatment he received sent him back home more determined than ever to break away from the protocol which restricted him in his service with the R.A.F.

An informal chat early in 1942 with an old American friend, Douglas Fairbanks Jnr., then an officer in the United States Navy Reserve and on a few days' leave ashore in England, seemed to point the way to a solution, and the Duke wondered if Fairbanks had any idea or advice to offer which might relieve his frustration. He wanted, he said, to find some sort of liaison assignment with the United States Forces where his royal rank might be less diligently protected and he would get a better opportunity to see some action. A meeting was subsequently arranged between the Duke and a senior American Air Force General. A week or so later they lunched together in a restaurant called 'Bon Viveur' off Curzon Street.

The sequel came some weeks afterwards.

Fairbanks, after another tour of sea duty, was expecting, on his next leave, to go to Coppins for the weekend, but on his arrival in London he received a letter from the Duke of Kent postponing the visit because, it said, he was going to Iceland.

Officially this was yet another tour of inspection to visit R.A.F. units in that country but it also had another purpose. In addition the Duke planned to inspect the American bases there as well and to have another meeting with the General— a meeting which he hoped would result in an American request for the assignment he wanted. 'I am just off to the frozen north,' he wrote. 'I will let you know the outcome when I get back.'

When Douglas Fairbanks received the letter it was lying on top of a newspaper. He saw the envelope with the familiar handwriting first; then he noticed the heavy black headline on the front page of the paper. It announced the death of the Duke of Kent.

On Tuesday, 25 August 1942, just after one o'clock on a calm, damp, grey afternoon, a Sunderland flying-boat took off from the R.A.F. base at Invergordon in Scotland.

The water of the wide Cromarty Firth was not good for take-off because it was too flat and, as the only surviving member of the crew said later, 'smooth like grey slate'. The Sunderland was fairly heavily laden with full petrol tanks, some depth charges, a crew of ten, a Commanding Officer and four passengers —the Duke of Kent, his secretary, his A.D.C. and his batman. It clambered with some difficulty into the sky and set off around the coast of Scotland northward towards Iceland.

Half an hour later, flying at the wrong height and on the wrong route, the seaplane crashed into the side of a low mountain on the Duke of Portland's Caithness Estate, right up in the north east of Scotland; a spot known locally as 'Eagle Rock'.

'The responsibility for this serious mistake in airmanship lay with the captain of the aircraft,' announced a Court of Inquiry afterwards. There was only one survivor of the crash—the gunner in the rear turret, thrown clear by the impact, which was of such force that the pieces of wrecked machinery, scattered all over the gorse, heather and bracken, were unrecognizable. A huge scar remained where the Sunderland had hit the slope, turned over and slid for two hundred yards on its back before it broke up.

It took a long time for the news to percolate south. A farmer and his son rounding up sheep in the thick mist, heard the noise of an aeroplane flying low overhead followed shortly afterwards by the tremendous reverberating din of an explosion which was so loud it was deafening. The son set out immediately for help and when a doctor and the search party arrived, it was not easy to find the aircraft, so dense was the mist. Even when they did, the bodies had to be carried for about five miles over rough and desolate moorland to reach the ambulances waiting at the nearest roadside.

It was not until evening that the telephones began to ring. The King who was at Balmoral was told about his brother's death when he was called away in the middle of dinner. 'This news came as a great shock to me and I had to break it to Elizabeth, Harry and Alice who were staying with us,' he wrote in his diary. Later he said to a friend: 'His death is a great shock to me as he was doing such good work and I shall miss him terribly. Thank God he did not suffer pain. I feel so desperately sad for poor Marina . . . her life was entirely bound up with his.'

Queen Mary heard what had happened at Badminton just after ten o'clock that night. 'I felt so stunned by the shock I could not believe it,' she said afterwards, but she had one immediate reaction. She announced, 'I must go to Marina tomorrow.'

And at Coppins it was Miss Fox who took the telephone call and broke the news to the Duchess of Kent.

6 | *Widowhood*

The shock of the Duke of Kent's death, so sudden and so unexpected, produced a reaction in his widow which was dramatic in its intensity.

At the funeral service in St George's Chapel, Windsor, it seemed at one moment that she would have hurled herself into the vault with her husband's body, had she not been held by the restraining arms of her sister-in-law, Queen Elizabeth.

In fact the Duchess had not wanted her husband's body placed in Windsor Chapel at all. He always said that he loathed the thought of being shut up in the gloomy royal vaults after he was dead, and how much better it was to have a grave in the open air. To comfort her she was promised that he would eventually be buried in the small royal cemetery in the grounds of Frogmore on the Windsor estate.

Although in public the Duchess kept her deepest grief under control, at home, where everything around her reminded her of the husband she had lost it was almost unbearable to watch. She had moments of wild weeping followed by periods of much more frightening apathy utterly unlike her usual nature. She would sit for hours staring blankly out of a window ignoring everybody or retreat into her bedroom and remain there for days.

It was obvious that something had to be done to bring her back to normality, and King George VI took action. First he telephoned his mother; and then he sent for Princess Olga.

The morning following the King's telephone call Queen Mary drove up to Iver in her great plum-coloured Daimler and walked into Coppins calm and erect. Unannounced, she went straight into the room where the widowed Duchess sat in her usual motionless position. No one knows the exact phrases Queen

Mary used to bring the Duchess of Kent out of her deep desola-
tion. But it was a talk, the elderly queen said later, in which
words such as 'self-pity', 'children' and 'duty' played their
part. These, combined with their mutual sense of loss, brought
the two royal ladies even closer than they had ever been before. And the visit was effective. Enough to bring the distraught
widow back into a world of reality. The arrival of Princess Olga
on 17 September, full of love and comfort, completed her return
to a comparatively normal life. Princess Olga was the obvious
choice when it became clear to King George VI that the
bereaved Duchess badly needed a member of her own family.

All of them were far away. Some in enemy territory. Her
mother was in Greece, which was under German occupation.
Her sister Elizabeth was in Germany itself and Count Toerring
was serving as an officer in the Army of the Third Reich. But
although Prince Paul was a political prisoner, he was under
British jurisdiction and his wife was the only one of the
Duchess's immediate family who could conceivably come to
her.

The King sent a cable to the Princess in Kenya and it was
transmitted to her by the British High Commissioner. She replied that she would come as soon as arrangements could be
made for her to travel.

The journey took a week. She went via Uganda, the Camer-
oons, Nigeria and up the West African coast to Portugal: and
the final leg was from Ireland to Poole Harbour. Princess Paul
used almost every known form of transport and was given
priority all the way—a necessary privilege granted on the King's
instructions. At that time women did not travel abroad unless
they were in the Services: and rarely even then.

It was only when he knew that she was actually on her way
that the King told the Duchess of Kent that she would soon see
her sister.

Their reunion was moving and emotional. It had been two
and a half years since they last met. Much had happened to
them both, and in many ways they were a comfort to each
other.

But several factors, as well as Queen Mary's loving support
and her sister's arrival, helped to complete the Duchess's road
to recovery.

The first was the great wave of sympathy which went out to
her from thousands and thousands of people all over the country. Many of the letters she received were from widows who had
also lost husbands whom they had loved. Reading them was a
tremendous consolation to her and answering each one of them
was a task which both distracted and helped.

To one message of condolence which she received from members of the House of Commons, she said: 'It is a source of great
pride and comfort to me to know that he died as he himself
would have wished, for his King and his country.'

But mainly it was her love for her children which did most to
assuage her grief. She had insisted on telling the two eldest
herself that their father was dead; a dramatic and moving
scene in which all three of them wept bitterly. And in the new
baby she found another great solace.

There was also the necessity to do her 'duty'—the word recalled to her by Queen Mary and which her maternal grandmother had set such store by. The Duchess of Kent made her
first public reappearance on 4 November, just about ten weeks
after her husband's death. In her naval uniform, looking sad,
dry-eyed and dignified, she visited a Wren training centre in
London; followed up by another less than two weeks later when
she inspected a detachment of W.R.N.S. drivers and motor-
cyclists.

And curiously one more unexpected factor emerged in the
first few months of her widowhood which was to help towards
her rehabilitation. This was the need to protect her sister.

The House of Commons has been the scene of many fierce
verbal battles fought among its green leather benches, and some
of the finest masters of invective in the world have crossed
words with each other there. But however bitter and heated the
arguments, it is extremely rare for them to end in physical
violence. Yet in the summer of 1943 there were shouts and
scuffles in the corridor leading to the House of Lords and two
angry M.P.s, arms whirling and fists flaying, fought each other
until one was on his knees and they were finally separated by
their colleagues.

And it all began with that consoling visit Princess Olga made
to the Duchess of Kent.

Less than four weeks after she arrived and for months

afterwards, constant verbal attacks were made in Parliament against the Duchess's sister Princess Olga and her husband. They were attacks which did not go undefended but they generated so much heat and fury that eventually they led to the exchange of blows.

The four M.P.s principally concerned were the Conservative Member for St Marylebone, Captain Alec Cunningham Reid; a Conservative who represented the Handsworth division of Birmingham named Commander Oliver Locker-Lampson; the Secretary of State for War, Mr Richard Law, now Lord Coleraine; and the Foreign Secretary, Mr Anthony Eden.

Captain Cunningham Reid began the attack in October 1942 by asking why Prince Paul 'after going over to the Axis', was allowed to take refuge in Kenya. And when he was told that the Prince's status was that of political prisoner 'subject to surveillance', the Captain went on to ask whether Princess Paul was also a political prisoner 'and if not, why not?' He brought up the subject of payment for her journey to England, and he suggested that she was a spy.

What were precautions worth he asked, 'when . . . the companion of this dangerous traitor is allowed to move about Kenya and this country . . . just as she wishes in a position to see, hear or say anything she likes?' He hoped, he said, that when the Minister replied he would not be reduced to sentimental excuses, because in a vital war such as this, privileged sentiment is no excuse for taking any unnecessary risks. . . . 'Bear in mind that the mother of the Princess was an exiled Russian Grand Duchess,' he went on, and 'Prince Paul has from the very start shown a keen desire to collaborate with the Germans; and he did so. . . . Princess Olga is his loyal wife. . . . We have deliberately brought this sinister woman over to the British Isles and have allowed her, to all intents and purposes, complete freedom.'

Mr Richard Law gave the Captain a curt reply. 'I do not really see why the honourable Member troubled the House with his speech,' he said, 'because any one of us could have got exactly the same thing by tuning in to "Lord Haw Haw" on the wireless. . . . I really do not see why he should ask these questions unless it is that he wants to restore his reputation by attacking a defenceless woman. . . . The Yugoslav Government understands, even if the honourable and gallant Member does not, the purposes for which the Princess came here.'

Captain Cunningham Reid had another go. 'If you are a quisling and you happen to be royalty, it appears that you are automatically trusted and forgiven . . .' he declared. He then repeated most of what he had said before and, referring again to Princess Olga, said: 'Her sympathies are anyhow with the Germans because of their enmity towards the Bolsheviks who have ill-treated her mother, a Russian Grand Duchess. . . .' He asked how Princess Olga's arrival in this country was reconciled with the fact that the Government had made a strict rule that no foreigner should be allowed into this country unless the direct national interest justified such a course, and continued on and on until he was rebuked by the Speaker for repeating himself.

When he was halted on a point of order—because a subject cannot be debated twice in the same session—Captain Cunningham Reid went to the almost unprecedented length of reprinting the Hansard report up to where he was stopped, and added the rest of the speech he had been unable to deliver, and circulated the lot to M.P.s and the Press.

A month later he was still at it, asking if Princess Olga had been given an exit permit and objecting to her being allowed to leave. 'Has not this lady been allowed to be in a position whereby she will be able to convey information to her quisling husband?' he asked.

By this time he had completely forfeited the sympathy of the House and Mr Anthony Eden, the Foreign Secretary, said sharply: 'The circumstances are well known. Princess Olga was the only sister of the Duchess of Kent who could come to this country at all and she came here with the Government's authority and approval, and I have no apology to make in the matter.' There were cheers from M.P.s and he sat down. He might also have added that Princess Olga had come at the King's express wish.

These verbal attacks on her sister and her brother-in-law were very distressing for the Duchess of Kent. Not only did it seem to emphasize the fact that she herself was not yet accepted in this country, but she was terrified that Princess Olga would see the reports.

Every day the Duchess scanned all the morning and evening newspapers to see if there was anything in them about those Commons debates. Any which included criticisms of Princess Olga or her husband she hid away from her sister. Sometimes, if Princess Olga came into a room unexpectedly, she stuffed the newspapers behind cushions or under low chairs. Or destroyed them altogether and pretended they had not arrived.

And in a way the unwelcome reports had considerable therapeutic value. In her concern lest her sister should read them the Duchess was diverted to some extent from concentrating on her own problems.

But the news leaked back to Kenya just the same and upset Prince Paul, already worn out and fatigued by his futile struggles in Yugoslavia. He became so ill that on New Year's Eve, after three months in England, Princess Paul left the Duchess and flew back to Kenya. Her husband's need was now greater than that of her widowed sister. In fact, Prince Paul's health was in such jeopardy that, through the intervention of General Smuts, he and his family were allowed to move to the comparative freedom of South Africa. They went to live in a rented hillside villa in the fashionable Mountain View district of Johannesburg, where they had a modest car, a ration of petrol and were sometimes able to travel to Cape Town and visit members of the Greek Royal Family who were living there.

And it might be thought that there they proved where their real loyalty lay for in February 1943, their eldest son, Alexander, who had reached the age of eighteen, joined the Royal Air Force and began training as a pilot in Pretoria. This did not pass unnoticed by Cunningham Reid; nor did the move. He commented disparagingly on the R.A.F.'s acceptance and he wanted to know who had requested the transfer of Prince Paul and whether other political prisoners could have the same facility 'should they desire to go abroad for the benefit of their health', and it was at this point that Commander Locker-Lampson leapt into the arena. He protested strongly against the abuse of Parliamentary time and counter-attacked by asking rather pointedly what disability Captain Cunningham Reid was suffering from 'when he left England in the blitz'; a reference to an abortive trip the Captain had made to New York in 1940 to see tobacco

heiress Mrs Doris Duke Cromwell, and discuss the evacuation of
some children.

In return Cunningham Reid called Locker-Lampson a cuckoo
'that makes itself a nuisance to other people's nests'. The argu-
ment continued in even stronger terms outside the debating
chamber and ended in the unseemly fight.

But Cunningham Reid went stubbornly on with his questions.
In August he asked whether Prince Paul's name had been given
as a war criminal; in November he suggested that the Prince
should be handed over to the Yugoslav Government 'until
such time as they may see fit to try him for treachery'; and in
December 1946 he inquired whether Prince Paul was in London
staying with the Mountbattens.

There was no support in the House of Commons for his campaign, but it was taken up by the press—through 1945, 1946
and 1947 when the Yugoslav National Assembly deprived both
Prince Paul and King Peter of their nationality and confiscated
their property.

But every time her brother-in-law was attacked in Parliament
the Duchess of Kent took it personally and she felt exactly
the same way when, after the war, he was mentioned disparagingly in the Press. The most vehement of the newspaper criticisms were written by John Gordon, a fiercely nationalistic
Scot with an independent mind, Editor-in-Chief of the *Sunday
Express* and an outspoken and widely-read columnist. He had
no personal vendetta against Prince Paul or the Duchess of
Kent, but he had an inbuilt distrust of 'foreigners'. He had not
been pleased when the Duke of Kent chose a Greek Princess
as a wife and would have much preferred him to follow his
brother Albert's example and marry a girl who was not only
technically a commoner, but a good Scottish lass as well.

And apart from the fact that Princess Marina was not British,
John Gordon was concerned because King George V had discussed politics with his Greek-born daughter-in-law and that
King George VI sometimes discussed with her topics such as any
events which took place in Greece or Yugoslavia about which
she might be expected to have special knowledge or information
because of her family connections.

To be considered a foreigner wounded the Duchess of Kent
deeply; and she thought the feeling was considerably more

widespread than it actually was. 'What must one do to make the English accept you?' she sometimes asked. 'In any other country in the world I would have become one of them; but however hard I try it seems impossible here.'

She was inordinately grateful for any signs of her personal acceptance. With remarkable humility she normally assumed that any cheering or waving she saw was not for herself but just part of the general enthusiasm common at the time towards the British Royal Family. She was always astounded when there was any evidence that the enthusiasm was specifically directed to her personally. Once, in 1945, when she was on holiday in Cornwall, she noticed a group of people smiled and waved when they recognized her. The Duchess was extraordinarily pleased and surprised. 'Did you see them? Did you see what they did?' she excitedly asked members of the party afterwards. 'I believe they really liked me.' And in 1953 when she was given an official reception at the Guildhall and a state drive through London after her successful visit to the Far East she relived the memory of it for months afterwards. This time there was no mistaking that the crowds who lined the route were there for her benefit and hers alone.

And never at any time did she consider living in any country but England. She loved Greece, of course, the place of her birth, and, as she said, 'a country truly blessed in beauty and character'. But England, which she had always liked and visited so frequently before her marriage was now her home.

Repeatedly she said: 'I could never live anywhere else.'

It was not until four years after the Duke's death that the Duchess could bring herself to visit the place where he died; although she had asked a friend to go for her on the first anniversary to say a prayer for him. But in 1946, accompanied by some friends and the doctor who had discovered his body, she walked the long distance over the rough moorland to where a wooden post marked the spot.

Most of the wreck of the aircraft had been cleared away but there were still some bits of the machine scattered among the rocks and heather and that long black scar remained bleak and bare and showed only too clearly what had happened. The sight of all this revived the Duchess's feeling of grief with such intensity that it was not until 1961, when all traces of the crash had disappeared, that she went again; this time with her elder son and Princess Alexandra to see the simple granite cross which she had arranged to be erected in memory of the Duke and those who died with him.

But for months after his funeral the Duchess of Kent visited the gloomy crypt at Windsor almost weekly to pray by the side of her husband; and was apparently one of the few members of the Royal Family who ever went down there. And on 20 December 1942, which would have been his fortieth birthday, she placed a wreath on his coffin made of his favourite clover-coloured carnations from the greenhouse at Iver.

Each time, in order to get access, she had to make an application for the key, which finally discouraged her from going so frequently. One can only suspect that it was with this very object in mind that there was this apparently unnecessary barrier (which could only have come as a result of direct orders from the King), and which was for her own good. And her wish that his body should be transferred to the Frogmore burial ground was not complied with, presumably for the same reason.

The Duchess of Kent never really got over her husband's death. 'She was lost without him,' said one of her royal relations afterwards. 'Her whole life revolved around him and she had no one else.'

For years afterwards it was necessary to temporarily move the Duke of Kent's photograph from any place or organization she was likely to visit, and all mention of him was censored from casual conversation or welcoming speeches. Seeing his picture or hearing his name would remind her again of how much she missed him and would upset her so much that all her latent distress would return undiminished.

Towards the end of her life this attitude changed and she was touched and moved by reminders of him instead of distressed. Any requests for her presence which also mentioned a tenuous connection with the late Duke were given priority. She was cautious, and she would investigate them thoroughly first, but once convinced that there had indeed been a link she would never refuse them.

Although she never ceased to mourn the husband she no longer had, the loss of the Duke moulded and strengthened the

Duchess of Kent's character in a way that nobody could have foreseen.

For the first time in her life she was forced to stand on her own feet and make her own decisions and with no one but herself to fall back on. She had always been sheltered from hard reality; first by her parents and then by her husband. For all her outward gloss, sophistication and self assurance, she still retained a certain amount of childlike naïvety and a lot of feminine helplessness. The fact that the Duke had been such a dominant character and that she had taken little or no part in the running of her household made the transition even harder.

Almost as if she were dedicating her life to him, she took on as many as possible of her dead husband's public duties and responsibilities. Between 1942 and 1943 she replaced him in nearly thirty of his former organizations.

Some—such as his position as Grand Master of the Free-masons—were impossible for her to take over. But in the case of the Royal Naval Film Corporation, for example, of which the Duke had been president, she became the Patron to continue the connection. She did not attend the routine 'all male' meetings but special social occasions were arranged to which she could come. Though she often thought that she was not doing enough for them.

Eventually Princess Marina was Colonel-in-Chief, Commandant, Patron, President or had some other connection with more than a hundred regiments, services, charities and hospitals; in organizations as diverse as the British School at Rome, the Iver, Denham and Langley Hospital and the University of Kent of which she was Chancellor. Not one of them was a nominal position but she was particularly assiduous in looking after anything which had even the slightest connection with the Duke.

Perhaps the clearest proof of this was the way the ultra-feminine Duchess with her dislike of complicated machinery took her husband's place as an unofficial factory inspector, a self-imposed task she began about six months after he died.

These visits were rarely if ever publicized, were kept as informal as possible and, as he did, she fitted them in whenever she had an available free morning or afternoon.

She went regularly three or four times a month; more often

than even the Duke had been able to manage because of his other commitments.

Her interest went far beyond a casual and cursory inspection. As has been said, because this task had taken up so much of her husband's time it was more a dedication than a duty and did not cease with the ending of the war. She went right on doing it until 1956, by which time Prince Philip had begun to take an interest in industry. It is doubtful whether she ever even told him that she was stopping because he was doing the same thing. But she felt it was much more a man's province, that he could show perhaps a greater technical interest and as long as it was upholding the tradition set by her husband she was content to hand over.

During the war, like the Duke, she visited factories in order to help the morale of the workers and make them feel that their contribution was just as important as those who were doing the fighting. Often before she went she would ask if there was anything in particular which needed doing when she got to a factory and in what way she could help.

In one light-engineering shop, where long hair was a hazard because it might easily be caught up in the machinery, it had proved difficult to make women workers wear their protective headgear in the proper manner so that not a wisp was showing. The Duchess was asked if she could make a point of speaking to girls who were correctly garbed and tell them how sensible they were. This she did; and within a week all the miscreants followed suit.

Another time, in 1943, she was due to go to the secret PLUTO (Pipe Line Under the Ocean) factory in East London. Flexible piping was being made in preparation for the invasion of France when it was used to supply petrol for armoured vehicles across the Channel. One of the shop stewards at this factory was a dedicated Communist who had been a cause of trouble until Russia became an ally. He was not fond of royalty. And it did not help that this royal Duchess had Romanov connections.

When she heard that he threatened to make a fuss if she visited the section where he worked, the Duchess made a special request to meet him. The result was almost inevitable; her personal charm brought her one more admirer regardless of politics.

After the war, the purpose of her industrial visits was to help

the export trade and give it much-needed encouragement; which
meant going to see firms manufacturing new plastics, clothing,
cosmetics, sports goods, chemicals and such-like.

In spite of her aversion to mechanical things, the Duchess of
Kent was fascinated and interested by nearly all of them. It
amazed her to be told that the maxim of a clothes manufacturer
was to make 'minimum sizes for the maximum people, with the
minimum waste', and she was intrigued, because of her interest
in the game, to watch tennis balls being made and see the intense trouble taken to ensure that all ping-pong balls were
identical. She was always astonished when she was shown small
and apparently insignificant objects worth a great deal of
money; such as a small bottle of ambergris for making scent
worth about £10,000 and a little heap of what looked like dirty
dross in a precious metal factory valued at something like a
quarter of a million pounds.

Sometimes the Duchess took Princess Alexandra with her and
they were both amused to be told that the most important per-
sonage in a cosmetics firm was apparently the package designer,
as the container and its box were worth more to them than its
contents.

Two or three times at the Duchess's suggestion, Princess
Elizabeth, daughter of Prince and Princess Paul, went with them
as well. One time, during Lent, the two girls accompanied the
Duchess of Kent to a small and exclusive chocolate and sweet
manufacturer in Soho. Both young princesses had made a vow
to give up eating chocolates for Lent but the sight of so many
delicious goodies proved too much for their self control. 'Do
you think it would be very sinful if we tried one or two—if we
extended Lent for two days?' they asked. And, on being reassured that it would not be they sampled more than one of the
factory's products.

Always the Duchess of Kent insisted on as little protocol as
possible. She was interested in people much more than material
things. And it was the workers she wanted to see, not the man-
agement.

The director of one firm made the mistake of bringing his
wife to the factory and presenting her to the astute Duchess.
It was an industrial concern in which, she had been warned
beforehand, there was a bad canteen. The director made every

excuse to prevent her seeing this; so she turned to the wife when they met and, in a woman-to-woman fashion, suggested that they should both go and look at the kitchen arrangements. 'Oh, but of course,' was the reply, to the discomfort of the husband. The Duchess's disgusted expression when she saw what they had been trying to hide resulted in an almost immediate improvement.

The Duchess of Kent's reactions, curiosity and intense interest made these informal and unpublicized visits invaluable both from the pleasure they gave to those whom she saw and talked to and the extra incentive they seemed to inspire. She went to scores and scores of factories over the years, almost unheralded and unsung, and few people ever realized how much effort and dedication she put into this.

Another of the tasks which the Duchess of Kent took over from her husband was the Presidency of the All England Lawn Tennis and Croquet Club, a job in which she became extremely involved. She always had been very interested in tennis and her family had played the game enthusiastically as far back as she could remember. Her mother played with the Tsar at Tsarskoe Selo; in Athens those rented summer houses always had a tennis court; and even in Switzerland she and her family played on hotel courts. But it was only when she took over at Wimbledon and regularly watched the world's top players—often accompanied by Queen Mary—that her enthusiasm became so great.

Rarely a day passed during Wimbledon fortnight when she was not there.

Some of the players would have been surprised if they had realized how much interest the Duchess took in them. Not only did she want to know the details of their careers but she also inquired about their parents' professions, and whether they were married or engaged. In addition she found out who their supporters were. If a player had a member of the family or a sweetheart in the stands, the Duchess spent almost as much time watching the expressions on their faces as she did the actual play.

If anyone was injured she sent relays of people into the dressing-rooms to find out the extent of the damage and the condition of the patient, and always at the end of a match showed as much concern for the loser as the winner.

N

Displays of anger, temperament or anguished yelps from frustrated players amused her—provided they did not go too far. Perhaps her favourite player was the Australian champion Rod Laver, and quite often she would follow him from court to court to watch him play.

And she had a great deal of fellow feeling for anyone who suffered from an attack of nerves. Once, when a new chairman escorted her to the Centre Court on the first day of the Championship she noticed that the players in the opening match consisted of a defending champion and a newcomer. 'Oh, they look nervous,' she commented—then turning to the novice chairman suddenly asked, 'Are you nervous too?' When he admitted that he was she reassured him: 'Don't worry. In about forty-eight hours everything will be going like a house on fire,' she said.

She was always very thoughtful about entering the Centre Court, or any other for that matter, while a game was in progress; she would peer over the entrance screen to watch until the players changed ends and her entry would not distract them. There was no fixed rule about it—it just happened and became a tradition—but whenever she took her place all the spectators would automatically rise to greet her.

And, both as Duchess of Kent and later as Princess Marina, she went round Wimbledon with fantastic diligence, peering into every room and making sure of meeting representatives from every section, as well as the players, groundsmen, referees and of course the ball-boys in whom she took intense interest; for they all came from the Shaftesbury Homes of which she was patron (another of the late Duke's interests which she had taken over). She showed the same concern for members of the St John Ambulance Brigade with which she also had a connection.

During the Wimbledon fortnight, the Duchess was the Royal Family's chief adviser on tennis. It was to her that they turned for any information; whether it was the state of the championship, how any player was doing, or if the weather was likely to stop play. She had to be kept very much in the picture.

But apart from that particular period she was just as interested in what was going on there during the rest of the year. She saw the members of the committee at least once annually and always met new officials. And she liked to hear all about any decisions they made. She was very much in favour of the resolve to make Wimbledon an Open Tennis Championship. When she heard that one international official opposed the idea, she said, 'Don't worry. Leave it to me. I'll convert him.' And of course she did.

The only thing she disliked about Wimbledon was that long walk out on to the Centre Court to present the prizes for the Singles Finals. Every year from her seat in the stand she made the same half-in-earnest joke. 'I think I'll present them from here this year.' And every year she would hear the same reply, 'Oh, Ma'am. But you can't.'

She was always extremely punctual and sometimes turned up well before the time she was expected. For it was one of the extraordinary things which happened after her husband's death that her former dilatory habits vanished completely. 'It was sad in a way; almost as if she deliberately tried to please him and in this manner was trying to pay a tribute to him,' says a member of her family.

7 | *The Kent Children*

The biggest practical problem the widowed Duchess of Kent had to face was the question of her finances.

Under the terms of the Civil List—the money voted by Parliament for the upkeep of the Royal Family—the Duke of Kent had received £10,000 a year as a bachelor; a sum which was increased after his marriage by an extra allowance of £15,000 totalling altogether an annual income of £25,000. At the time of the Duke's death this was £10,000 a year less than the annuity received by the Duke of Gloucester whose income had been increased because of his 'additional duties' during the minority of Princess Elizabeth.

When King George V died in 1936 he divided most of his fortune between his children. The exact amount he bequeathed has not been made public though there have been guesses that each of his sons received something like three-quarters of a million pounds. This seems to have been an exaggeration. According to one member of the family, although the King left a great deal of money, when it had been shared out the final legacy each of his sons received was 'not all that much'.

The Duke of Kent spent a large part of his portion on amassing his collection of antique furniture, pictures and silver—all of which, as it turned out, were a wise investment. With the rest of the money he bought a certain amount of stock and securities. But he was not a rich man. The Civil List allowance ceased at his death. Coppins was left to his elder son and heir; and most of the money was placed in trust for his children.

It never occurred to him—or apparently to anybody else—that he needed to make special provision for his wife.

It has been widely, almost universally believed—even among members of the Royal Family itself—that the Duchess of Kent received an R.A.F. pension of £398 a year as the widow of an Air Commodore. She did not. She refused from the first to accept it.

Her decision may have been influenced by her own private and personal reasons, or perhaps, as has been suggested, because she wanted to contribute it as a part of the war effort. In any case, the Duchess never thought that she would need it. She was confident that as a working member of the Royal Family some income would be made available to her by the government.

At that time the widowed Queen Mary received an annual income of £70,000; Princess Beatrice (Queen Victoria's only surviving daughter), the Princess Royal, and sixteen-year-old Princess Elizabeth, all received £6,000 a year.

There was no provision on the Civil List drawn up at the beginning of the reign of King George VI for the widows of younger sons. By precedent they had formerly always been provided for as and when the need arose. At the beginning of the nineteenth century the Duchess of York (George III's daughter-in-law) received a grant of £4,000 on her own account which was in addition to the Duke's annual £26,000. And two nieces of George III—the Duchess of Mecklenburg and Princess Mary of Teck (Queen Mary's mother)—received allowances. Princess Mary's, for example, rose from £3,000 in 1850 to £5,000 in 1889. Two of Queen Victoria's widowed daughters-in-law, the Duchess of Albany and the Duchess of Edinburgh, each received £6,000 annually. And one must remember that until 1917 the Duchess of Edinburgh also had her own large income from the Russian Imperial Apanages.

But the practice of providing for members of the Royal Family whenever necessary often became the subject of political controversy in Parliament. In this century, therefore, there has been a tendency to embody all financial provisions relating to the Royal Family in the Civil List at the outset of a reign—to avoid embroiling the Royal Family in parliamentary controversy for the rest of it.

The Duchesses of Edinburgh and Albany were still included in the Civil List made at the beginning of the reign of King George

V. But the Duchess of Edinburgh died in 1920 (a few months after the death of the Grand Duchess Vladimir) and the Duchess of Albany in 1922. By the time King George VI ascended the Throne neither were alive and when his Civil List was drawn up, by an oversight the subject of allowances for widows was omitted.

There is not much doubt that if an application had been made to Parliament shortly after the Duke's death requesting a Civil List allowance for the Duchess, it would very likely have been granted without question. But, because the war was still in progress she was advised not to apply immediately for a grant and there was a long delay. On 24 February 1944, when the Conservative Member for the Putney and Otley Division of West Riding, Sir Granville Gibson, asked whether any decision had been arrived at about a day for the discussion of the Civil List, Mr Anthony Eden replied: 'I cannot make an announcement upon that until the next series of sittings.'

But it was not until two years later, after the war had ended and when there was a Labour Government, that the Civil List was discussed. And then not specifically in relation to the Duchess of Kent. Major John Morrison, Conservative M.P. for Salisbury, brought up the subject on 5 February 1946 when he asked the Prime Minister, Mr Clement Attlee, whether, 'in view of the increase in the cost of living', he would review 'the sums payable under the Civil List in recognition of valuable work'.

The Prime Minister, apparently referring to pensions paid to members of the Royal Household, pointed out that some new and existing pensions had been increased and that he intended to continue this policy. When Earl Winterton joined in to suggest that 'in view of the fact that no party issue arises on this' a committee should be set up to advise the House on how the pensions should be dealt with, Mr Attlee replied: 'That is another matter but I should like to consider it.'

And there it rested. But as a result, the beautiful and elegant Duchess of Kent, one of the busiest members of the Royal Family, and more in demand than anyone else, except for the King and Queen, had no public income whatsoever. She found herself in desperate financial straits—three children to look after and educate, a large establishment to run, and above all a standard to live up to.

Somehow the Duchess achieved it. But not without the loss of many of the possessions that both she and the Duke valued so highly. In March 1947 the Duchess of Kent was forced to sell the bulk of the art treasures collected by her husband.

During a three-day auction at Christie's, old English furniture, porcelain and what were called 'objects of art' went under the hammer. Period William and Mary, Queen Anne, Georgian and Regency furniture; many pieces made by Heppelwhite and Chippendale. A vast collection of English porcelain; Worcester, Derby, Coalport, Rockingham, Minton and Spode. Sèvres candlelabra. A Limoges dinner service. Dresden figures. Examples of Chinese enamelled porcelain; Ming, famille rose and famille verte. Queen Anne and Georgian silver. Objects in lapis lazuli, jade, Egyptian stone and Indian gold. Cut glass chandeliers. More than sixty pictures and drawings. And a few bizarre items which looked suspiciously like unwanted wedding gifts.

The sale fetched more than £92,000 and proved that the Duke of Kent had not only been what one art expert called 'a gifted and imaginative connoisseur' but a shrewd one. Those three pictures by Claude de Lorrain which he bought in 1940 were sold for nearly twice what he paid for them. Someone estimated that the profit on the whole sale was £50,000.

The Duchess was reported afterwards as saying that the sum she received was not much of a price to pay for her humiliation. But in fact in private she still bravely held her head high and ridiculed stories that she had been offered a contract to star in a Hollywood film. 'As if I were short of money,' she once wrote scathingly to a friend. 'But if you deny things publicly people think there must be something in them.'

As a result of the implication that her finances were at a low ebb, the Duchess did receive a great many invitations to go to America which included both commercial propositions and requests to stay at various houses all over the United States. There were so many, and the rumours that she would be going across the Atlantic became so strong, that in the end the British Ambassador in Washington was forced to issue a denial that the Duchess of Kent intended leaving England.

In many ways, both financially and otherwise, the Duchess

received tremendous support, both from King George VI and Queen Mary, but grace and favour donations, however kindly meant and however gracefully given, are no substitute for an independent income. The Duchess's economies became more and more apparent, and she fell back into the habits which she had been forced to learn in Paris.

To some, who did not and could not realize her situation, she was at times considered mean. She could not afford to pay high wages to her servants. She rarely entertained on an elaborate scale. She pioneered the royal wearing of off-the-peg cotton dresses—in which she and Princess Alexandra looked so elegant that it became a fashion followed by the present Queen and Princess Margaret and eventually Princess Anne. Sometimes the Duchess would order an elaborate dress for a special occasion, wear it once and then return it to be re-sold privately —which of course it always was: there were plenty of wealthy women glad to own a gown which had been chosen by the well-dressed Duchess.

For eleven years, from 1942 to 1953, during which time she performed innumerable official duties, the Duchess of Kent received no income at all from the State.

It was not until the beginning of a new reign under Queen Elizabeth II in 1952 that the Civil List was reviewed again.

When it was finally passed by a Select Committee and approved by the Commons it contained, under Clause 9, a new addition. Not the hoped-for annuity for the Duchess of Kent; but a fund of 'up to £25,000' was put at the disposal of the Sovereign for the benefit of those members of the Royal Family not provided for under the Civil List but who undertook public duties.

At the time this sum was agreed there were four or five members of the Royal Family potentially admissible for a share under the terms of reference. One was, of course, the Duchess of Kent; two others were her elder son and her daughter, who, when they were old enough would be called upon to take part in the royal round. In the event, the Duchess received approximately £5,000 annually. It did not solve her problems and was no substitute for an annuity; but it helped. And in addition she was bequeathed a small annuity after Queen Mary's death in 1953.

But although the Duchess of Kent suffered from lack of money she was never without friends.

Some widows tend to get neglected and left alone after the death of their husbands. Acquaintances disappear, invitations lessen, and loneliness takes over. But this did not happen to the Duchess of Kent. If anything Coppins became more crowded than ever, and a mass of visitors descended on her there.

One of the first was Mrs Eleanor Roosevelt, the wife of the United States President, who came to Britain on a semi-secret official visit in 1942. She went down to Iver to inspect her husband's new godson, taking with her a crate of oranges as a christening gift. Another was General Smuts who had been so kind to the Duchess's elder sister and brother-in-law. And Winston Churchill turned up regularly for private visits.

Then there were members of her family, such as King George II of Greece, in exile once more after fleeing with his Prime Minister over the mountains of Crete away from the pursuing Germans. Afterwards he went to Cairo and later South Africa. The Grand Duchess Xenia was also often at Coppins; and so was the Tsarina's sister Victoria, the Dowager Marchioness of Milford Haven, and Queen Wilhelmina of Holland with Princess Juliana.

And the younger generation went too—her cousin Prince Philip had nearly always spent part of his holidays at Coppins; the young Marquis of Milford Haven; Princess Elizabeth and Princess Margaret.

There was one summer party on the Coppins estate at which many of them spent a happy afternoon playing village fête games—such as a three-legged egg and spoon race in which the Duchess and her partner were narrowly beaten by Princess Margaret tethered to a young officer on leave. Another time, when Prince Philip was there, they experimented to find out how long a line they could make with one person sitting on some stone steps and the rest perched in turn on each other's knees. They managed to stretch it to about twenty people before the 'snake' collapsed. And nearly always, when the weather was fine, they played tennis.

To all her visitors the Duchess gave a warm welcome. Because she talked to the young as if they were adults, always kept secrets, and never passed on malicious gossip, she became a sort of beloved Universal Aunt to whom they could confide without fear of being ridiculed and whom they could always ask for advice.

Often she acted as a go-between when some delicate negotiation had to be handled and more than once she interceded when one or other of the younger members of the family got into some sort of scrape and were likely to suffer parental wrath.

For instance, one of those who sought her help was Princess Alexandra, the daughter of the Duchess's cousin, the former King Alexander of Greece (the one who was killed by a monkey bite) and Madame Manos, now known as Princess Aspasia. Princess Alexandra of Greece, at the age of twenty-one, had met the exiled King Peter of Yugoslavia—two and a half years younger than herself—at a diplomatic cocktail party given for Greeks and Yugoslavs. They wanted to marry, in spite of the fact that in many quarters it was felt that the King should delay any question of marriage until he was older and his political future was settled. 'Marina was the first one to whom I admitted my feelings,' said the Greek Princess later, and to King Peter, she said: 'Marina has been more wonderful than I can begin to tell you. She has helped us in every way possible, and I know that Uncle Bertie sees things from our point of view now, since Marina talked to him about us.'

Behind the scenes the Duchess's influence with King George VI had eased the way to the couple's marriage and with great accuracy she was able to foretell for them the probable date of their wedding, which eventually took place in the Yugoslav Embassy in London on 20 March 1944.

During the war, but not because of it, the Duchess of Kent lost three relations who had each played a part in her family saga. Both Grand Duke Boris and Grand Duke Dmitri died in 1943: the former living comfortably on the Riviera, well off and well looked after; the latter in a Swiss sanatorium, killed at last by the tuberculosis which had threatened him for so long.

Grand Duke Dmitri had one short-lived marriage with an American heiress named Audrey Emery by whom he had a son. He was planning to re-wed when he was overtaken by his illness. At fifty-nine he was still as handsome, amusing, elegant and charming as ever. Before his death, and when he knew he did not have long to live, Grand Duke Dmitri, who had always been loath to discuss the murder of Rasputin after the Revolution, referred to it once more. 'If I had my time all over again,' he said, 'I would still do the same.'

And there had been an even greater bereavement back in 1940 when Prince Christopher, her father's youngest brother and her own favourite uncle, who had shared so much of her life before her marriage, died in Rome and was buried in Athens.

But the present was more important than the past. It was to her children that the Duchess of Kent turned to most and they were a constant source of delight and joy to her. She loved them devotedly and was immensely proud of them. She was also extremely conscious of the fact that she had to be both father and mother, and she tried to take her husband's place in their lives as much as she could, and paid a lot of attention to them.

Much more than most mothers at that period, she treated them as grown-up people, even when they were very young. They had a great deal of freedom at home though, like her mother Princess Nicholas, the Duchess of Kent had strong views about the importance of good manners.

Her children returned her admiration and devotion. Once, at breakfast, not long after their father died, Prince Edward, aged seven, and Princess Alexandra, six, sat looking intently at the Duchess of Kent for some minutes and then turned to a guest staying with them and said: 'Aren't we lucky to have such a beautiful mother?'

The end of the war meant that the Duchess of Kent could at last meet her mother and sisters again. First she travelled to Munich to see her sister Elizabeth. A year later there was a grand family reunion in Greece after Prince and Princess Paul returned from South Africa. Afterwards the Duchess's elder sister and her husband settled in Paris and later divided their time between there and Italy—where Prince Paul had inherited an estate near Florence from one of his Demidoff relations. And the constant visits between the three sisters and their mother were resumed.

Often the Duchess took one or more of her children with her on her own trips abroad. Her sisters did the same when they came to England. Five of them—the Duchess of Kent's two eldest, Princess Elizabeth's son and daughter and Princess Olga's daughter—were all much the same age, and all of them got on well together.

One of the reasons why members of any royal family stick so closely together and tend towards nepotism in their choice of courtiers is the feeling of instability they almost inevitably feel in the presence of outsiders. Over and over again those who have apparently been their closest and most devoted friends have, for one reason or another, failed to stand by them in moments of stress or have, inadvertently or deliberately, been indiscreet. But once loyalty has been proved beyond doubt Kings and Princes are often the most faithful of allies. But even with this in mind the Duchess of Kent—and her entire family—displayed an unusually deep attachment to those on whom they could rely.

One of these was Kate Fox and her faithfulness was returned with love and gratitude for the whole of her life. The Duchess, her sisters and her mother, saw her frequently, and often invited her to stay with them.

But because Miss Fox lived in England it was her 'baby' Marina whom she saw most. Every week they met and as the Norland nurse grew older and more frail it was the Duchess who went out to Miss Fox's flat at Belsize Park rather than give her the trouble of travelling to Iver. Their relationship never changed; and Miss Fox never stopped fussing over the Duchess of Kent, and on occasions bossing her about. 'Powder your nose, Marina. It's shiny,' she sometimes said. Or, 'You look tired; have your supper on a tray tonight and go to bed early.'

Eventually it became necessary for Miss Fox to leave her flat and, at the Duchess's suggestion, she moved into Iver Hospital where she could be better looked after and nearer to her former 'charge'. It was there, after the Duchess of Kent spent the day with her, that Miss Fox died in November 1949.

In her will she gave instructions for the return of most of the many valuable gifts she had received to the original donors or their families. Her linen teacloth on which she had embroidered the signatures of so many Kings and Queens went to Princess Nicholas—and also the diamond bracelet which had once been a present from the Grand Duchess Vladimir.

The silver tea service which the three sisters had given their nurse went to Princess Paul, whose elder son received a tie pin which had once been worn by the Grand Duke Vladimir, and her daughter Elizabeth had a pendant which had been given by the Tsar to Princess Paul—and which she in her turn had given to Miss Fox on the morning of her wedding day in Belgrade.

Countess Toerring's two children also received mementoes. Her son, Hans Veit, received a green jade brooch which Queen Olga had presented long ago to Miss Fox; her daughter, Helen, a diamond brooch in the shape of the Imperial double-headed eagle—once a present from the last Tsarina of Russia.

The Duke of Kent got back some of the gifts his father had given to Miss Fox; and among the objects for Princess Alexandra there was that aquamarine pendant which the Duchess gave her former nurse as a souvenir of her wedding. All letters and photographs were faithfully returned to the families concerned.

But it was to the Duchess of Kent in whom Kate Fox placed her greatest trust. After distributing more than £3,000 for various people and purposes the rest of her estate went to the Duchess 'to be applied by her according to the wishes I have made known to her. . . .'

After the funeral of Miss Fox at Warlingham, the Duchess and Princess Paul called on another old friend, Miss Fox's sister Jessie, who had been present at Princess Marina's birth. Jessie was bed-ridden but still living in the house she had been brought up in and the Duchess of Kent insisted on going into the kitchen to see if an old Ideal boiler was still there which had intrigued her as a child—and was delighted to find that it was.

As her own family grew up the Duchess of Kent took more and more delight in them. They all went on long carefree holidays together: to the Kent coast or to Scotland where they could be completely informal. The Duchess had always loved Scotland ever since she first went to Balmoral as a prospective bride and was initiated into the intricacies of Scottish dancing. She liked the mountains and she liked the peace she found there.

Quite often she and her family stayed at Birkhall and, dressed in waterproof slacks and a sweater, she would go fly-fishing for trout while the children played at the side of the river. Then the two older ones would build a fire among the rocks at the water's edge and sit round while the Duchess cooked masses of bacon and eggs in a large frying-pan, making all sorts of jokes as she did so.

Her children, as the result of the care and freedom with which she brought them up, became unselfconscious, lively, natural and extremely good-mannered, and they led a much more normal life than most royal children ever had before them.

When she grew older Princess Alexandra was a pupil at a boarding school at Heathfield, near Ascot, the first British Princess to be given an ordinary school career, a precedent followed later by Princess Anne. And in the winter of 1953–4 she went to Paris where she stayed with the family of the French Pretender, the Comte de Paris, whose sister had married her great uncle Christopher (after the death of his first wife). Like her mother Princess Alexandra attended a finishing school there and studied French and music.

The Duke of Kent went to Eton for a while as his father had wished, and then to Le Rosay in Switzerland to learn French. After that he attended the Royal Military Academy Sandhurst and became a Lieutenant in the Royal Scots Greys. At times the Duchess felt very emotional when she looked at him— for in looks her elder son resembled his father so much.

The youngest of the three, Prince Michael, also went to Eton. And in 1968, the year of her death, the Duchess was pleased when, as a Lieutenant in the 11th Hussars, Prince Michael was seconded to a department of Military Intelligence responsible for liaison with foreign military attachés—thus, in a way, following his father's example of having connection with the diplomatic service.

Some of his relations think that he is very much like his grandfather, Prince Nicholas. And he is the only member of the Royal Family who has learned to speak Russian, and extremely interested in Russian history, art and culture. He also speaks French and German fluently—taking after his multilingual forebears.

The Duchess, though she was strict with her children where manners were concerned, was remarkably easy-going in other ways. She was never anxious, for example, when either of the boys were out late at night. 'Don't you ever sit up and wait for them ? Or worry whether they will have an accident, like I do ?' asked one of her friends.

'Certainly not,' said the Duchess. 'Why should I ? I go to bed and go to sleep, like any sensible person.'

And to prevent them suffering like she had from inexperience she began to train them for public appearances when they were young.

In 1952, when he was only sixteen, the Duke of Kent accompanied his mother on her first long official tour, a State visit to Malaya and the Far East. It was at her suggestion that he went along. It was obvious to the Duchess that he would have to take on an increasing amount of royal duties and she wanted to prepare him as much as she could. Throughout the tour she guided her son, gave him advice, and warned him of pitfalls—but so gently and tactfully that he hardly noticed she was doing it. She also made sure that he enjoyed himself and went off on all-male expeditions without her—such as one trip from Hong Kong to the border of Communist China.

The Duchess herself had hoped to do some painting during this tour and Winston Churchill insisted that she must borrow his easel—a heavy, old-fashioned and complicated affair—to take with her. Out of politeness she took it. But it took so long to erect and she had so little free time that it was never used. And it was so cumbersome and unwieldy that carting it about from place to place became something of a nightmare.

It was not then a particularly safe time for anyone to visit Malaya; the country was troubled by terrorists. Planters and their wives went about in armoured cars and slept with pistols under their pillows. Every village was a fortress. There were constant bomb explosions and attacks. The jungle was full of menace and every road and track was potentially dangerous. When the Duchess travelled by road she was protected overhead by R.A.F. helicopters, and the roof of her car covered with a bright red eiderdown to identify it—a precaution which some members of her suite felt singled her out rather more conspicuously as a target. But the Duchess was not afraid. Never once did she show a sign of fear at any time.

Her courage was proved by an incident which took place that October in Singapore. A party was arranged at Government House to celebrate the Duke of Kent's seventeenth birthday. A special cake was made and he was given a Malayan *kris*, a dagger with a long wavy blade, with which to cut it. And he was shown the way the knife should be used—Malayan style with a swirl and an overhead flourish.

The Duke swung the knife as instructed, but to everyone's horror he struck his mother in the eye. A stream of blood spurted from her face and ran down her dress and for one dreadful moment the white-faced young Duke thought that he had killed her, or anyway blinded her. In fact he had not damaged the eye itself but nicked a corner; and the amount of blood was disproportionate to the size of the cut, as they found out after the Duchess had been rushed to the cloakroom to have the wound attended to.

But she herself remained perfectly calm during the whole incident. All she was concerned about was the shock it must have caused her son. 'Don't bother about me,' she kept saying. 'I'm perfectly all right. There is no need to fuss. But where is Eddie? Please fetch him. I must let him know that he has not hurt me. I don't want to spoil his evening.'

Later, after she had changed her dress and with a plaster over her eye, she insisted on going on with the evening's celebration as if nothing had happened at all.

In the same way she flew through storms, which usually had most people cowering in their seats, without showing a flicker of emotion—though there was one time when she was annoyed because an airline stewardess woke her up to say that they were flying through a severe storm. 'If I'd been left alone I wouldn't have known anything at all about it,' she said.

The Duchess very much enjoyed her Far East tour and wrote long and detailed letters to Queen Mary about her experiences. Princess Olga happened to be in England at the time and the Queen invited her to Marlborough House to read the letter to her so that they could share the Duchess of Kent's news together.

Two years later the Duchess took Princess Alexandra with her to Canada and the United States; and early in 1959 to Latin America. Again with the idea of letting her have some experience of a royal tour.

During the Canadian visit the Duchess of Kent took a few hours off to visit one of her Russian relations—the Tsar's sister, the Grand Duchess Olga Alexandrovna—whom she had last seen in Tsarskoe Selo before the Revolution: the same Grand

Duchess who had entertained the very young Princess Marina and her sisters when they went to play with the Emperor's children.

The Grand Duchess lived in a four-roomed red-brick cottage at Cooksville about ten miles from Toronto and was difficult to find. The Duchess and two companions travelled on rough unmade roads to get there. Her visit to such an out-of-the-way place stirred up a lot of excitement. The neighbours crowded round; and the Grand Duchess Olga was delighted to see her.

'Wasn't it sweet of Marina to come and see her old Aunt whom she could not even remember,' she wrote afterwards. 'Marina is really a lovely person and so friendly and sweet. She looked in our little house and ate some sandwiches in the kitchen.' The Grand Duchess regretted, though, that there were so many people about that it was impossible to have what she called 'a good intimate talk'.

On her part the Duchess of Kent was rather appalled at the condition in which her mother's cousin was living—the ugly, squalid untidy house with hens scrabbling in the dust outside and wandering in and out of the house. 'Especially after all the grandeur she was used to!' the Duchess commented.

She enjoyed this tour as well and also the later visit to Latin America. 'I am very lucky to be able to travel like this and see so many exciting places,' she once said. She loved travelling and going abroad, although curiously the one place she did not want to go to was the West Indies although she had spent part of her honeymoon there. The newly-married royal couple had been so hounded by crowds and sightseers that it spoilt everything and they were never left alone long enough to appreciate their surroundings. The effects of the experience had left her with the feeling that she never wished to go back.

For Princess Alexandra the Latin-American trip was the prelude to her first solo tour abroad which took her nearly two months and started with a visit to Queensland for its centenary celebrations which began on 18 August 1959. Afterwards she went to twenty-two other cities and towns in Queensland and then to other parts of Australia, including New South Wales and Victoria. On the way home she called at Thailand and Cambodia and made brief stops at Delhi, Teheran and Istanbul—a formidable programme for a girl aged twenty-two, but

o

one which she accomplished with enormous success. Her informality and naturalness—and above all the charm with which she coped with every situation whether it was planned or otherwise, endeared her to everyone she met. And she herself thought often about her father both before and during the tour and referred to him several times.

The Duchess of Kent was thrilled by her daughter's achievement. 'I am indeed overwhelmed with pride about Alexandra possessing the wonderful gift of spreading happiness around her. It has made her tour something greater than a triumph and is very moving for me,' she wrote to a friend. And she was extremely gratified when the princess became more and more in demand as a royal representative at important functions and was the Queen's special representative at the Independence celebrations of the Federation of Nigeria in October 1960.

She was always pleased at every complimentary reference to her daughter and looked at her lovingly when they were both together at some silk-gowned and glittering royal affair. But she never took any credit to herself for the emergence of the young Princess out of her hoydenish chrysalis into an elegant and extremely good-looking young woman. 'Breeding will out,' she would say. 'Breeding will out.'

It was a phrase the Duchess often used and not only about her daughter; for, in spite of all her pleasant informality, her infectious laugh and her self-mockery, to nearly all those who knew her, Princess Marina Duchess of Kent was always surrounded by an unconscious aura of royalty. She knew she was royal; and it showed. She accepted her lineage and birth without arrogance, but even those in close daily contact with her were as aware of it as though it were an invisible glass barrier surrounding her. They knew just how far they could go in terms of friendship.

There were limits to intimacy and very few, apart from her family, were allowed to pass those limits.

And with it went her strange humility. Her royal and imperial descent was a thing apart: she was born with it and proud that she possessed it. Her own personal characteristics were entirely different; about those she was extremely humble indeed.

The Last Decade

In 1957, when he was twenty-two, the young Duke of Kent met a girl whose freshness, liveliness and candour gave her the same sweet invigorating charm as the winds from her native Yorkshire moors. She was two years older than he was. And her name was Katharine Worsley, the youngest child and only daughter of the Lord Lieutenant of Yorkshire, baronet Sir William Worsley, whose family is one of the few which can be traced back with some certainty to the time of the Norman conquest, came originally from Lancashire, and has certain republican connections—one of Sir William's ancestors married a grand-daughter of Oliver Cromwell.

The Duke of Kent fell in love with Miss Worsley, in the deep and single-minded fashion of his Romanov great-uncles, and wanted to marry her.

There was a great deal of gossip at the time, both in London and Yorkshire, that the Duchess of Kent was opposed to her son's marriage. The general feeling was that the regal Duchess would have preferred her elder son to form an alliance with a European royal family and choose a girl who would almost certainly have been one of his kinswomen.

But this was not so. When the Duchess met Miss Worsley she liked her immediately. The only grounds for her reluctance to agree to the marriage were the difference in their ages and the fact that the Duchess considered her son to be too young and inexperienced and not ready at that time to settle down with a wife and family.

The Duke loved his mother and did not wish to upset her. At her suggestion he and Miss Worsley agreed to a year's separation. He went to Germany with his regiment. She went to Canada to stay with her eldest brother.

If they still felt the same way at the end of that time, said the Duchess of Kent, she would withdraw any objections and do all she could to help them.

Twelve months later the young couple were, if anything, more in love than ever; and Miss Worsley's engagement to the Duke of Kent was announced in March 1961. 'We are all very happy about it as he has loved Katharine for four years,' wrote the Duchess to a friend. 'It is a good beginning I feel, and she is a pretty, sweet, person, so I thank God for another great blessing. But how the years pass. It seems only the other day he was a little boy.'

The Duke of Kent and Miss Worsley were married on 8 June in the Cathedral at York. Like most mothers the Duchess of Kent wept a little during the service, but shortly after the wedding she gave several clear indications of how highly she regarded her son's bride. For a start, she announced that she was reverting back to her girlhood title and wished to be known in future as Princess Marina, Duchess of Kent. Then she moved out of Coppins and into grace and favour apartments in Kensington Palace which had once been promised to herself and her husband—and the same place in which one of those former Dukes of Kent had lived. Princess Marina must have felt some pangs of nostalgia and affection as she left the house in which she had spent the happiest years of her married life, but they did not show. She was as calm and outwardly unemotional as if she were going away on a holiday; and accepted the change in her circumstances with the attitude of a fatalist. 'She knew she had to go and it was the best and most sensible thing to do. It was as simple as that,' said a friend afterwards.

And the Princess herself instructed her daughter-in-law in the intricacies of royal etiquette and protocol, helped her to choose clothes and took almost as much pride and pleasure in the new Duchess of Kent's success and popularity as she had in her own daughter's début, and referred to her frequently and affectionately in public. An incident which took place in June 1962 when the Duke and Duchess of Kent were shortly expecting their first child is typical of Princess Marina's whole attitude.

At her son's request she went over to Coppins for the event. Like any prospective new father he was feeling nervous and agitated and he knew that her calmness and confidence would be a tremendous help. But Princess Marina felt that not even this was enough. In consequence Princess Alexandra, who was spending the evening at a friend's house, received a telephone call when she was in the middle of dinner. It was from her mother. 'Come at once,' Princess Marina said. 'Kate is starting to have her baby. And she needs all her family with her.'

And after the Duke and Duchess's second baby was born on 28 April 1964, Princess Marina wrote to another friend: 'We are delighted with my first grand-daughter, especially as Katharine longed for a girl.'

In their turn the Duke and his young wife pleased Princess Marina immensely when their son, the Earl of St Andrews, was called George after his grandfather; and their daughter named Helen (after Princess Nicholas) Marina Lucy.

When twenty-six year old Princess Alexandra was married two years later in April 1963, her choice of husband received her mother's unhesitating approval and blessing. There was talk at one time that Princess Marina would have been pleased if her daughter had become the wife of the Duke of Abercorn's heir, the Marquis of Hamilton—a young man whom Princess Alexandra had known most of her life and whose sister was her lady-in-waiting; but although they were good friends there was no deep affection on either side.

In any case Princess Marina could hardly have hoped for a more perfect son-in-law than the one she got—the Honourable Angus Ogilvy, second son of the 9th Earl of Airlie, whose grandmother she had known and liked so well.

He too comes from a family of ancient lineage—though with strong royalist rather than roundhead connections—and is a descendant of one of the seven great hereditary chiefs of Scotland. One of his ancestors was made Ambassador to Denmark in 1491; another escaped execution in the seventeenth century by escaping the night before he was due to be beheaded dressed in his sister's clothes; and a third fled to France after the Battle of Culloden and raised his own regiment known as 'Ogilvy's'. When he met Princess Alexandra Mr Ogilvy had already made his own way in the City; and was a director of a large number of companies with such diverse interests as cattle breeding, gold mines and supermarkets. He charmed Princess Marina, amused her and teased her and was very much the kind of man she understood; he was also strong-minded, refused to accept a title and was obviously well able to care for her beloved daughter.

After their marriage Mr Ogilvy and Princess Alexandra rented Thatched House Lodge, another of the Crown properties in Richmond Park, which was on a long lease to Clare Duchess of Sutherland. They lead as near a normal life as is possible for any member of the Royal Family, are happily married and intend to stay that way. So long separations are out, and if Mr Ogilvy goes on a business trip as often as not his wife goes with him, and like him flies tourist class. Although whenever he can he accompanies Princess Alexandra on her royal duties, they neither of them talk much about their official life when they are at home together. 'I don't bore her with my daily routine and she doesn't bore me with hers,' he once said. It was an attitude Princess Marina very much understood and she rejoiced that her daughter's home life was, in some ways, remarkably like her own and very much centred on the children.

For to her great delight Princess Alexandra made her a grand-mother twice over again: with a son born on 29 February 1964 and, in the Airlie family tradition, called James after the one-time Ambassador to Denmark who also happened to be the first Lord Ogilvy; and a daughter named Marina Victoria Alexandra born two years later on 31 July 1966.

Her four grandchildren—all of them exceptionally beautiful to look at—were Princess Marina's pride and joy; and in the way that her own grandmothers had spoilt and made a fuss of her, she did the same to them and often repeated amusing incidents in which they had been involved—such as the time when Master James Ogilvy, after being told that his father was going on a business trip to Chile said: 'Chile? Well then you'd better take a cardigan!'

These new additions to her family helped to compensate Princess Marina for those she had lost.

One of her greatest sorrows had been the unexpected death in 1955, when only fifty-one, of her sister Elizabeth. Countess Toerring, a gay, sweet and amusing person, was the least known and most retiring of the three sisters. But the other two often said that she had by far the nicest nature of them all. They never ceased to miss her.

A year afterwards Countess Toerring's daughter Helen

married the Archduke Ferdinand of Austria and placed her
bridal bouquet on her mother's grave. And a daughter born of
this marriage, another Elizabeth, was one of the attendants at
the wedding of Princess Alexandra.

There was another great tragedy in the family when Princess
Paul's second son, Nicholas, aged twenty-five, a handsome,
popular boy, was killed in a car crash near Coppins in 1954.

Then there were the older ones who had gone. Grand Duke
Andrei, aged seventy-eight and the last surviving Russian
Grand Duke, died in 1956. 'Poor Andrei,' said Princess Nicholas
afterwards of her brother. 'He had such promise. And he ruined
his own life.'

And Princess Nicholas herself died a year later in Athens at
the age of seventy-five.

There were also troubles for Princess Marina of a different
kind. And ones with which she was familiar. Her financial
affairs.

In 1960 she was forced to have another sale, and at Sotheby's
on 20 June her collection of rare and beautiful objects made by
the Russian Court jeweller Carl Fabergé was auctioned for more
than £9,000. Buttons, buckles, parasol and cane handles, snuff
boxes, ash trays, frames, clocks, bell pushes, cigarette cases,
fans, even thermometers, many jewelled and enamelled and all
made with exquisite care.

Among them was a silver and cut glass centrepiece—a wedding present to her mother from the Dragoon Guards at
Tsarskoe Selo—and a magnificent canteen of silver which her
parents had used long ago in Greece for those weekly Thursday
family dinner parties.

In September 1964—exactly twenty-five years after she
should have accompanied her husband there—Princess Marina
went to Australia: a journey by far the most poignant and
sentimental of all her official tasks.

Before she went she studied every single speech the late Duke
of Kent had made during the time he was preparing for his term
as Governor-General. Again she re-read all the books about the
Dominion which she and her husband had once studied together.
Again she invited Australians to visit her. One was the man who
had been Prime Minister in 1939, was Prime Minister once
more and had since been knighted—Sir Robert Menzies, who

frequently went to dine with her at Kensington Palace and discuss the prospective tour.

But if Princess Marina did not have a husband to share in her preparations, she did have her daughter Princess Alexandra still bubbling over with enthusiasm for Australia after her own successful visit five years previously.

And there was one thing more. At Government House, Canberra, where she stayed, Princess Marina saw for the first time some of the furnishings chosen by her husband and still in use: the blue satin-covered sofas, the silk tweed curtains, the Grecian rugs—and even some of those expensive pink sheets.

'Well I'm here at last,' she said, just after she arrived. 'It's taken me twenty-five years to get here. War and tragedy prevented it. That's what war does to a person.'

Princess Marina's tour was just as much of a triumph as that of her daughter. With much of the same informality—though never, as happened with one extrovert visiting dignitary, upsetting the carefully planned arrangements.

She pleased Australians by going out of her way to speak to ordinary people waiting in the crowds; by talking to members of the Guards of Honour (not always a common practice among royalty); and by cheerfully putting up with uncomfortable situations—such as insisting on planting a tree when it was pouring with rain in order not to keep photographers waiting.

'That's marvellous. Just what we want,' they said as she posed for a picture in raincoat, headscarf and stout shoes. 'Good on you,' said Princess Marina.

And over and over again she paused to study traces of where her daughter had been such as inspecting a tree planted by Princess Alexandra or a plaque she had unveiled. 'It's interesting to see what the family's been doing,' she said.

It is quite extraordinary to realize that in her youth Princess Marina never thought that she was at all good-looking. She admired her sisters' features but never considered that her own were anything out of the ordinary. During her girlhood in Paris, though both Princess Olga and Princess Elizabeth told her she was pretty—and so did her parents—she never believed them. And she was so modest that not even at the height of her beauty,

The Duchess of Kent looks at her own exhibit 'Por-
trait of a Young Man' at the opening of the 50th
Anniversary Exhibition of the Women's International
Art Club.

A view from the Chateau de Malbosc, Grasse, by the
Duchess of Kent entitled 'Autumn Leaves'

Sketch of Mrs Ralli, done
in 1937

The 91st Annual Exhibition
of the Society of Women
Painters in 1952. The Duchess
of Kent is looking at a portrait of her sister, Princess
Paul of Yugoslavia

A painting of Princess Alexandra by the Duchess of
Kent, 1959

during her marriage, was she ever conscious of her lovely appearance.

She was still very handsome and attractive even in her later years; as beautifully dressed as always and, with the mobility of her facial expressions and the sparkle with which she talked, just as charming as she had been in her youth. She had also lost nearly all the nervousness which she used to experience and was often as vivacious and assured in public as she could be in private.

One example of this is a speech she made in Canterbury in July 1966 at the opening of a new library in the Cathedral. 'To judge by a rather cursory glance at the history of the Canterbury Cathedral library: it seems to have been dogged by disaster from the start!' she said. 'And I am afraid that successive deans and chapters—not to mention *archbishops*—cannot be acquitted of aiding and abetting the successive blows which have fallen upon different parts of this great institution! Book after book seems to have vanished from the Library's shelves only to adorn those of the College Libraries at Oxford and Cambridge. . . .'

The way in which her expressive face acted out her words, the heavy stress she gave to the mention of archbishops and the meaningful glance directed at the Archbishop of Canterbury sitting by her side transformed what might have been just a light-hearted remark into a wildly funny piece of humour. And her personality entranced some of the boys of Kings School in the audience, who were not even born until at least ten years after she reached the height of her beauty, 'She's so amusing and attractive,' said one.

Princess Marina always had great sympathy with the trials and problems of the young and when in 1966 she became Chancellor of the new University of Kent she had an opportunity to air her views which she directed particularly to the first generation of students who attended the university.

'I hope you will not take it amiss if I give you a few words of warning,' she said. 'New universities are arising with the object that as many boys and girls as possible should have the advantage of a university education. But this should not mean that universities are to become mere forcing-houses for particular professions or studies, nor that the high standards of our existing universities should be allowed to decline. A university degree should not only qualify a student for his or her future job; it should teach that student how to make use of leisure; how to become a good citizen; and how to value all that is best in every aspect of life.'

And she went on: 'It seems to me that a good deal of nonsense is said and written about the young nowadays. Far more attention is given to their failings than to their very real virtues. What is not so often recognized is that young people, in questioning authority as their parents did in their time, are taking an entirely natural and indeed intelligent line. In doing so, however, they in their turn must realize that without authority the world would revert to jungle. Authority there must be, but there must be understanding too; and that is one reason why I welcomed—when I first heard of it—the decision to build this University on a collegiate plan.

'One has often heard university life criticized today because of the difficulty which undergraduates find in making friends with those who are there to teach them. This is a two-way process of course, but it demands a high degree of patience and a good deal of time from hard-worked teachers if it is to be achieved. I am quite certain that the collegiate plan does much to encourage this relationship, and that if students can meet and discuss their problems with their own teachers in their leisure hours, as opposed to their working hours, it is of tremendous benefit not just to the student but to those who are set above them as well.'

The Princess was 'exceedingly proud' at being chosen as first Chancellor of the University. She took pains to stress that she lacked the qualifications she thought she should have had for the appointment; and that she had been disappointed that she did not go to a university herself. But, with her usual diligence she put herself out to make sure that her position was not just a nominal title.

One of the things she did was to give a party for students at Kensington Palace. There was not room for them all so seventy guests were selected by students among themselves and the Princess was quite appalled and horrified when somebody suggested that they should be instructed how to behave and what to wear. 'No certainly not,' she said. 'Not on any account must they be told. They must come as they wish and behave as they wish.' As she confidently expected, the students were extremely well-mannered yet natural: though she laughed a lot when she asked one of them if he had any particular friends at the party and he said that he was not sure. 'It is difficult to recognize anybody. We all had a haircut this morning.'

But there was rarely any pomp and ceremony at Kensington Palace: like Queen Mary, who took less than twenty-five minutes to get through informal meals, Princess Marina's own mealtimes were short and unelaborate. But if the Prime Minister came to lunch, which he did quite often, or she had other guests, then everything had to be exactly right and she took great pains to see that it was.

Acting as hostess on her own when always before it had been her husband who had looked after the arrangements was another hurdle Princess Marina had to overcome when she became a widow. Because of her inexperience she was, for years, rather a nervous hostess.

During the festivities which surrounded the Queen's coronation she once gave a big party at Coppins to which the whole of the Royal Family and many overseas notabilities, such as Queen Salote of Tonga, had been invited. For most of the day beforehand she was in what somebody described as 'a terrific tizzy' and was in just as great a panic as any ordinary person would be with such an imposing guest list.

But of course when they all arrived not a trace of her 'tizzy' remained and she was as apparently cool and controlled as the most consistent and sophisticated party-giver.

Except with a handful of people with whom she was on really intimate terms, Princess Marina was not always an easy person to entertain herself. She would often veto other suggested guests, either because she had seen them too recently or else because she did not wish to meet them for one reason or another.

At dinner parties she dutifully and charmingly paid equal attention to her neighbours on either side but if, as frequently happens in London social life, somebody started discussing personalities and said anything even slightly malicious she very quickly put a stop to it. 'That was a catty thing to say,' she would remark, or, 'I am sure that is not right. How could you say such a thing?' which, as someone said, is apt to dampen an evening in which everybody is longing to gossip.

Yet it was a rare, and many think her most splendid quality.
Princess Marina did not make friends easily. She was basically
cautious; it took her a long time to accept anyone new. Her
closest friends were her sisters and the few intimates whom she
had known since she was a child. But once she had accepted
someone she did it wholeheartedly, with no reserve and with
complete and unswerving loyalty. No matter what damaging
comments anyone made afterwards she would disbelieve, ignore
and, after the first few words when she realized what was happening, would not hear any more.

Even in a cosy twosome with one of her life-long companions
she was the same; if they attempted to hand on some choice
morsel of scandal about anyone she knew and liked, she would
put up her hand and say firmly, 'Stop. I refuse to listen—whatever it is I am sure it is not true.' This fierce loyalty extended to
everyone who had known her parents or her grandparents, and
it went far beyond hating to listen to criticism. When it was a
question of doing something for somebody else then her self-
admitted indolence and lack of application vanished with the
wind and she had the implacable determination and energy of a
bulldozer.

Always Princess Marina clung to old friends and old associa-
tions and she made a point of cherishing anyone who had a
connection with her past or with her family.

One such instance concerned the daughter of Madame Komstadius who had helped her mother with the children's home in
Paris. In 1968 she was ill in a nursing home in a London suburb
which was too far away for many of her friends to visit her
easily—though Princess Marina herself went as often as possible. With tremendous difficulty—because the nursing home
she had in mind was full—Princess Marina, only a few months
before she died, arranged for her friend to be transferred nearer
to Kensington Palace.

This was only a small instance perhaps, but it is typical of
many such acts of kindness she performed, not one of which was
ever known outside the people concerned.

But there was very little that she did not notice. In common
with the present Queen, Princess Marina was extraordinarily
observant. At a luncheon or banquet or any function her eyes
would flicker everywhere, missing nothing. Of those who were

presented to her she noticed every detail, shoes, dress, hand-bag, even the number and type of rings they wore. And she was generous with her praise where other women were concerned. If she thought they looked pretty or were wearing a colour which suited them she never hesitated to say so.

And it would be misleading to give the impression that Princess Marina frequently blighted a party. If she was relaxed and sure of her companions, she was easy to please and amuse. She had a disarming, childlike quality for enjoyment and never lost her enthusiasm for party games which, through the years, she entered into with as much gusto as she had when she was a little girl.

There was one game called 'Conversations' which nearly always reduced her to fits of laughter: in this, two people each representing a well-known character would come into a room and in their normal voices start a conversation with one another. The rest had to guess whom they were impersonating. They were always unlikely pairs such as Queen Mary and the Duchess of Windsor; or Mahatma Gandhi and Winston Churchill.

Sometimes when it was her turn Princess Marina would partner one of her sisters and they would both collapse in help-less giggles in the middle. Before the death of Princess Elizabeth the three of them always laughed easily and frequently to-gether; in the pleasure of each other's company everything around them seemed to be amusing and gay. 'Oh, how we laughed,' she would say afterwards, or, 'We never stopped laughing the whole time.'

She was a wonderful member of the audience for any theatri-cal production which was at all funny. If she saw a romping bedroom farce for example, in which the wife was with a lover and her husband turned up unexpectedly Princess Marina would say delightedly, 'What a situation! What a situation!'; and if it were comic enough she literally doubled up with laughter.

Princess Marina's taste in opera was also on the popular side. She liked the romantic composers such as Verdi, Wagner and Puccini. She went a great deal to Covent Garden and every year to Glyndebourne.

Her choice of reading matter was very like her husband's—she preferred biographies and memoirs to anything at all weighty, political, or abstract. Repeatedly she had books by authors she admired such as Laurens van der Post. She enjoyed reading *Dearest Child* (the edited letters which Queen Victoria wrote to her eldest daughter, who later became the Empress Frederick.) At the time she died she was in the middle of reading Harold Nicolson's *Life and Letters*; shortly before that she had been engrossed by Robert Massie's *Nicholas and Alexandra*, a biography of her relatives the last Tsar and Tsarina of Russia.

And she became more television-minded—very often eating her supper from a 'television tray'.

Like many people she was addicted to 'The Forsyte Saga' which she saw when it was first shown on BBC 2. She made sure that she did not miss any episode and told all her friends to watch it. She liked the Maigret series and when it ended, and was put on in London as a stage play, she made a point of seeing it and going backstage afterwards to see Rupert Davies the actor who portrayed the French detective. She also liked watching 'Doctor Finlay's Casebook' and always meant to arrange a meeting with Bill Simpson, who played the part of Finlay, though she never got around to doing it.

But, except when it came to helping one of her friends, Princess Marina found it difficult to concentrate tremendously hard. Even her painting intrigued her only spasmodically. As she said herself, she was too indolent and easy-going to become really proficient. Yet she had a great talent for producing an accurate likeness and did one very good sketch of the Queen who is not at all easy to portray.

Once she was defeated in an attempt to draw a portrait of one of her friends—they both said afterwards that the final result resembled nothing so much as a sheep; and a rather worried sheep at that. She had one more try and then gave it up. Probably her best portrait was a black and white sketch of Mrs Lilia Ralli which the knowledgeable Prince Paul said was her finest, though she never liked very much herself.

There was one time when, encouraged by an artistic friend, she seriously considered going to classes at the Royal College of Art or the Slade so that she could become more than a gifted amateur painter and develop her strong talent up to professional standards. But she needed somebody like her husband who was strong-minded enough to stir her out of her natural, easy-going

ways and persuade her to carry out the suggestion to its conclusion.

Another time, not long after the Duke of Kent's death, and
an additional example of the effort she made to take over everything he did, she decided to learn to drive. But that idea too,
was doomed to failure. She was in no state to concentrate and
she never had been mechanically minded so it proved impossible
to teach her easily. Eventually she gave up the idea altogether.

She knew that she was not particularly clever and was often
conscious of her lack of university education and the sketchiness
of the intermittent lessons during her nomadic girlhood. Unless
she was sure of her ground she was diffident about pronouncing
any very strong opinions.

She did not realize quite how much information she had
accumulated and how her eager curiosity had given her a much
wider range of knowledge, extending over a vast and varied field
of activity, than most.

When she was invited to be Chancellor of the University of
Kent her first reaction was of sheer stupefaction. 'They must be
mad,' she said. 'Surely they want somebody like a don.'

Latterly, Princess Marina became increasingly interested in
visiting museums and art galleries. Nearly every weekend,
accompanied by a woman companion, she visited in turn such
institutions as the Tate Gallery, the Victoria and Albert
Museum, the National Gallery and the British Museum. And
when the Tutankhamen treasures were on show in Paris on loan
from Cairo, with two friends she went over on a day trip to see
the spectacular objects from Pharaoh's tomb, and also lunch
with Prince and Princess Paul.

Princess Marina went to some of the museums several times:
but the one she returned to most often was the British Museum.
Each time, Princess Marina went back again and again to look
at the Elgin Marbles—the magnificent carvings which had once
adorned the Parthenon in Athens, the city where she was
born.

And gradually she changed the habits of her younger days.
More and more she preferred the company of just one of her
intimates instead of a group. 'Isn't it nice, just sitting here
on our own having tea and talking cosily,' she would say. When
she was in Paris it would be the same. Formerly her visits always

meant an excuse for a party when a dozen or more of her French friends would get together to meet her. Here again she made it clear that she preferred to see only one close friend at a time— and of course her surviving sister.

Very belatedly, after all the years, Princess Marina began to take an interest in gardening. She found a great deal of pleasure in pottering around her garden at Kensington Palace. And sometimes she went on expeditions to see famous gardens such as Sissinghurst which had been created by Sir Harold Nicolson's wife, the writer Victoria Sackville-West.

The Princess very much liked living at Kensington Palace and it amused her at intervals to rearrange the furniture, getting one of her friends to help her push the pieces around— a chore they did not always appreciate as quite a lot of the objects were rather heavy. But she preferred to do it herself rather than get a servant to assist.

In the same way she disliked the fuss of having police out-riders when she was going to perform some official duty. 'Do I *have* to have them?' she sometimes asked. And only when it was pointed out that without them traffic might hold her up and make her late for an appointment, did she realize the necessity for it.

She liked going shopping in Kensington, either by herself or with a woman companion. She took tremendous care whenever she was buying presents; and every Christmas there was always a great whirlwind of activity in the Palace when Princess Marina was preparing gifts for her family and especially those for her grandchildren.

Strangely, although Princess Marina was noted as a beautiful and elegant woman, this was not the kind of reputation that she particularly wanted. She preferred to be thought of as a cosy person. And though she was interested in clothes she did not really like dressing up for grand occasions. Even in London, more often than not she would wear tweeds—though on her they always looked distinguished.

Nor was she fond of hats. She much preferred a scarf or a light veil. Sometimes on country car journeys she would not wear one and just put it on at the last minute. Once or twice— though never for an official function—she forgot to put on a hat at all, and then had to hastily retrieve one. And one time, at a débutante ball, she found her tiara so heavy and uncomfortable that she unpinned it and left it perched on the piano for the rest of the evening.

Like her mother, Princess Marina was devoted to animals. It had upset her when her first dog 'Kiffy' had been left behind in Athens in the care of a servant when they went into exile. And she was pleased when, after her marriage, the Duke bought a dog, a beautiful chow.

But one of her greatest joys in her later years was a Pekinese called Chin, who slept in her room and greeted her ecstatically whenever she came home after being out without him.

Every day, generally entirely alone, Princess Marina took her dog for a walk in Kensington Gardens; and frequently came back with some amusing story of an adventure which had taken place.

Once, as she was returning to her own private gate, she noticed a man in a Tyrolean hat waiting with a camera poised. At first she thought it was a newspaper photographer and was slightly upset because it meant the end of her privacy and that she would in future have to find a different route. As she got nearer she realized that he was not a cameraman but an American tourist and she thought he was probably going to ask her to stand still for a picture. But not at all. As she drew close, he politely addressed her as 'Ma'am' and asked her to take a photograph of himself, his wife and his sister sitting on a park bench. The Princess with great gusts of laughter recounted the incident afterwards, giving a flawless imitation of the visitor's Mid-Western accent and giggling at her own discomfiture as she prepared to be gracious and pose for him, only to find a camera thrust into her hands.

'I wouldn't have known how to focus it,' she commented, 'if I hadn't owned one myself of the same make.' Someone asked her why she had not mentioned who she was. 'Oh, I didn't think of it,' she said.

Another incident which took place some years back at a big film première was one she often described amusingly. As she walked down the steps of the dress circle in the glare of spotlights, there was a tremendous roll of drums. Thinking that it was the beginning of the National Anthem she stood stock still in the limelight for what seemed an eternity until the drumming

P

ended—the orchestra went on to play a popular tune. That too she often recalled, giving a comic rendering of her own feelings and expressions which would have done more than justice to a professional comedienne.

There were apparent contradictions in Princess Marina's character because she would sometimes assume a different personality to different friends. Those who were English or American looked upon her as a rather mystical person with occasional moods of depression which came straight out of a Chekhov play and were attributed to the fact that she was three-quarters Russian with that strong Romanov streak which so stubbornly persists through all the descendants of that dynasty. To her mid-European friends she appeared calm, temperate and placid with an acceptance of all that happened to her which she made no attempt to protest or struggle against.

It has been said that her cousin King George II of Greece consulted a fortune-teller once a fortnight, but the Princess herself was not in the least inclined this way. She was much more of a fatalist. She once gave a long lecture to a friend who believed in the Greek superstition that a hat on the bed meant a death in the house and told her not to be so silly.

Towards the end of her life Princess Marina became increasingly interested in spastic organizations and various aspects of mental welfare, and she had a rare gift for being able to talk to handicapped children in a way which few other visitors could emulate.

She would arrive at some home or institution in a vast motorcar complete with outriders and accompanied by the usual royal cavalcade; the Lord Lieutenant, the Chief Constable, the local Mayor, the Town Clerk, the Chairman of the Rural District Council and possibly one or two others—with their wives. But given half a chance, with a knowing look which was not quite a wink, she would break away from them and send them all on a separate procession of their own while she went off, comparatively unfettered.

Officials of such organizations, some of them anti-establishment and quick to spot feigned interest or phoney sympathy, were impressed by the genuine interest and natural manner in a person who, as someone said, was 'Royalty personified'.

At first the most severely malformed cases were kept away

from her but a curious: 'What is going on in that room' or 'Who is in there?' meant that she eventually went everywhere. Never once did she show that quick flicker of revulsion which even the best intentioned visitors sometimes give before they pull themselves together—although sometimes her inquisitiveness led her to look at untidy cupboards and glory-holes which were not meant for prying royal eyes.

'Ah, I can understand why you didn't want to show me that,' she would say with mock seriousness.

Princess Marina was what one official called 'quick on the uptake' and observant; and burrowed industriously on all her visits to find out the cause of disabilities and what could be done to cure them. But she liked plain old-fashioned English, not medical jargon. If someone told her that a child was 'educationally sub-normal' it meant nothing to her. Rephrasing it to: 'this child is slow to learn' brought quick reaction and a 'What can you do about it?' from the Princess.

Once, when an official made an unusually hard-hitting speech about conditions in mental hospitals in her presence and apologized afterwards she said: 'I know it was a tough speech but I only wish I had been able to say it myself. That's what these people need to be told.'

Sometimes Princess Marina would be very near to tears when she talked to some grossly handicapped five-year-old infant but she never gushed over the children and talked in a way that made them feel she was their friend and not an over-powering strange lady visitor.

She was always more concerned about younger patients, and talked constantly about her own grandchildren, saying over and over again, 'Oh, how thankful I am that they are normal.'

During the onslaught of her final illness Princess Marina often treated her disability as a joke in spite of the alarm and discomfort she must have felt when, as sometimes happened, her left leg gave way under her and she stumbled. Ruefully she would look at it and say 'Poor little thing. It hasn't done too badly. After all it has supported me for sixty years.'

Never at any time had she pandered to its weakness and never would she confess that she was tired however far she walked or however energetically she had played tennis. And she had

tramped uncomplainingly for miles on it over that rough moorland to see the site where her husband met his death. Only those
who loved her watched carefully and when they saw signs of
strain made some excuse to stop and rest.

It is believed that Princess Marina never knew how serious
her last illness was. She attributed the pain she had to rheumatism and was depressed when, after planning to go to Florence
to stay with Prince and Princess Paul, as she normally did, her
doctors, that summer of 1968, advised her not to go.

But she did have one holiday that year to which she had been
looking forward a long time—a three-week visit to Kenya,
Uganda and Tanzania on safari, with Prince Michael and two
others. A visit that was so informal that she did not take an
evening dress; and Prince Michael, to his mother's amusement,
temporarily grew a beard.

When she went into hospital, in Norman Hartnell's dressmaking salon in Bruton Street a half-finished white and silver
evening dress hung in a wardrobe, waiting until she should be
well enough to have another fitting. And over and over again
when she was home again Princess Marina counted her blessings.
'I am so much better off than those poor spastic patients,' she
said. 'I have my family, a comfortable house and a nurse to look
after me. And I have had a wonderful life. They have nothing
at all.'

She died as gracefully as she had lived. With dignity, without
fuss; and mercifully without pain or any of the distressing symp-
toms which might have occurred had she stayed too long on
earth.

Princess Marina's last conscious day, 25 August 1968, was a
very happy one. It was a sunny Sunday, and although Prince
Michael was away for the weekend, she had a friend staying
with her, and Princess Alexandra, with her husband, motored
over from Richmond to Kensington Palace for luncheon. As
always, to have them all around her gave Princess Marina a
great deal of pleasure; and she looked so young and vivacious
that Princess Alexandra commented on it and said that her
mother did not look a day over thirty-five.

When they had gone, Princess Marina spent the afternoon
sitting in the Palace garden with her friend, reading the Sunday

newspapers and wrestling with the crossword puzzles; the pair
of them wrangled gently over the clues and, in disgust, left some
of the puzzles half completed by tea-time.

Early that evening there was a television programme in which
Malcolm Muggeridge, who fascinated Princess Marina, was
holding forth. They watched that, then she had her bath, and
ate her supper in a dressing-gown. Once more they looked at
television. This time at one of a series of detective stories and
they spent a lot of the time discussing which of the suspects was
the villain.

The only untoward happening was that, as she went to bed
that night Princess Marina stumbled and fell.

And there was one more event that Sunday. In the morning
during a brief service, she said prayers for her dead husband;
for it was the anniversary of his death and exactly twenty-six
years since that aeroplane crash in Scotland. Just after nine
o'clock the following morning Princess Marina said: 'I feel tired.
I think I will go to sleep'; a sleep from which she never
awakened.

Princess Alexandra telephoned Princess Olga in Florence that
same day to say that her mother was unconscious and she
begged her aunt to come at once. Princess Marina's sister
arrived that evening and sat by her bedside throughout most
of the night. Once Princess Marina opened her eyes and seemed
to feel her sister's presence.

But Princess Marina never recovered consciousness. She died
on the morning of 27 August. And one of her friends, remember-
ing her last happy Sunday, said afterwards, 'It was just as if her
husband had come to fetch her.' And Princess Olga said: 'Now
I am alone.'

The night before Princess Marina was buried, on the instructions of the Queen, the body of the late Duke of Kent was taken
from the vaults of St George's Chapel. And he was at last
placed, as she had wished, in the small private burial ground
behind the mausoleum at Frogmore which holds the tombs of
Queen Victoria and the Prince Consort. It is just a plain green
lawn among the trees not far from Windsor Castle, with a scattering of simple graves each with a planted border of flowers.
Not quite so beautiful as the hill at Tatoi perhaps, but almost as
secluded, open to sunlight and fresh air; and a great contrast

to the grand and gloomy crypt where the Duke had lain so long.

The following day on 30 August, Princess Marina and her husband were buried side by side.

She left a sum of £17,398 after liabilities and death duties were paid—one of the smallest fortunes ever bequeathed by a member of the Royal Family.

A memorial service for H.R.H. Princess Marina, Duchess of Kent, was held in Westminster Abbey on 25 October 1968, two months after her death. It was televised to millions, but among the two thousand mourners present were members of the British, Greek, Danish, Russian and Yugoslav Royal Families. There were people who had known her since childhood; those who remembered the day she had walked up the aisle of the Abbey as a radiantly beautiful bride; those who had also been her husband's friends; and those whose families had been involved with her own since before she was born. These included relatives of the last Emperor and Empress of Russia; descendants of the Grand Duchess Xenia and King Ferdinand of Bulgaria. Also there were two representatives from a garage at Iver, many who were connected with all aspects of her official life: and some who never knew her at all, but thought of her always with affection and admiration.

To them all the Dean of Westminster said: 'Into the hands of Almighty God . . . we commend his servant Marina, with thanksgiving upon our remembrance of her grace and beauty, her spirit of spontaneity, her courage in adversity, her unswerving service to this land of her adoption, her faithfulness in friendship, her percipient sympathy with sufferers, her love and knowledge of music and the arts, her knowledgeable patronage of so many human activities; not least do we thank God for the mutual affection which was established between her and our people, and for her own loving family.'

List of Offices held by Princess Marina

The Queen's Regiment	Colonel in Chief	1966
(formerly the Queen's Own Royal West Kent Regiment)	Colonel in Chief	1947
The Queen's Regimental Association	Patron	1967
The Essex & Kent Scottish	Colonel in Chief	1954
The Devonshire & Dorset Regiment	Colonel in Chief	1958
(formerly the Dorset Regiment)	Colonel in Chief	1953
Devonshire & Dorset Officers Club	Patron	
Corps of Royal Electrical & Mechanical Engineers	Colonel in Chief	1963
299 (Royal Buckinghamshire Yeomanry, Queen's Own Oxfordshire Hussars & Berkshire) Field Regiment Royal Artillery (T.A.)	Hon. Colonel	1961
Bucks Battalions Old Comrades' Association	Patron	1957
Women's Royal Naval Service	Chief Commandant	1940
Women's Royal Naval Service Benevolent Trust	President	1945
Wrens—Association of	Patron	1946
Women's Royal Australian Naval Service	Hon. Commandant	1954
Alexandra Rose Day	President	1936

All England Lawn Tennis & Croquet Club	President	1943
Anglo-Hellenic League	President and Chief Patron	1942
Armed Forces Art Society	Patron	1958
Army Ski Association	Patron	1950
Artists' General Benevolent Institution	Patron	1942
Association of Civil Service Art Clubs	Patron	1955
Association of Kentish Men & Men of Kent & Fair Maids of Kent	Patron	1942
Bethlem Royal Hospital & the Maudsley Hospital	Patron	1955
Bristol Old Vic Trust	Patron	1964
British Epilepsy Association	Patron	1959
British Red Cross Society, County of London Branch, Kensington Division	Patron	1956
British Sailors' Society (Prince of Wales Sea Training School)	Patron	1942
British School of Rome	President	1965
Buckinghamshire Historic Churches Trust	Patron	1957
Bucks County Show	Patron	
Caldecott Community	Patron	
Central School of Speech and Drama	Patroness	1935
Chelsea Play Centre for Children	Patron	
Chest and Heart Association	President	1943
Civil Service Orchestra	Patron	1946
Clothworkers' Company	Hon. Freewoman	1942
Combined Services Lawn Tennis Association	Patron	1949
Derwen Cripples' Training College, Oswestry	Patron	1943

Elizabeth Garrett Anderson Hospital	Patron	1935
Embankment Fellowship Centre	Patron	1953
Friends of the Fitzwilliam Museum, Cambridge	Patron	1968
Glaziers' Company	Hon. Freewoman	1943
International Social Service of Great Britain	Patron	1963
Iver, Denham & Langley Cottage Hospital	Patron	1943
Kandahar Ski Club	Patroness	1945
Kent Council of Social Service	Patron	1949
Kent County Nursing Association	Patron	
Kent County Ophthalmic & Aural Hospital, Maidstone	Patron	1942
Kent County Playing Fields Association	Patron	
King Edward Memorial Hospital, Ealing	Patron	1943
McGill Society of Great Britain	Hon. Member	1962
Memorial Hospital, Shooters Hill	Patron	1948
Mental After Care Association	Patron	1958
Merioneth Nursing Association	Patron	1943
Musicians' Company	Hon. Freewoman	1943
National Association for Mental Health	Patron	1946
National Benevolent Institution	Patron	1943
Old Vic	President	1957
People's Dispensary for Sick Animals	Patron	1943
Professional Nurses & Midwives Conference	Patron	1957
Queen Adelaide Naval Fund	Patron	

Robert Jones & Agnes Hunt Orthopaedic Hospital, Oswestry	Patron	1943
Rochester Cathedral, Friends of	Patron	1945
Royal Air Force Benevolent Fund	President	1943
Royal Alexandra & Albert School	Vice-President	1948
Royal Choral Society	President	1942
Royal Geographical Society	Hon. President	1943
Royal National Hospital for Rheumatic Diseases, Bath	Patron	1948
Royal National Lifeboat Institution	President	1942
Royal Naval & Royal Marine Branch & Special Duties Officers' Benevolent Fund	Patron	1942
Royal Naval Benevolent Trust	Patron	1942
Royal School for the Blind, Leatherhead	Patron	1943
Royal South Hants Hospital	Patron	1942
Royal Wanstead School	Patron	1943
St. George's Hospital	Patron	1948
St. John Ambulance Brigade for Wales	Commandant-in-Chief of Nursing Corps & Divisions for Wales.	
Seamen's Mission	Patron	1940
Shaftesbury Homes & 'Arethusa' Training Ship	Patron	1943
Society of Women Artists	Patron	
Soldiers', Sailors' & Airmen's Families Association	Vice-Patron	
S.O.S. Society	Patron	1957
Spastics Society	Patron	1963
Tavistock Clinic	Patron	1942
University College Hospital	Patron	1942
University of Kent at Canterbury	Chancellor	1962

War Widows' Guild of Australia	Patron	1948
Women's Holiday Fund	Patroness	1935
Women's International Art Club	Patron	1947
Working Ladies' Guild	President	1945
Y.W.C.A. Central Club for Women & Girls	Hon. President	1937

Bibliography

Mabell Countess of Airlie, *Thatched With Gold*

Grand Duke Alexander of Russia, *Once a Grand Duke*, Cassell, 1932

Queen Alexandra of Yugoslavia, *For a King's Love*, Odhams Press, 1956

Anon, *Russian Court Memoirs*, Herbert Jenkins, 1937

Anon (Stopford), *The Russian Diary of an Englishman*, Heinemann, 1919

Admiral Sir Reginald Bacon, *From 1900 Onwards*

Consuelo Vanderbilt Balsan, *The Glitter and the Gold*

E. F. Benson, *As We Were*, Longmans, 1930

E. F. Benson, *Our Family Affairs*, Cassell, 1920

Lord Bertie of Thame, *The Diary of Lord Bertie of Thame*

John Wheeler-Bennet, *King George VI*, Macmillan, 1958

(Ed) E. J. Bing, *The Letters of Tsar Nicholas and Empress Marie*, Ivor Nicholson and Watson Ltd, London, 1937

Sir George Buchanan, *My Mission to Russia*, Cassell

Meriel Buchanan, *Victorian Gallery*, Cassell, 1956

Meriel Buchanan, *Diplomacy and Foreign Courts*, Hutchinson, 1928

Prince von Bülow, *Memoirs*, Putnam, 1931

Baroness Sophie Buxhoeveden, *The Life & Tragedy of Empress Alexandra Feodorovna*, Longmans Green and Co., 1928

M. C. Carey, *Princess Mary*, Nisbett, 1922

Prince Christopher of Greece, *Memoirs*, The Right Book Club, 1938

Captain Walter Christmas, *The Life of King George of Greece*, Eveleigh Nash, 1914

Edna Woolman Chase and Ilka Chase, *Always in Vogue*, Gollancz, 1954

Winston S. Churchill, *The Second World War* Vol III, Cassell, 1950

Count Ciano, *Ciano's Diary*, 1939–1943, Heinemann

Lady Cynthia Colville, *Crowded Life*

The Marchioness Curzon of Kedleston, *Reminiscences*

Grand Duke Cyril, *My Life in Russia's Service—Then and Now*, Selwyn & Blount, 1939

Daisy Princess of Pless, Autobiography, John Murray, 1928

Lili Dehn, *The Real Tsaritsa*, Thornton Butterworth, 1922

Anthony Eden, *The Eden Memoirs*, Cassell, 1965

Jennifer Ellis, *The Duchess of Kent*, Odhams Press, 1952

Grace Ellison, *The Life Story of Princess Marina*, Heinemann, 1934

Herbert T. Fitch, *Memoirs of a Royal Detective*, Hurst & Blackett, 1936

Roger Fulford, *Dearest Child*, Evans Bros., 1965

David Lloyd George, *War Memoirs,* Odhams Press, 1938

Prince George of Greece, *The Cretan Drama*, Robert Speller, New York 1959

Elinor Glyn, *Romantic Adventure*, Ivor Nicholson & Watson, 1936

John Gore, *King George V*

Lord Grantley, *Silver Spoon*, Hutchinson, 1954

Sir Nevile Henderson, *Failure of a Mission,* 129

James Pope-Hennessy, *Queen Mary*, Allen and Unwin, 1959

J. B. Hoptner, *Yugoslavia in Crisis 1934–1941*, Columbia University Press, 1962

Thomas Jones, *A Diary with Letters 1931–1950*, Oxford University Press, 1954

Tamara Karsavina, *Theatre Street*, Constable, 1950

Princess Romanovsky-Krassinska, *Dancing in St Petersburg*, Doubleday, 1961

Alexander Kerensky, *The Kerensky Memoirs,* Cassell, 1965

Mark Kerr, *Land, Sea and Air*, Longmans Green & Co., 1927

Air Vice Marshal Sir Arthur Gould Lee, *The Royal House of Greece*, Ward Lock, 1948

Air Vice Marshal Sir Arthur Gould Lee (Ed) *The Empress Frederick Writes to Sophie,* Faber & Faber, 1955

Air Vice Marshal Sir Arthur Gould Lee, *Helen Queen Mother of Rumania,* Faber & Faber

Sir Sydney Lee, *King Edward VII*, Macmillan, 1925

Elizabeth Longford, *Victoria R.I.*, Weidenfeld & Nicolson, 1964

Maurice Leudet, *Nicolas II Intime*, F. Juven, Paris 1898

Vladimir Lazarevski (Trans. and annot.) *Archives Secrètes de L'Empereur Nicolas II*, Payot, Paris 1928

Queen Marie of Rumania, *The Story of My Life*, Cassell, 1934

Grand Duchess Marie of Russia, *Things I Remember*, Cassell, 1930

Vera Laughton Mathews, *Blue Tapestry*, Hollis & Carter, 1949

Compton Mackenzie, *My Life and Times Octave 5*, Chatto and Windus, 1966

Grand Duchess Marie of Russia, *A Princess in Exile*

Philip Magnus, *King Edward the Seventh*, John Murray, 1964

W. Miller, *Greek Life in Town & Country*, Geo. Newnes, 1905

A. A. Mossolov, *At the Court of the Last Tsar*, Methuen, 1935

Prince Nicholas of Greece, *Political Memoirs 1914–17*, 1928

Prince Nicholas of Greece, *My Fifty Years*, Hutchinson, 1926

Harold Nicolson, *King George the Fifth*, Constable, 1952

Countess Nostitz, *Romance and Revolutions*, Hutchinson 1937

Serge Obolensky, *One Man in His Time*, Hutchinson, 1960

Sidney Cunliffe-Owen, *Elisabeth Queen of the Belgians*, Jenkins, 1954

Walburga Lady Paget, *Embassies of Other Days*, Hutchinson, 1923

Maurice Paléologue, *An Ambassador's Memoirs*, Hutchinson, 1923

Princess Paley, *Memories of Russia 1916–1919*, Herbert Jenkins, 1924

Bernard Pares, *My Russian Memoirs*, Cape, 1931

King Peter II of Yugoslavia, *A King's Heritage*, Cassell, 1955

Sir Frederick Ponsonby (ed), *The Letters of the Empress Frederick*

Princess Catherine Radziwill, *The Intimate Life of the Last Tsarina*, Cassell, 1932

Princess Catherine Radziwill, *Memories of Forty Years*, Cassell, 1915

Princess Catherine Radziwill, *Nicholas II Last of the Tsars*, Cassell, 1931

William Howard Russell, *The Prince of Wales's Tour 1877*

Baroness Agnes de Stoeckl, *My Dear Marquis*, John Murray

Edgar Sheppard, *HRH The Duke of Cambridge*, Longmans

Demetrios Sicilianos, *Old and New Athens*, Putnam, 1960

The Duke of Sutherland, *Looking Back*

Prince Serge Shekerbatov, *The Artist in Old Russia*, Chekov, New York

The Letters of the Tsaritsa to the Tsar 1914–1916, Duckworth, 1923

The Letters of the Tsar to the Tsaritsa 1914–1917, John Lane, 1929

Lalla Vandervelde, *Monarchs & Millionaires*, Thornton Butterworth, 1925

Count Paul Vassili, *Behind the Veil at the Russian Court*, Cassell, 1913

Ian Vorres, *The Last Grand Duchess*, Hutchinson, 1964

Nourah Waterhouse, *Private and Official*, Jonathan Cape, 1942

Mrs George Cornwallis-West, *Reminiscences of Lady Randolph Churchill*, Edward Arnold, 1908

Rebecca West, *Black Lamb and Grey Falcon*, Macmillan, 1941

The Duchess of Windsor, *The Heart Has Its Reasons*

The Duke of Windsor, *A King's Story*

The Duke of Windsor, *Windsor Revisited*, Houghton Mifflin, Boston 1960

Prince Serge Wolkonsky, *My Reminiscences*, Hutchinson

Prince Felix Youssoupoff, *Lost Splendour*, Cape, 1953

Also:

Documents of British Foreign Policy 1919–1939 First Series Vol. III, Vol. XII, HMSO

Oxford Slavonic Papers Vol XII, Clarendon Press, 1965

Krasny Archives Vols. 21, 22, 25, 26, Moscow 1926/1927

Parliamentary Papers Vols. 971, 1771, HMSO

Hansard

And the following newspapers and periodicals:

Daily Express, Daily Mail, Daily Mirror, Daily Sketch, Daily Telegraph, Daily Worker, Evening Standard, Evening News, Le Figaro, Manchester Guardian, News of the World, New York Daily Tribune, New York Herald Tribune, New York World, Rand Daily Mail, Star, Sunday Chronicle, Sunday Dispatch, Sunday Express, The Times

The Candid Friend, The Gentlewoman, The Norlander, Norland Quarterly, Lady's Pictorial, Woman's Pictorial, The Tatler

Public Record Office Documents.

	2282
FO 372/	3068
	3069
	2999
FO 371/	7585
	4683
	4684
	4685
	2878
	3150

Index

Index

Nicholas, Prince of Greece—*contd.*
Princess Marina, 118–19; G.C.B., 119;
and Princess Marina's bridal attendants, 121; at her wedding, 127, 128;
at birth of her first child, 141; in
Paris, 145; his death in Athens, 147;
his tomb at Tatoi, 147
Nicholas, Prince of Yugoslavia, 101,
130, 203
Nicholas, Princess, 25; her beauty, 25,
26, 34; personal details, 25–6, 34; her
travels, 26; and Prince Nicholas, 26;
and Prince Max of Baden, 26, 114;
engaged to Prince Nicholas, 26; her
marriage, 27; and massacre of Russian
Imperial family, 65; and her mother's
death, 79; her marriage and honeymoon, 27–8; in Denmark, 27; her
first arrival in Greece, 28–9; her first
and second daughters born, 30; at
Nicholas Palace, 31, 33; and her
children, 31; the royal routine, 31,
48; journeys abroad, 31, 37–43; her
third daughter born, 31; seriously ill,
31; at a health spa, 32; at the christening, 32; and Princess Andrew, 34;
focus of Greek society, 34–5; her
'court' (or salon), 35; and charities,
35; supported Miss Fox, 39; and
Grand Duke Vladimir's death, and
the Grand Duchess, 43; and Grand
Duchess Vladimir's threat, 44–5; and
Balkan War, 45; in Salonika, 45;
recalled from Belgrade, 46; and education of her children, 49; and Princess
Marina's disability, 50; in attack on
Athens, 52; and King Constantine I's
departure, 53; left Athens, 54; in
Switzerland, 63, 78; and execution of
Tsar and family, 65; and her mother's
death, 79; returned to Greece, 82;
worked in war hospitals, 84; left
Greece, 84; on Riviera, 85; in Paris,
87; Palermo, 87, 89–90; in France,
93, sold jewels, 93; 94; her Home
for Russian Children, 94–5; supported Grand Duke Kirill's claim to
Tsardom, 96; and Grand Duke
Boris's morganatic wife, 97; her
contented and united family, 97; to
Yugoslavia, 97; to England annually,
97–8; a strict parent, 99, 191; at
Bohinj, 101; and Princess Marina's
engagement, 117; Belgrade, King
Alexander's funeral, 122; her wedding
gift to Princess Marina, 127; at
Princess Marina's wedding, 127, 128;
at birth of Princess Marina's first
child, 141; in Paris, 145; and Prince
Nicholas's death, 147; lived on in

Athens suburb, 147, 164, 170; at
Grand Duke Kirill's deathbed, 148;
in Yugoslavia, 154; during the
Second World War, in Greece, 164–5;
and Prince Andrew, 165; Miss Fox's
legacies to, 192; on Grand Duke
Andrei's death, 203; her own death,
203; her tomb at Tatoi, 147
Nigerian Independence celebrations,
198
Norland Institute (*see also* Fox, Miss
K.), 30, 31–2, 37, 39, 142
Novorossisk, 76

Ogilvy, Hon. Angus, 201–2, 216
Ogilvy, Hon. James, 202
Ogilvy, Hon. Marina, 202
Okhrana (Russian Imperial secret
police), 58
Olav, Prince of Norway, 108, 109, 166
Olga Alexandrovna, Grand Duchess of
Russia, 43, 64, 76, 196–7
Olga Nicholaevna, Grand Duchess of
Russia, 43, 64, 69
Olga, Princess of Greece, her birth, 30;
her nanny (Miss K. Fox, *q.v.*), 30, 36;
at Nicholas Palace, 31; childhood and
upbringing, 33–4, 36, 40; and her
cousins, 34, 35; and sisters, 36;
journeys abroad, 31, 37–43, 44; and
the seaside, 37–8; London, and
Buckingham Palace, 38–9; Vladimir
Palace (St Petersburg), 39–41; Christmases in Russia, Greece and Coburg,
42; and summers at Tsarskoe Selo,
42; and the Russian grand duchesses,
43; and Tsarevitch Alexis, 43; and
Balkan War I, 44; to Russia and
Paris, 44; in Russia after King
George I's death, 47; returned to
Greece, 48; education resumed, 49;
visits to Greek islands, 50; at
Kiphissia, 50; in attack on Athens,
52; left Athens, 54; Switzerland, 63,
78; mourning Tsar and family, 65;
her drawing, and continued education, 78; and Grand Duchess Vladimir's death, 80; returned to Greece,
82; at Tatoi, 84; and war charities,
84; left Greece, 84; on Riviera, 85;
engaged, 85–6; in Paris, 87; Palermo,
87, 89–90; the London Season, 90;
her 'coming-out', 90; met and married
Prince Paul of Yugoslavia, 90–1;
her wedding at Belgrade, 92; in
Paris, 92; to England annually, 98,
102; her first child born, 98; in Belgrade, 101; her second child born,
101; in England, 115, 116; on
Count Toerring, 115; and Princess